Investing in Information Technology
Managing the Decision-Making Process

Titles in the IBM McGraw-Hill Series

Open Systems and IBM: Integration and Convergence
Pamela Gray   ISBN 0-07-707750-4

OS/2 Presentation Manager Programming: Hints and Tips
Bryan Goodyer   ISBN 0-07-707776-8

The IBM RISC System/6000
Clive Harris   ISBN 0-07-707668-0

The IBM RISC System/6000 User Guide
Mike Leaver and Hardev Sanghera   ISBN 0-07-707687-7

PC User's Guide: Simple Steps to Powerful Personal Computing
Peter Turner   ISBN 0-07-707421-1

Dynamic Factory Automation: Creating Flexible Systems for
Competitive Manufacturing
Alastair Ross   ISBN 0-07-707440-8

MVS Systems Programming
Dave Elder-Vass   ISBN 0-07-707767-9

The New Organization: Growing the Culture of Organizational
Networking
Colin Hastings   ISBN 0-07-707784-9

Commonsense Computer Security 2nd Edition: Your Practical
Guide to Information Protection
Martin Smith   ISBN 0-07-707805-5

CICS Concepts and Uses: A Management Guide
Jim Geraghty   ISBN 0-07-707751-2

Risk Management for Software Projects
Alex Down, Michael Coleman and Peter Absolon ISBN 0-07-707816-0

Investing in Information Technology: Managing the decision-making
process
Geoff Hogbin and David Thomas   ISBN 0-07-707957-1

The Advanced Programmer's Guide to AIX 3.x
Phil Colledge   ISBN 0-07-707663-X

The CICS Programmer's Guide to FEPI
Robert Harris   ISBN 0-07-707793-8

Details of these titles in the series are available from:

The Product Manager, Professional Books
McGraw-Hill Book Company Europe
Shoppenhangers Road, Maidenhead, Berkshire, SL6 2QL
Telephone: 0628 23432 Fax: 0628 770224

Geoff Hogbin and David V. Thomas

Investing in Information Technology

Managing the Decision-making Process

McGRAW-HILL BOOK COMPANY

London · New York · St Louis · San Francisco · Auckland
Bogotá · Caracas · Lisbon · Madrid · Mexico · Milan
Montreal · New Delhi · Panama · Paris · San Juan · São Paulo
Singapore · Sydney · Tokyo · Toronto

Published by
McGRAW-HILL Book Company Europe
Shoppenhangers Road, Maidenhead, Berkshire, SL6 2QL, England
Tel 0628 23432; Fax 0628 770224

British Library Cataloguing-in-Publication Data

Hogbin, Geoff
  Investing in Information Technology:
  Managing the Decision-making Process.—
  (McGraw-Hill/IBM Series)
  I. Title II. Thomas, David III. Series
  658.4038

ISBN 0-07-707757-1

Library of Congress Cataloging-in-Publication Data

Hogbin, Geoff
  Investing in information technology: managing the decision-making
process/Geoff Hogbin and David V. Thomas.
      p.   cm.—(The IBM McGraw-Hill series)
  Includes bibliographical references and index.
  ISBN 0-07-707757-1
  1. Information technology—Decision making. 2. Capital
investments—Decision making. 3. Information technology—Great
Britain—Decision making—Case studies. I. Thomas, David V.
II. Title. III. Series.
  HD30.2.H636
858.4'038—dc20   93-39047
                                                                   CIP

2345 CUP 9654

Typeset by Paston Press Ltd, Loddon, Norfolk
and printed and bound in Great Britain at the University Press, Cambridge

To Sylvia and Greta . . .
and to our investments in the future:
Tim, Jo and Andy
Alexis and Lorna

Contents

Foreword

The IBM McGraw-Hill Series

IBM UK and McGraw-Hill Europe have worked together to publish this series of books which provides an up-to-date and authoritative insight into the wide range of products and services available, and offers strategic business advice. Some of the books have a broader business bias, others are written with a more technical perspective. What they have in common is that their authors — some from IBM, some independent consultants — are experts in their field.

Apart from assisting where possible with the accuracy of the writing, IBM UK has not sought to inhibit the editorial freedom of the series, and therefore the views expressed in the books are those of the authors, and not necessarily those of IBM.

Where IBM has lent its expertise is in assisting McGraw-Hill to identify potential titles whose publication would help advance knowledge and increase awareness of computing topics. Hopefully these titles will also serve to widen the debate about the important information technology issues of today and of the future — such as open systems, networking and the use of technology to give companies a competitive edge in their market.

IBM UK is pleased to be associated with McGraw-Hill in this series.

Sir Anthony Cleaver
Chairman
IBM United Kingdom Limited

Foreword to this book

In our consulting business we often find that evaluating IT is an unwelcome after-thought. Yet value is a critical dimension of IT strategic planning. The topic is key to the manager of the IT function and critical for the business manager. Building the investment case and making the right decision is not easy, but managing the benefits through to their full achievement is even more often beset with uncertainty. Failure to do either penalizes the business resulting in dissatisfaction with the service provided by the IT function.

In the process of decision-making and managing the consequences of the investment, there is a shared responsibility for success between the IT manager and the business manager. The difficulties and uncertainties of the total process demand a knowledge of the strategic and tactical issues. Both roles need this understanding as well as access to methods and skills, if full value is to be squeezed from each investment.

The authors, typical of many in the IBM Consulting Group, have built up years of experience by planning IT investments in all the major industry segments. Their book takes a panoramic view of investment decision-making and stakes out how to do it well. It uses down-to-earth examples and text to describe how to build a business case and to illuminate the practice of managing value from IT. It is likely to become an essential handbook for executives, managers and professionals.

Robert M. Howe
IBM Vice-President and General Manager
IBM Consulting Group

Foreword to this book

Acknowledgements

While the responsibility for the contents of this book rests with the authors, many others have contributed to specific topics.

Colleagues from IBM consulting groups have readily shared their expertise. In particular we acknowledge that of Bill Amos, Steve Davis, David Garcia, David Hankin, John Hawkes, John Hicks, Colin Lawrence, Richard Littell, Christine Lissoni, Colin Watts, and of others who have contributed less visibly.

Those named above have also contributed by reviewing individual chapters of the book, as have other colleagues; Tim Lincoln, Roger Bagnall and Ian Little. Outside IBM UK, we have appreciated personal comments on parts of the text from Ken Jacobs, IBM Advanced Business Institute, Dallas, Prem Agrawal, IBM Canada and Gordon Channon and Andrew Hogbin, International Distillers and Vintners Ltd. Where appropriate, the source of case material has been acknowledged and we are particularly grateful for input from Bruce Don, Oxford Regional Health Authority and Graham Hughes, Wacker Chemicals Limited.

Part 1
Investment decisions in context

You have decided to invest in this book! Our aim is that it will help you to decide how to invest profitably in information processing, through the application of technology.

Making a decision to buy can be fraught with uncertainty and unexpected complexity, which may be good for authors and for consultants, but it does not help in making good decisions. Making decisions can be expensive and the results of bad decisions can range from disappointment to disaster, which is generally good for no one but one's competitors. The purpose of this book is to unravel some of the complexity, reduce the uncertainty and to point the way to investment appraisal techniques that work. It is written primarily for those who have the responsibility for producing business cases, for non-specialist readers and for forward-looking managers who expect to use and to benefit from the use of information technology (IT).

There are three basic questions to be answered about an investment.

1 Does this investment potentially represent value for money, or could I obtain the *benefit* (not the product) for less cost?
2 Is this investment what I really want, or could I spend my money on something else more in line with my current goals?
3 Has the investment been managed well, or could it have been done more effectively?

These questions will recur repeatedly throughout the book. It is our aim that, by the end of the book, you will be in a position to answer them in your own situation.

For decades, much has been written on the topic of investment decisions, embracing more than just the technology (that is, hardware and software) purchased to process information. This book confines itself to reviewing how successful decisions have been made about IT in the late 1980s. It discusses and proposes how good decisions can continue to be made in the 1990s.

The book is in two parts. Part 1, Chapters 1–9, considers the overall planning framework within which project planning often takes place and investigates the key issues of aligning IT with the enterprise. It reviews factors affecting the

1

ongoing investment in IT resources. The influence of IT architectures on the business case is discussed, and finally a method is described for building a business case. Part 1 should be read by those requiring a more strategic view of IT investments. If the topics of Part 1 are not your immediate interest, then after reading Chapter 1, and any chapters of specific interest, go straight to Part 2. Part 2 looks closely at the investment decision-making process for a specific IT project. It does this in five stages, from the project's inception as an idea to its review as a successful change in the enterprise. A guide to the topics covered in the chapters of this book is provided in Fig. P1.

Downbeat views of the value of information technology abound. The weekly press reports, 'Much of the £10bn invested by UK companies in technology each year is giving no real payback because of a lack of understanding between IT staff and business executives'.[1] A leading IT author states, 'There is no evidence that US business' massive investments in IT over the past decade have significantly improved productivity or economic performance'.[2] Ask any business manager's view of the value of IT and the answer is more likely to be cautious than it is to be ecstatic.

And yet the investment continues. In 1991, Price Waterhouse reported the expectation of a 7% increase in real terms in 1992, in spite of severe budget constraints.[3] Many enterprises depend on IT for survival. Where a central IT department does not or cannot satisfy user requirements, then business managers will invest their own budgets in IT. Presumably, in these cases at least, they can find no better alternative to help them achieve their objectives. However, the stakes are high. With a spend of £10 billion per annum in the United Kingdom alone, and hundreds of millions of PC users worldwide, searching questions about the value of IT do need to be asked.

Confident assertions about the value of IT, whether good or bad, reflect some aspects of the true position, but often they are generalizations which hide some real and important issues. Common experience should lead us to expect some examples of the application of IT to have been outstandingly good, some examples to have been outstandingly bad and a majority to have been somewhere in between.

For example, Hochstrasser and Griffiths,[4] researchers in the Kobler Unit, Imperial College, London, found that 60% of their surveyed enterprises considered their IT investments to have an average or above average return on capital. However, they noted that even within an organization there can be disagreement about the true value of large-scale IT investments, with more positive views being found in those companies having stricter standards of IT evaluation. Over 50% of companies in their survey had improved internal efficiency by speeding up business cycles and had taken on more work with the same resources. Further, 60% of the companies had improved their effectiveness by improving future scenario predictions, but only 22% found IT as helpful in opening up new markets.

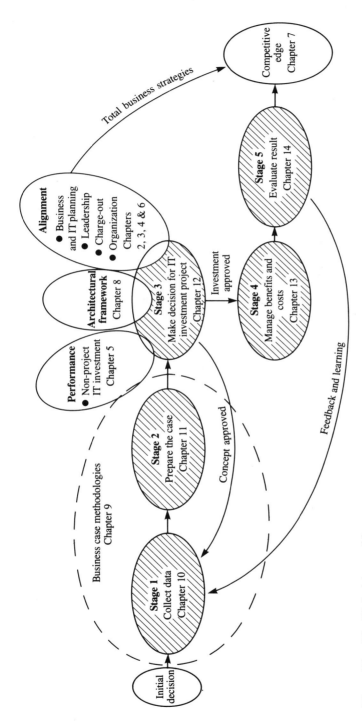

Figure P1. The IT decision-making process.

Overall, investigating the correlation between IT investment and market leaders, Hochstrasser and Griffiths found that the leaders had a more positive and proactive approach to managing and exploiting IT, particularly in the areas of communication and decision support.

A survey by A. T. Kearney and the Chartered Institute of Management Accountants (CIMA)[5] reaches similar conclusions, stating that, 'Companies are deriving greater benefit from their IT installations than they were in 1984'. From a case example, Keen[2] concludes:

> All large firms must change their cost structures by reducing unit costs, eliminating unnecessary jobs and staff, and cutting out organizational layers without sacrificing customer service and quality. Pervasive investment in IT – e.g., in electronic data interchange, computer-integrated manufacturing and telecommunications – can substitute technology for people in all the above areas, afford major longer-term opportunities to avoid costs and help to generate additional revenues without proportionately increasing staff costs.

This is supported by estimates published by the Organization for Economic Cooperation and Development,[6] showing that, 'Industrialized economies need to grow by about 2.5 per cent a year to maintain employment levels as labour-saving technology is introduced . . .'. (This link with unemployment might, for some, provide a reason for stemming an increased investment in technology, rather than justifying it.) Whatever the general finding regarding the value of IT, each enterprise, for each investment and each year, still needs to demonstrate to its own satisfaction that decisions to invest in IT are sound.

This book is about practice rather than theory. The methods outlined in this book have been used to prepare quantified investment proposals. However, neither the processes nor the case studies are offered as a panacea. The methods are a combination of pragmatic techniques and holistic frameworks which have been and can be applied to make good investment decisions. We have drawn on the internal processes of IBM United Kingdom Ltd, but based our work substantially on our consultancy assignments with IBM clients over a period of 12 years. (Examples from IBM are offered by way of illustration and not to promote a preferred approach.) Success in determining the value of IT lies in the more consistent and diligent application of what is known and practised, rather than in new or complex methods of appraisal.

We have not, in general, distinguished between the investment decision processes of different sizes or types of enterprise. It is not that we do not recognize the differences, but that we see them as differences of emphasis and as differences in the way common principles are applied. In the larger enterprise, issues are often more complex, skills more specialized and successive decision activities more distinct. In the smaller enterprise, one person has a wider range of responsibilities and fewer people have to understand the reason for the investment. The decision-making style will be more clearly that of the CEO, probably with a greater emphasis on gut feeling and with less need for an overhead of coordinated planning. Both planning and communications will still be needed, but will be less formalized.

Therefore, in our analysis for larger enterprises, we have in the main covered the ground for small enterprises too. In any case, we have not set out to be prescriptive, because cultural differences distinguish even large enterprises from each other. The five stages described in Part 2, and many of the techniques and checklists within them, are applicable to both small and large enterprises. As Thurston commented, when discussing the best approach to planning for small companies,[7]

> That depends on the style and ability of the CEO (often the owner), on the level of involvement of others in managerial decisions, on the complexity of the business, and on other considerations . . . I do not intend to give a single, prescriptive approach to planning . . . But I will advance some ideas from which you may pick and choose. In part, you may find confirmation for what you are doing.

Many managers feel the need for a prescriptive approach, a simple clear business case methodology. Such cannot be designed to meet the requirements of all enterprises, and even if it could then its successful application would still be uncertain. Good decisions and successful projects depend on the understanding and participation of those affected by the decision process. At the end of Chapter 1 we consider how the problem has changed over the last 20 years and how it will change in the next 10. First we must consider some important aspects of investment decisions.

References

1 Jason Hobby, *Computer Weekly*, October 1991.
2 Peter G. W. Keen, *Shaping the Future*, Harvard Business School Press, Harvard, 1991.
3 *Information Technology Review 1991/92*, Price Waterhouse, London, 1991.
4 Beat Hochstrasser and Catherine Griffiths, *Controlling IT Investment: Strategy and Management*, Chapman & Hall, London, 1991.
5 *Breaking the Barriers; IT Effectiveness in Great Britain and Ireland; Management Perspective*, A. T. Kearney Limited, Stickley House, 130 Wilton Road, London SW1V 1LQ, UK, 1990.
6 K. Maguire, *Daily Telegraph*, 24 February, 1993.
7 Philip H. Thurston, Should small companies make formal plans?, *Harvard Business Review*, September–October 1983.

1
The nature of investment decisions

1.1   The scope of the investment decision

The increasing opportunities which seem to be offered by information technology raise questions about its use. Typical questions are:

- What investment should we be making?
- What financial criteria should we use?
- Can financial savings be identified?
- Will the savings be achieved?
- Will earlier investment be protected in subsequent stages?
- Who else has done it?
- How fast should the investment proceed?
- What if we delay or do nothing?

An enterprise will make its investment decisions based on marketing and competitive needs, business risk and financial criteria. The financial aspects of investments are often regarded as 'the bottom line', and to evaluate investments future cash flows and profitability can be analysed.

In reaching a decision to invest, executive management will consider factors other than financial. How well the proposals fit with the direction of the business, the level and timing of implementation and the acceptability and the usability of new applications of technology are all important.

Ultimately, the quality of management available for implementation of the investment will affect how well financial objectives are achieved. Even management with a good track record may need new skills and techniques for a significant new type of investment.

Investments, and not least those in IT, are about creating change. Money, of course, is important as an enabler. But people are a more important factor. Catching the imagination and applying the creative energy of a mixture of individuals, welded into a team by a good leader, is what really counts in making effective investments.

Thus we also need to consider the size and complexity of the projects and their

6

impact on people's normal working patterns as well as the rate and nature of change in the environment external to the enterprise; these could affect the financial criteria applied to the investment. The business case must necessarily be based on a viable project plan.

In our experience, when evaluating a proposed investment, as much value comes from the process of evaluation as from the result it gives.

For these reasons, investment appraisal is not simply a process of manipulating numbers. This is only one component of the decision-making process, a process which involves people and their individual and corporate assessment of where the greater benefit for the enterprise lies in the future.

1.2   Types of investment decision

Many of the potential applications of new technology can be hard to cost-justify. They appear to promise sound benefits, but their quantification remains elusive. It may be felt in some industries and enterprises that the benefits may not be quantifiable, and possibly not attainable. Often this difficulty arises from a low appreciation of the application and of its potential effect on the enterprise and from the lack of established cost justification techniques within the enterprise. The application of technology often introduces new concepts, and these need to be thought through and reduced to simple terms.

Several terms may be used to express the positive effects of an investment project, such as savings, benefits and value. We have used the term 'benefits' to include savings and value, of which some can be quantified and some cannot, although it is desirable, as far as possible, to quantify project benefits. So benefits may be used to position the project results on a scale ranging from financial or tangible to soft or intangible.

The problem of quantifying the benefits and costs of a project has many facets. The nature of the problem varies and, while there are some general principles that can be followed, it is the characteristics of an investment decision which determine the most effective approach. For example, an IT investment decision can be characterized by:

- the function which the proposed systems will provide
- the maturity of the IT application
- the stage in the project life cycle.

1.2.1   *Application function*

The nature of information technology support to the business is changing. It cannot so readily be justified in straight financial terms. In this view an IT business application is classified by the function it delivers, into one of four types:

- Operational transaction processing systems, which result in *direct cost savings*, for example, order processing. These often collect data which will be of value elsewhere.
- Systems which manage resources across the organization, again often with *measurable cost savings*, for example, inventory and production facilities. Here, the ability to collect and collate data across systems is important.
- Systems which are aimed at *improving a company's growth and market share*, for example, those which feature a 'tie-in' service for customers.
- Applications of *great strategic importance* to the business, which are often a combination of the first three and which may be accepted on the basis of their intangible benefits, for example office systems which save individuals' time, but more importantly speed up communications across departments and increase the level of service which can be provided to customers.

Quantifying benefits cannot by itself provide a sufficient and satisfactory way to assess priorities between competing projects, particularly when both are of strategic significance. Nevertheless, it is important that, within business cases for all projects, 'best efforts' are made to quantify benefits, because in doing so the objectives of the project are sharpened and the scope is better defined.

1.2.2 *Application maturity*

This characteristic addresses the likely economic justification of an investment project, and places an IT application in one of three categories. With experience and in the course of time, for any enterprise, some applications will migrate across the categories, which are:

- **Clearly justified** These investments are generally in an established technology, with few project risks, relating to high-volume repetitive operations. Responsibility for the costs incurred and the savings to be achieved can be readily assigned to specific areas of the business and managed. The enterprise may well have been through earlier implementations and have experience of their subsequent appraisal.

   Typical information systems will involve processing large numbers of transactions for the main operations of the business. Savings will be expressed in terms of cost reduction and cost avoidance of materials, people, buildings, plant, equipment etc. Aggressive financial criteria can be met.
- **May be justified** In this category, project risks, in terms of size, complexity and technology, will be greater. Hard or tangible benefits will be quantifiable and under management control. Soft or intangible benefits, while of less certain achievement, could be of more importance in the overall decision. The benefits are likely to depend more on the perception and understanding of senior management and an assessment of the enterprise's position in the external environment, with and without the investment.

These applications produce smaller productivity improvements from non-clerical office-based staff (i.e. professionals and managers) across all functions and divisions. They improve the level of service provided by units within the enterprise to each other, and by the enterprise to its clients. They provide information for management control, planning and decision-making. Savings will often be expressed in terms of the competitive advantage and as the potential for an increase in sales and revenue income.

- **Not justified**   Applications in this category may well be technically feasible and even strategically desirable. Currently, they are just not economic. The volumes of transactions (and hence equipment utilization) may be too low. The storage requirements may be very large, with a low level of activity of the information stored. The cost of developing the systems may be out of proportion to the value to be derived. The projects might present high risks, as the technology may be new and untried.

   However, applications in this area can attract a lot of interest and indeed need constant re-evaluation. Many organizations will devote 1–2% (and some as much as 10%) of their IT budget investing in research projects, in developing new products and services or in joint ventures with IT suppliers.

Over a period of time, as the business grows and as technology advances, some computer applications will migrate from the 'not justified' category to 'clearly justified'. The way in which an investment is defined might well move it across the category boundaries. Indeed, the category of a project is, within limits, somewhat arbitrary, but within any category the requirements for its financial justification may be different. For example, a 'not justified' application involving a new technology could well be justified as a prototype project. A 'may be justified' application, with better project management skills and coordination between users and systems specialists, could move firmly into the 'clearly justified' category. Historically, applications involving database management techniques would have been 'not justified' in the 1960s, but are now in 'clearly justified'. Similarly, office automation applications, once 'may be justified', have moved into 'clearly justified'.

Understanding an application's position in these categories helps to establish realistic expectations of its benefits and to select techniques for their assessment.

1.2.3 Project stage

As a project proceeds from its inception, through its early planning stages and into its implementation, so the costs and benefits associated with it change in nature. It is no good hoping that early planning activity will produce totally dependable figures. As costs are incurred, management systems need to be set up to control them.

The words 'conceptualize', 'calculate' and 'control' help to set the right level of expectation for the nature of costs and benefits as the project unfolds. Under-standing this classification is of fundamental importance to financial appraisal. It is developed further in Chapters 4 and 10. But first we must consider the nature of the 'business case' and provide a historical perspective of IT investment appraisal.

1.3   What is a business case?

1.3.1   Its purpose and scope

To bring about a major change, an organization will need to make an investment. *The business case is the rationale for the investment.* Sometimes change can be achieved by diverting existing resources to bring it about. When a change is of some significance, it can only be brought about by making additional resources available and by implementing it through a project. A project is a management tool for moving an enterprise from its current internal structure, in terms of its products, organization, production facilities, management systems etc., to a new structure, to achieve the goals it has set for itself for the future. The project will generally be initiated by a project proposal containing a business case. This will contain the financial implications of the project, so that its merit can be appraised against financial criteria. The relationship between the project proposal, the business case and the financial case is shown in Fig. 1.1. In practice, there is rarely a clear distinction between them and no mutually exclusive definitions of the three are offered here.

Thus, *a business case is normally produced to support any major change or investment in the business.* It might be either to increase the level of ongoing resources used in the business (for example an increase in headcount to accommo-date increases in business volumes), or to make a one-off investment in order to reduce the level of ongoing resources used, or to change the products and services being offered.

The business case for a project can have one of several aims:

1   To assist with setting the scope and objectives of the project.
2   To determine the financial viability of the project.
3   To assist in decision-making about the future of the project.

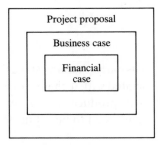

Figure 1.1.   Positioning the business case.

Furthermore, the type of investment being proposed will affect the contents of a business case. The level of detail which is possible and appropriate depends on the stage of the project, and on how much resource is actually being committed in the next phase. A business case which is prepared to enable a decision to be made to commit substantial resources is likely to involve other groups (and in some instances suppliers) in preparing estimates, implementation plans and alternatives.

The main focus of our interest is on the IT project. Significant change often involves IT, but implies other solutions as well, such as the redesign of business processes in the office, or integrated manufacturing techniques in the factory. Such total solutions, adding to the complexity of producing quantified business cases, are an issue of the 1990s.

1.3.2 *What the business case will not do*

This book is concerned with making the business case before the project starts and auditing the benefits after it is completed. A 'good' decision to invest might be made, which considers and balances all factors pertinent to achieving the investment objectives. However, neither the business case nor the decision will ensure that the benefits are delivered. To do this, the IT project needs to be managed to a successful conclusion (for which some important factors are discussed in Chapter 13).

1.3.3 *The value of the financial case*

It is important that IT projects are appraised within the context of the changes they may bring about to the business plan. Ultimately, what matters is the beneficial effect that a project has on budgets and profits. Where the estimated benefits of a project are consciously applied to revenue, expense or capital budgets upon implementation, the term 'budget-based justification' is commonly used. Intangible benefits that are not quantified cannot, of course, be treated in this way, but their direct contribution to the business plan is very relevant.

Sometimes the question is asked, 'Do all projects need a quantified business case, that is a financial case which meets financial criteria?' The danger is that a good and necessary project may be turned down because the required figures cannot be produced with sufficient credibility. The need for a financial case forces a focus on short term factors. Not all costs and benefits can be quantified, which means that a financial case never provides a complete picture of what the project might achieve, even in financial terms.

In these circumstances, the best effort should be made to estimate what quantified savings might arise. The process clarifies the project manager's planning and objective setting. There is a stronger element of realism brought into the users' requirements and priorities. The accountant will ask what the project saves, if no one else does.

However, there might be instances where a full investment appraisal is not warranted. Where the need to proceed is unavoidable, or the cost of making an appraisal is large relative to the investment, then there is a clear case for not following normal procedures. Here, the evaluation of alternative implementations is likely to be a realistic approach or abbreviated procedures will be used for smaller proposals, and this is typically the approach found in smaller business units.

Even when a good return on investment (ROI) is forecast for a project, one should not imagine that this will necessarily be the main decision criterion. 'Will it work?', always follows hard after 'What's the bottom line?'

CASE STUDY

Dr Frank, a geophysicist, employed by an American oil company, went to a trade show. There he saw a technology which was used in the medical industry to extract data from a source and to present it on a high-resolution workstation. The image was presented in three dimensions and it could be rotated, exploded or imploded. The program also had an opacity function. This stripped away layers of data to enable hidden features, such as organs of the body, to be viewed.

Dr Frank realized that this technology was equally applicable to visualizing an oil reservoir. It promised to be a revolutionary tool for improving the business process of finding and extracting oil; its potential scope was division-wide in his enterprise. For his use, the application program would need modifying by the vendor, at a cost of $30 000. He was not certain, at this stage, that the application could be modified to meet his requirements, nor could he quantify how much better insight it would give into oil field maps and reservoirs. The downside risk was relatively small, but the consequences of missing out on such a potentially attractive technique could, in his view, be significant.

Dr Frank was concerned that he might be forced to consider all the costs and benefits of the application on a division-wide basis and identify its impact on systems platforms and infrastuctures. However, he asked his IS department for $30 000, simply to provide for the modification.

As the annual IT budget was $155 million this seemed a modest investment request for an idea with such strategic potential. Concurrent with Dr Frank's request, a proposal for an $8 million infrastructure investment was being presented by IS to divisional managers.

The IS answer was, 'We can't help; you have missed the cut-off for the planning cycle; we have not budgeted for your request; your workstation is incompatible with corporate standards'. The result was a frustrated line manager who felt even more that he should have his own IT budget and facilities.

This case exemplifies issues which recur repeatedly throughout our book. According to our earlier classifications, this application proposal is strategic, not (currently) justified and conceptual. Its formulation has not meshed with business and IT planning cycles; it appears to run counter to IS policies and procedures; it does not seem to have a documented financial case. But an experienced and skilled professional backs it.

This book analyses the decision-making process and describes how to prepare a business case for IT applications. It can help a geophysicist, or other user, to present a proposal for an IT investment and to understand better the environment in which the investment request will be considered. The aim of the book is to help good ideas come to life, and to shine the light of reality on others. We return to this case study in Chapters 3 and 12.

1.4   The history of investment appraisal

Has the nature of investment decisions changed – are they now more difficult than in former years? Many leading users of IT, but far from all, have abandoned the inclusion of tangible savings in investment cases. Tough questions can be asked of numerical statements, which can be hard to defend. No sponsor wants a project fall at this hurdle. It is argued that numbers are only a 'comfort factor'; and they can be manipulated to provide whatever degree of comfort is required.

Overall, the differences in the nature of today's investments, compared with those of the past (Table 1.1), are of less significance than some suggest. Many of the problems are the same. The new challenges are no reason, in most instances, for not trying to produce a quantified case. Financial evaluation should not be dropped, but rather should have other methods added to it.

Table 1.1   History of investment appraisal

Investment appraisal was	Investment appraisal is
Mainly financial	Holistic
Cost savings/tactical	Opportunity/strategic
Projects available <2 years ROI	Projects available >3 years ROI
Single business area	Multi/cross-functional
Small, then monolithic systems	Modular and incremental systems
In the IT Department	Within business departments
Technically risky	Organizationally risky
Standalone systems	Interdependent and infrastructure
Pre-project	Post-project
Project management	Change/benefits management

What of the future? Some of the factors which professionals expect will play a more important part in investment decisions are:

Systems integration
Computer aided software engineering (CASE) in its maturity
PCs, local area networks (LANs), and downsizing
Networks and communications
Progressive systems design with modelling and prototyping
IT services (for example, facilities management)
Object-oriented programming
Architectures

However, these are technical factors and relate to IT solutions. In business terms, commentators identify other issues. The worldwide recession of the early 1990s forced a focus on more local, shorter term, quicker return investments. The rate of change and scale of change can be expected to increase, if current trends continue. Change will be less by migration and more by transformation; for the leaders, less by reaction, more by proaction. More enterprises will adopt higher risk strategies with a consequent demand for better skills in project and change management and a sharper business judgement. Product development cycles and deadlines will continue to reduce, while enterprise alliances and partnerships will increase. Scarce in-house skills will be supplemented by outsourcing.

Increasingly, the value and response provided by the IT Department will be scrutinized and some business managers will take more control of their systems and asociated technology.

The survey by A. T. Kearney and CIMA[1] found that 'Successful users are more likely to have fully interdependent business and IT plans than unsuccessful users'. This fits with our experience, and the issues are explained in the following two chapters.

Reference

1 *Breaking the Barriers; IT Effectiveness in Great Britain and Ireland; A Management Perspective*, A. T. Kearney Limited, Stickley House, 130 Wilton Road, London SW1V 1LQ, UK, 1990.

2
Planning and investment decisions

2.1 Aligning IT with the business

> 1988's main cause of grey hair in the dp department was 'integrating IT with
> corporate strategy'. For the first time, a technical concern with making the
> computer work has been ousted by a management concern with making it work
> for the company.[1]

Three years and a recession later this key issue had been overtaken by the concern
of IT cost containment.[2] Our introduction acknowledged the question, which is
frequently asked by Chief Executive Officers (CEOs), 'Am I getting value for
money from the use my organization makes of IT?' However, the need for IT to
be aligned with the business is still central to the discussion of value.

Although this topic emerged in the 1989 Price Waterhouse Review, it is hardly
new. Herbert and Hartog, identified it in the mid 1980s, but it has been with us
since at least the late 1970s.[3] The question still remains as to how IT can be
integrated with the corporate strategy.

It is not likely that there will be only one way to align IT with the business, which
if applied will guarantee the necessary alignment, particularly over any period of
time. However, there are four key factors which taken together will result in IT
supporting the real needs of the business. They are:

- Business and IT planning
- Leadership of the Information Technology Department (ITD)
- Charging out the costs of IT to the user departments
- Organization of the ITD

The value of IT depends on its measurable impact on the enterprise. This has
two dimensions, from its impact on the enterprise in future (the plan) and from the
results of implementing the plan (feedback and management control). Therefore,
as a foundation to obtaining value from IT investments, the next two chapters
discuss aspects of business and IT planning which relate to the planning-based
evaluation of those investments. If business plans and IT plans are interlocked, IT
is likely to be well aligned with the business.

Readers not needing to review business planning should skim this chapter and proceed to Chapter 3.

2.2   Complementary planning procedures

Planning procedures which bring together IT projects and business plans address the issue of integration and also make an important, even unique, contribution to the quantification and achievement of IT project benefits and to establishing IT priorities. The need to integrate planning and investment procedures and to manage benefits is a fundamental proposition of this book. This discussion of business and IT planning lays the foundation for our approach to effective benefits management in Chapter 13.

A component of planning will be the development of an IT strategy. This gives one way of aligning IT with business needs, although taken alone it will not give a sufficient basis for measuring the value of IT. Strategy is dealt with in Chapter 4.

2.2.1   The business planning cycle

The business plan describes the resources which will be needed and used by the whole organization, or by a unit or individual within it, to deliver the products and services required by a user (or customer) within a period of time.

Most enterprises plan their future to a greater or lesser degree, even if only to the extent of preparing budgets for the next 12 months, or a proposed cash flow for the bank. The changes needed to move from one year's plan to the next will be implemented by direct management action (such as a reorganization), by education and training (for example in the use of new procedures) and by means of projects. IT projects may be implemented using the resources managed by line managers or through the resources of specialist groups, such as IT departments. In the latter case, the investments in people and equipment may be large and may substantially alter the enterprise's way of operating.

The business case provides a measure of how far an individual project might 'work for the company', in bringing about change and in helping to redraw the business plan.

Many companies have developed their own approach to business planning; some have adopted a proprietary methodology. In most cases, business planning has arisen from, and been centred on, financial planning. Business planning is taken here to include both the preparation of quantified budgets for a 12-month period and corporate planning, which provides qualitative statements of direction over a longer period. The terminology and time frames used for business planning can vary widely across different enterprises. Therefore these, and some of the characteristics of a typical planning cycle, are illustrated in Fig. 2.1 and described below.

1 January Year 1

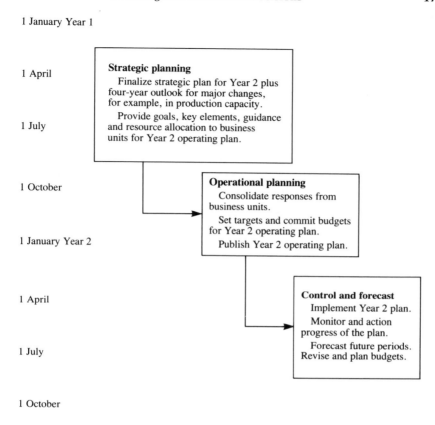

1 April

1 July

1 October

1 January Year 2

1 April

1 July

1 October

1 January Year 3

Figure 2.1. The business planning cycle.

2.2.2 *The strategic plan*

The overall shape of the company, typically for the next five years, will be laid out in the *corporate* or *strategic plan*. Much of this plan will be descriptive, with 'where-we-need-to-be' statements. The plan will generally be based on and contain an analysis of the organizations' products and services and the prevailing and forecast future business environment. This will include reviews of markets, competitors, customers and suppliers and of the availability and quality of major resources, such as personnel. Legal, political, economic and social frameworks and trends will be assessed.

The plan will set out the main goals and strategies to be followed and will need to identify all the main areas for investment. The driving forces, main parameters and base statistics for the plan are likely to come from plans for products and services, from reviews of markets and from the resultant corporate marketing plans. The resources required to meet these goals and plans will vary widely with the nature of the products and services and the mission of the enterprise. For product-based companies, research and development will be important, particularly where the products incorporate advanced technology. In a manufacturing enterprise, production capacity plans and proposals will form a major part of the corporate plan. In enterprises which provide services, staffing is likely to be a larger part of the plan, with headcount and deployment being key parameters. It is at this level that issues such as productivity need initially to be addressed, for if this is not done at the corporate plan level, more detailed plans for achieving it, for example through IT, are likely to be poorly directed and less effective.

The corporate plan will be underpinned with five-year financial projections. Key items, such as revenue, cost and expenses, capital requirements and profit forecasts, will be mapped out, but only in very broad terms. The output of the strategic plan will typically propose a set of strategies for the main functions of the enterprise, such as marketing, manufacturing, finance, personnel and research and development. This plan also will contain proposals for the key parameters of the business and for the deployment of the main resources of the business, particularly for the next 24 months. These will be inputs to the operating plan.

This strategic planning process will have stimulated forward thinking and will have laid the foundation for more detailed planning and for subsequent control over a period of years. It will have helped to define the affordable structure and resources deemed necessary to achieve the projected revenue stream and profit goals. It will have revealed the shortcomings and exposures of objectives that would otherwise have been unrealistic hopes. The one certainty about this year's strategic plan, is that next year it will have been modified to meet emerging challenges. Its effective implementation, through operational plans, will depend on the consensus and commitment of executive management to the strategic plan and to the planning processes, and to the communication of this plan to functional heads.

2.2.3   *The operating plan*

The operating plan consists essentially of the 12 month budgets but generally has a rolling 24 month outlook. The use of a rolling plan is vital to achieve flexibility; changes will be made more frequently to the plan for months 13 to 24 than to the committed part of the plan. The operating plan breaks down the overall resources set by the strategic plan to departments and to projects. The plan can be prepared top–down, as a 'tablet of stone' by a central function, such as finance, but more normally the planning will be interactive, and prepared partly bottom–up. The main structure may be set by the financial or business planners, but input will be taken from functional managers, particularly in 'agreeing' the details of the final budgets. The budgets for the next 12-month period are often derived by simply extending the last 12 months by a given percentage.

More advanced approaches to budget setting might be used, such as zero-based, probabilistic and three-level budgeting. In zero-based budgeting, last year's budgets are set aside and new budgets built up on the basis of new targets and new methods. The underlying philosophy of 'Let's start again', is similar to that of business process re-engineering. Probabilistic and three-level budgeting envisage alternative outcomes to the plan, according to probabilities or to pessimistic, realistic and optimistic budget estimates. Each aims to achieve more realistic budgets and targets.

The operating plan will have a financial plan as a major component. The financial plan will typically contain the following items: an income/expense summary and a balance sheet.

Income/expense summary

This comprises the following items:

Revenue
Cost of revenue
Gross profit
Expenses and other deductions
Net earnings before tax
Gross profit and margin percentages
Expense to revenue ratio as a percentage

Revenue projections will be supported by non-financial numerical forecasts of product and service volumes and prices, and of market and competitive trends. Expenses will be built up from (or broken down to) proposed departmental budgets. They will be significantly affected by the changes that management are proposing to make in terms of manufacturing processes and technology, the operation of new buildings and associated facilities and the employment, organization and remuneration of people, to mention but a few typical areas of potential change. Expenses associated with developing and running information systems will be incorporated into the operating plan.

Balance sheet

This includes:

Capital additions/disposals
Inventory
Accounts receivable/payable
Cash flow

An equally wide range of considerations will affect the balance sheet projections. The sources and uses of funds will be set out and the effects of varying costs of money may be assessed. Items on the balance sheet will be directly affected by proposed investments, including those in information technology. Each investment will involve cash flow and the use of resources.

It is here, in the operating plan, that the effect of each proposed investment will be set out. The overall effect of investments needs to be visibly and, as far as possible, measurably beneficial. It is at the end of this planning stage that new investments will be committed, and it is now that their value needs to be established.

2.2.4   *Plan implementation and revision*

The final stage of the business planning cycle is reached during the plan's implementation. Regular (monthly) measurements are made of the plan achievement, to facilitate management control and remedial action at all levels, to provide a basis for the year-end outlook and, where necessary, to lead into in-period amendments to the plan. The sequence of month-end reviews will vary from company to company.

Overall, both the strategic and operating plans are prepared to meet important deadlines according to an annual calendar of activities. Whether the planning process has a top–down or bottom–up emphasis, three key principles must be applied: it must be a process which involves live negotiation and trade-offs to achieve a committed plan; it must be constructed to capture opportunities and to provide early warning of potential problems; and it must aim to achieve the optimum balance between being a structured and continuous process, while providing the ability for the business to respond to customer and market dynamics.

The specifics of this planning framework may not be appropriate for all types and sizes of organization. However, application of the principles is essential as a basis for aligning IT with the business and for managing the benefits of IT projects.

2.3   IT planning

One of the strategies within the corporate strategy will be that of the function responsible for information technology. In the 1970s the IT function was generally known as the Data Processing (DP) or Computer Department. In the 1980s these names were broadened to, among others, Management Information Services (MIS) and Information Systems (IS) Departments. All of these may still be used in the 1990s, but the most favoured title now seems to be the Information Technology (IT) Department. For the purpose of this book we have adopted the latter and used the abbreviation 'ITD' where we refer specifically to the function and department. For the head of this function we have used the title Chief Information Officer (CIO).

We use the term 'ITD strategy' to mean that part of the business strategy which is the responsibility of the ITD. (The term IT strategy often has other connotations, as discussed in Chapter 4.)

2.3.1 *ITD strategic planning*

The overall parameters of the ITD planning will, or should, be set by the corporate strategy, as for any other function. Conversely, opportunities offered by IT will enable significant change to be brought about, and this can influence the corporate strategy. However, the main factors to be considered in planning for IT are:

1   The ITD exists to provide an information processing service to the enterprise (and sometimes outside the enterprise).
    The ITD needs to be driven by its customers, the great majority of whom will be within the enterprise. Good interaction with them is essential, both at policy and at personal levels. the ITD will need to be responsive and sensitive to the needs and personalities of its customers. On the other hand, its customers will need to recognize that an economical and effective service can only be provided within the context of some rules and constraints. All service functions operate this way: the cafeteria will have its service hours and menu constraints, each maintaining a balance between potential demand and cost of supply.
    Success for the ITD lies in gaining the right balance of the tensions implied by these forces for the prevailing circumstances.
2   Part of the IT service will be ongoing, but a significant part will be aimed at creating change, and this will require some new investments. If history is any guide, the demand for IT services to create change will continue to outstrip the affordable supply. Therefore, the opportunities for new investment in IT will have to be prioritized.
3   Like many other resources, those associated with processing information cannot quickly be turned on and off. This means that business needs must be considered in the longer term so that systems and infrastructure developments can be planned.
4   Items 2 and 3 lead to the need to relate investment proposals to corporate goals and priorities.
5   To establish IT priorities, a sound and credible process is required for assessing and approving investment proposals. Part 2 of this book sets out such a process.
6   Finally, to realize the benefits of the investment, there needs to be an executive and management commitment which results in actions to achieve them.

These factors will mould the policies and directions of the ITD's strategic plan.
    Specifically, the plan will need to provide, among other things, for the location

and capacity of computing power over the years. It will need to address improvement in the quality and productivity of the delivery of ITD services, whether in operations or development. In general terms, it will need to address how the ITD will support the business through IT applications and systems solutions, through technical strategies for hardware, software and networks, and through the organization and management of these resources and of personnel. This will be a four to five year view. The details of how this will be achieved, over a two-year time frame, will be in the operational plan.

These descriptions will provide support for the financial and other resources to be allocated to ITD, for the purpose of maintaining existing services and for developing new services. Broad cost levels will be set, together with any major constraints and dependencies. It is from this strategy plan that the ITD annual plan, or two-year rolling operational plan, will be derived.

2.3.2 ITD operational planning

The ITD's annual planning process will define the new investments and the annual budgets for that function. Both of these will be arrived at after interaction between the ITD plan and the general business plan. In IBM UK, requirements will be built up from those of line and staff management and from UK, European and US corporate functions. In any organization, the planning cycle will mesh with that of the business, following the time-scale of Fig. 2.1. The plan is likely to be agreed within the ITD in October, booked with corporate planning in November and in December concurrence with the content sought from other functions, as appropriate. As for other major functions, plans are of a 'chicken and egg' nature, and for this reason the planning process has to be both iterative and continuous.

The planning is often carried out by a small group or by an individual within the ITD. Typically, the group consists of IT specialists assigned to planning. The group will often coordinate application development, technical infrastructure and personnel and other resource plans. The group might include financial planning specialists to ensure interlock with corporate financial planning, to provide capital planning and appraisal and to track expense budgets. The planning group might also have responsibilty for coordinating the measurement and tracking of benefits previously lodged with user managers at project appraisal time. The precise arrangements for planning depend considerably on the size of the ITD and on its role in the organization.

2.3.3 ITD resource allocation and investment planning

The resources allocated by the strategic plan to the ITD for its annual operating plan will be used for four purposes (Table 2.1). The operating plan must ensure that there is a balanced distribution of these resources and investments to meet

Table 2.1　IT resource requirements

- Investments for projects to provide new systems and IT services
- IT infrastructure needed to facilitate efficient provision of new services
- Investment to maintain or to improve the delivery of existing IT services
- Ongoing cost of running existing IT services

---

these needs. New investments must be affordable in both scope and time-scale and be capable of being prioritized.

In justifying IT resources, either from a zero base or as an incremental increase on the previous year, it is desirable to separate these four elements.

The two base levels of resource allocated to ITD are those required to operate and to maintain the existing IT service levels for the future business volumes of current products (that is tomorrow's business at today's service levels). A relative reduction in this resource level can be expected (indeed, demanded!), provided that appropriate investments are made, for example in new technology or in productivity or quality projects. These investments need to be justified and to result in an identifiable reduction in resources, relative to a stable business environment. Targets for year-on-year cost reduction and quality improvements must be set and achieved.

In addition to maintaining service levels from IT, there will be a continuing demand from the business for improvements. These will be needed to accommodate increasing complexities, to support new products and services, and to achieve economies in the use of other major resources, such as people, cash, premises, plant and material. The benefits from these projects will be business benefits, and they must be identified and managed by appropriate business managers within non-ITD functions.

To continue to deliver these improvements efficiently and effectively, the ITD will need to make a further investment to develop the IT infrastructure, in hardware, in systems software and in networks. There will need to be an ongoing investment in training and developing people, and probably in real estate and associated facilities as well. This investment will be over and above the direct investment needed for the projects set up to deliver the improvements and the benefits. The investment will need to be identified and managed by the ITD management.

It is the sum of these four resource requirements (Table 2.1), with their supporting investment proposals, which will be the ITD input first, in broad terms, to the strategic plan and then, in more detail, to the operating plan. Business cases are most often prepared for new systems projects. Sometimes they may not be prepared at all for infrastructure projects or for investments needed to maintain existing services. If a business case is provided, it is likely to be at the level of appraising the options for spending money, rather than any serious attempt to identify those benefits that can be managed out of the investment. In this situation it is little wonder that the value of this investment, or of IT in general, is questioned.

In summary, it is important that the funds available to the ITD are enough to provide a balanced and sustainable allocation across all four areas and that some investments will result in cost savings in the provision of the IT service. The six key steps of the investment planning process are:

1   Establish the *total* affordable ITD resource.
2   Determine the base resource required.
3   Calculate the resource available for investment, and particularly that available for development, as person years.
4   Identify and prioritize the infrastructure investment portfolio.
5   Prioritize the application investment portfolio.
6   Construct a plan which can realistically be implemented.

The main outputs from the operational planning process are threefold. Firstly, investments will be presented as a prioritized portfolio of development projects. Typically, this portfolio will include applications that are already under development, projects that aim to maintain technical currency, improvements and developments to the technical infrastructure and new application developments.

As part of the plan, a brief description is needed for each project but fuller documentation, particularly for larger projects, is required before project authorization and commitment in the plan period.

Secondly, there will be a machine and services plan, which will provide the basis for a prioritized schedule of the capital purchases that are needed to support all new investment areas, and the dates by which funding will be required. This will provide the basis for the capital expenditure plan.

Thirdly, the application development projects will give rise to project schedules, with dates for key project milestones, and to resource plans showing the monthly utilization of manpower, equipment and expenses, again with monthly budgets and controls for all key items in the plan.

Before leaving the subject of the operational plan, two issues warrant comment. The total spend on IT will in most cases, and sometimes as a matter of policy, be considerably more than that made by the ITD. Other business units may devote significant levels of resource to IT and make sizeable investments in its development. Most organizations establish guidelines which determine the level of resource or investment that can be committed by non-IT departments. Within these, investments in hardware will be relatively easy to control. Software expenses and the time spent by individuals in developing and setting up local systems will be harder to monitor and control. These expenses will only be managed to the extent that they are provided for within the existing business planning and control procedures.

Even the best plans are never stable for long. During the plan period, assumptions made about costs, revenues and volumes and the availability of capital will be validated or changed. Manufacturing facilities might come on stream late; product launches might be delayed; new taxation might change cost profiles; and new competitors might enter the market. The management systems of the planning process will need to allow for changes to budgets in the light of monthly and quarterly reviews. However, it is these changes to plans which can frustrate attempts to maintain the alignment of business and IT plans.

This description of the operational planning process highlights the importance of the IT project and the way in which it is planned, documented and evaluated. It is through projects that many new investments will be made and controlled. It is vital to understand the role of the project life cycle and how it needs to interact with the business planning cycle. This theme will be further developed in Chapter 4. In Chapter 3, we shall describe how different organizations implement the planning processes discussed above, in order to illustrate further important considerations and variations in IT planning.

References

1 *Information Technology Review 1989/90*, Price Waterhouse, London, 1989.
2 *Information Technology Review 1992/93*, Price Waterhouse, London, 1992.
3 M. Herbert and C. Hartog, MIS rates the issues, *Datamation*, November 1986.

3
Case studies of IT planning

A planning framework and procedures help to achieve the alignment of IT with the business, but still more can be done through good communication between the people and groups involved. This chapter describes three situations. They round off our discussion so far of business and IT planning, and set the scene for the topics of later chapters. The first example will illustrate some relevant aspects of IT investment planning within IBM UK. The second draws on public sector practice. Both enterprises are in a state of change; the tide of devolution is flowing strongly for the provision of IT services, but within the context of centralized corporate IT planning. The third example has been chosen to illustrate IT planning in a smaller business unit.

3.1   IT planning in IBM UK

IBM UK had about 14 000 employees in 1992, with plans to reduce by 2000 in 1993. It manufactures and markets a wide range of IT products through various sales channels and has recently expanded its consultancy services.

Within IBM UK, the IT Department was positioned within the Corporate Staffs until 1992, together with finance and other associated departments. The IT function was then known as United Kingdom International Information Services (UKIIS). In 1992, UKIIS became IBM Information Services Limited (ISL) and was established as a subsidary of IBM United Kingdom Holdings Limited. IBM ISL now offers services for managing and running computer systems and application development to IBM UK, IBM Europe and other companies and organizations wishing to outsource all or part of their IT operations.

IBM ISL consists of some 1400 personnel, of which approximately 200 are engaged in development work. It is responsible for providing most IT services in the UK and selected services to IBM Europe. ISL develops new services to meet the functional requirements of the UK company and also to provide systems which are implemented internationally across Europe. The reverse also applies, and ISL implements systems in the UK which have been the development responsibilty of groups in other countries. Some requirements for new systems will also be generated by corporate functions. These and European requirements are coordinated through the European Business Systems Management Board.

While IBM has clear and continuing planning procedures, the detailed implementation changes from year to year to meet the needs of the business. Four periods are discussed below.

1   In the early 1980s the IT development resource, available for IBM UK systems, was initially assigned to the main business functions by the business and finance planning groups and finally agreed between UKIIS and the business functions. Resource was also allocated for IT infrastructure developments. Requests for IT development, originating from users or from the Application Development group, were submitted to the UKIIS Requirements Planning group. Requests were prioritized by this group, in conjunction with Application Development, according to a clear set of rules, agreed with business and finance planning. Developments tended to be driven up and initiated from within UKIIS.

2   At the end of the 1980s, from 1987 to 1989, the responsibility for setting application development for IT was transferred to a Business Case Review Board (BCRB). This Board consisted of senior representatives from UKIIS, Business Plans and Finance Planning. Project proposals from the functions, prepared with the assistance of UKIIS, were reviewed by the Board. This interlocked IT project proposals with the company planning process, but was administratively cumbersome and, through its lack of business involvement, failed to give an appropriate priority to several projects of strategic importance.

3   In 1990, a Business Systems Management Board was instituted, consisting of directors from line and staff functions. Responsibility for all IT matters was delegated by the Management Committee to the Board. The three annual meetings of this Board were timed to interlock with the company's strategic planning conferences and with the parallel European Business Systems Management Board, emphasizing a top–down approach to planning.

4   In 1992, UKIIS was incorporated into the new company IBM ISL, as noted earlier. The title of the BSMB was changed to the Business Systems Management Council (BSMC). New responsibilities were assigned for managing the IT investment process and the IT project portfolio. Bids for IT projects from line managers, ISL business/IT consultants and from ISL architecture groups, were set against available skills and resources. The portfolio manager built and maintained an integrated IT plan according to priorities agreed by the BSMC.

Organizational changes have been made in IBM to link IT developments closely to business strategies and to ensure that IT resources are used efficiently. It is the responsibility of the BSMC to ensure that the business receives value for money from the investment in IT. It is in the meetings of this council, and in subsequent staff work, that IT plans and priorities are interlocked and aligned, in terms of resources and time-scales, with overall business and financial plans.

3.2   IT planning in the public sector

The Department of Health establishes its revenue budgets and capital plans for approval by the Treasury and Parliament. It does this from submissions provided by the 14 Regional Health Authorities (RHAs), regarding the funds they require year-on-year to meet their statutory health care targets. Regional Health Authority practices for IT investment planning vary considerably, but the arrangements in Oxford RHA can be cited to give an insight into the process. The Oxford RHA employs some 45 000 people, and is responsible for achieving the public health targets set by government and its own strategic plans. It is responsible for the full range of health care facilities required to service public needs. It has an annual spend of approximately £950 million to fund hospital and community health care services.

Within this region, capital planning for IT was only at regional level, prior to 1991. Capital expenditure plans for individual units within the Region were short term. Capital was allocated annually on the basis of 'the loudest shout'. Capital allocation for IT competed with capital for basic health facilities, such as hospitals. Thus the major capital requirements of the operating units were provided by the RHA. For IT, this capital allocation was applied to the replacement and enhancement of existing information systems as well as the procurement and development of new systems. It covered all expenses for new major developments and equipment, including software and personnel, that is, all one-off project costs. (The revenue expense covers the running and maintenance costs of systems and is not supported from the region.) Major development proposals, prepared mainly by Regional Computer Unit (RCU) staff, were submitted to the Regional Computer Unit Manager, who, with the agreement of a Regional Computer Policy Steering Committee, set priorities and allocated capital resources.

This had changed significantly by 1991. The principle of purchaser/provider, formulated in the Department of Health's policy guidelines, 'Working for Patients', was being applied. The region's IT services had been reorganized. Within the policy guidelines, and following the Regional IT strategic plan, individual health and administrative units began to develop their own IT strategic plans. Contracts for IT services were raised across the region between users and IT departments in the local units, and between them and the central providers of IT in the RCU, as well as other suppliers.

The RCU was cast in a supplier role, and developed contracts for system maintenance and support and for developments. Requirements planning for the region became the role of the RHA Information Division, a small regional HQ function responsible for coordinating the 'purchasing' of IT services across the region. This group has prepared an information strategy setting the policies and directions for information handling in the region and a three year rolling plan for capital expenditure of some £27 million. Currently, they hold most of the skills needed to identify and prioritize requirements for, and to project manage, large systems developments, but detailed elements of these responsibilities will be devolved to operating units within the region, in due course. Indeed, several units have already drawn up their own IT strategies, under the regional IT strategy umbrella. Thus, over a three-year period (maximum) it is intended that control of IT development and services will pass to the operating units of the region, within the region's strategy framework. These units will plan IT investments and purchase the service they require from the most appropriate source.

In summary, over a three-year period it is planned to achieve devolution of authority for funding, other than for certain infrastructure investments, for example shared telecommunications facilities; a fund to promote innovation; and funding for the RHA's own HQ systems. Funding arrangements will provide balanced investment throughout the region, recognizing the pace of change that can be accommodated in different areas and the advantages that focused invest-ment can bring.[1] Units within the RHA will be establishing their own business-led information strategies based on their business plans, incorporating a three year rolling plan, with a process for building annual investment plans and prioritizing and initiating systems projects.

This case study illustrates how many organizations achieve a strategic alignment of IT with the business through a more focused investment in IT which is in line with the priorities of business units.

3.3   IT planning in smaller organizations

For this example we shall take a business unit of 50 people which has successfully used (and expanded the use of), over a period of five years, Siemens Nixdorf mainframe computers with a fully integrated package software, covering order processing, stock control, financial accounting and word processing.

Wacker Chemicals Limited, as the UK subsidiary of the German company Wacker Chemie GmbH, has provided the sales organization for five main product divisions. Three of the divisions handle traditional bulk chemicals of polyvinyl chloride (PVC), silicones and vinyl acetate polymers and organic intermediates. Two divisions specialize in semiconductors and in materials, namely, engineered ceramics and ceramic materials. Each UK sales division has an ultimate sales profit role.

Prior to 1988, IT was highly centralized, mainly in Munich. In 1988, a processor was installed in the United Kingdom with nine local terminals for the traditional application of sales order processing and invoicing; 90% of UK invoices were raised in this country, whether for local stocked items or for goods shipped direct from parent company factories. Sales data were key-entered into a local system and then again in Munich, from telexes sent to the parent company for internal order processing. More recently, a direct link has been established using the International Network Services GE Mark III facility to establish twice daily two-way data transmission, utilizing new software. This development was required by the business's need to be more responsive and to be more efficient by reducing duplicated effort. A total of 22 terminals are now installed.

Business planning in Wacker is traditional. In March and April the parent company sets the overall marketing and manufacturing scenarios with broad estimates of sales targets for each major product division. This continues with the operating divisions and subsidiaries building, bottom–up, their own financial outlook in projected profit and loss accounts and cash flows. For the UK Company Secretary and Accountant, IT expenditure is one more item in the overall business equation.

Individual financial cases are not a formal requirement of the group, for proposed investments. Overall capital spend has to meet corporate ROI criteria and to enable achievement of the Wacker strategic objective for the ratio of equity to total assets in the UK company. However, for local control and reassurance, a normal accounting appraisal will be made, including an assessment of savings and an evaluation of the net present value of an investment. The level of investment is a business judgement made by the Company Secretary and Accountant and the Managing Director. The size and nature of the business enables them to be involved in all aspects of the business and thus to drive investment decisions in this way.

Where specialist skills are needed there is an interface with professionals and technical specialists in the group head office. For example, for the recent major investment in IT, staff of the parent ITD were involved in the systems feasibility study and shepherded the proposals though the technical appraisal process.

Decision-making might seem less formalized than for bigger business units, but the questions are the same for all. Has the investment proved worthwhile? Does it support the business?

Staff are delighted with the terminals, each having hands-on access to the systems. The facilities have removed administrative grind. Staff are less hard-pressed, giving flexibility and leaving time to address new opportunities. The vulnerability of the old systems has been removed and the controls required by BS5750 (for quality) are in place. The increasing flow of information required by head office can be met, with minimum disruption. Product codes and the chart of accounts have been rationalized. For Wacker Chemicals, revenue has grown by 15% over three years, and it is more professional in the service it provides to customers – with no growth in staff numbers. Today's business problems could not have been handled without the investment in IT systems.

Realistic planning, together with strong involvement and leadership in IT development by the Company Secretary and Accountant and by the Managing Director, has helped Wacker Chemicals Limited to answer both questions positively.

3.4 Discussion

The case study at the end of Chapter 1 can now be seen in the context of business planning and of the above examples of IT planning. Our descriptions of corporate planning processes could, at this stage, simply add to Dr Frank's frustration! The next chapter will provide some relief, however, in discussing the relationship between individual project proposals, planning processes and IT resource allocation. For requests placed on central resources (where the IT investment is not better funded by a departmental budget) it is desirable for the project champion to understand the environment and the politics of decision-making. More than this, the champion will need to provide a business case for the project, and to illustrate this the example is discussed again in Chapter 12.

Of the three case studies in this chapter, the first shows that, even for an enterprise (IBM UK) with a well-established planning framework, there is the need for regular reviews of, and changes to, planning and decision processes, to ensure that business objectives are being met. However, until 1992 the **role** of the ITD did not change significantly; organizational effectiveness was enhanced in small, continuous steps.

This contrasts with the second case study (Regional Health). Here, some IT resources and funding were devolved and contracts set up between service suppliers and users, paralleling other business practices. Funding parts of the IT infrastructure centrally, as a business asset rather than a cost, and business applications separately, follows the advice of Keen.[2] Organizational effectiveness flowed from transformed relationships. The approach increased the need for coordinated IT strategies, the value of which is discussed in Chapter 4.

In the first two case studies, committees and procedures are used to achieve a corporate understanding of IT investment. In the smaller business unit of the third example (Wacker), or in any small enterprise, these devices are not so necessary. The reason for the investment is more immediately apparent to the decision-makers; its impact falls largely within their area of operations and accountability. But even small businesses can apply the five stages described in Part 2 to make good investment decisions.

References

1 *Information Strategy in the Oxford Region; Policy Framework*, Oxford Regional Health Authority, Old Road, Headington, Oxford OX3 7LF, 1991.
2 Peter G. W. Keen, *Shaping the Future*, Harvard Business School Press, Harvard, 1991.

4
Planning for profitable projects

4.1   Investment projects

We have considered the basics of business planning and some aspects of IT planning that relate to IT investment approval. We now look at the IT investment project and its relationship to business planning and how both relate to an IT strategy. This discusses the context in which investment decisions are made. If your immediate interest lies in determining the value of an IT project, please read this first section, then skip to Part 2 of the book and return to the rest of this chapter later.

The project is a key management tool for introducing change into the business plan, from one year to the next. It may not always be clear whether the change requires a business project or an IT project, and the distinction between the two is increasingly arbitrary. The same principles apply to both; the differences arise in the assignment of project responsibilities and resources. Some IT projects will only concern the ITD, but most IT projects will (or should) be initiated by business functions. In this case, they became a business project with a strong IT component and with a need for ITD project skills and resources. While recognizing the business nature of most IT projects, for convenience we use the term 'IT project' for projects that are mainly about the application of IT.

In some cases, investment programmes can run for three or four years, for example those concerned with business transformation. The application of IT is part of a larger investment, and this will be increasingly so through the 1990s. Such investment programmes might be seen as a steady process of change, using experience learned on the way to determine the rate and direction of change, rather than creating change through the traditional project. However, there is still a strong case for using a series of projects of manageable size to achieve the change and to realize its benefits.

Therefore the nature of the project and its relationship to planning and investment is worth understanding. More than that, it will not be possible to make a full and proper business case for IT without considering the project.

Table 4.1 The IT project life cycle

Phase	Description	Benefits level
Pre-phase 0	*Initial business proposal.*	Benefits in 'concept'.
Phase 0	Feasibility and project plan, with a *full business case.* Business case committed.	Benefits can be 'calculated'.
Phase 1	Requirements definition	
Phase 2	Systems design. Develop prototypes. *Business case confirmed.*	
Phase 3	Programming and development.	
Phase 4	Test, install and change working practices.	
Phase 5	Review project completion and *audit of results.*	Benefits need to be 'controlled'.

4.1.1 *Project structure and life cycle*

The special characteristics of a project which make it a key tool for implementing change are

- It has a beginning and an end.
- It has agreed levels of resources allocated to it.
- It has a deliverable which is defined in its objectives.
- It proceeds by phased approval.

A task will be given the status of a project, and managed as such, when it is intended to accomplish a significant change.

A practical and comprehensive account of project management is to be found in a series of booklets published by the Institute of Management (IM).[1] The typical phases of any project are described in Book 2 of the series as planning, construction, commissioning and run-up.

IT projects are no different; a more detailed presentation of the above four phases, expressed in traditional IT terminology, is in Table 4.1. Here seven phases are recognized; two for planning (pre-phase 0 and phase 0), three for construction (phases 1, 2 and 3), one for commissioning and run-up (phase 4) and one for audit and review (phase 5). Other project frameworks exist, but we have chosen these well-established phases for IT projects to help in our later discussion of project benefits. (We have retained the nomenclature of 'Pre-phase 0' and 'Phase 0' to emphasize that two essential planning phases exist, before the project is finally committed.) Moreover, recent 'procedures' for project management have focused more on the required management disciplines than on project phases.

Willcocks and Lester, in investigating how IT systems are evaluated,[2] identified five stages in the evaluation cycle, and their model is shown in Fig. 4.1. This gives more emphasis to the later project stages and to the need for feedback to complete the project life cycle. It does not identify the two planning stages (Table 4.1), nor

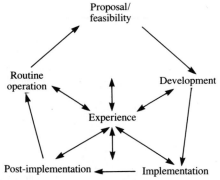

Figure 4.1.   The project evaluation cycle.[2]

the most useful distinction between commissioning and run up of the IM structure.

To be successful a project needs to be structured as shown in Table 4.1, or in a similar way, so that the relevant skills and resources can be applied to each phase and so that the progress of each phase can be monitored. A project also needs to be assigned to a sponsor or an owner and to have a manager nominated, who is responsible for its planning and implementation. Project resources will be taken from both the business and from the ITD. While the ITD is likely to take the lead in project management, support will be needed from line managers and, increasingly, line managers will take a more dominant role in project management. Line managers manage processes within an organizational hierarchy. The majority will need to aquire new skills to manage or work in a project, where team working and equality of authority predominate. To address this, many enterprises are providing management education in project management. However, a single responsibility for managing either a project or a process, but not both, is invariably more effective, if not always practicable.

4.1.2   *The investment planning dilemma*

Projects compete for resources within the business and with each other, mainly in the areas of capital and manpower. The purpose of the business case is to establish what resource is needed to implement the project and what benefits will flow from it. Until the cost and benefits are firm there is a reluctance to commit resources to the project, because, once committed, resources can be difficult to de-commit. However, good estimates for project costs and benefits cannot easily be made until some resource has been committed to the project.

This dilemma is addressed by recognizing that project appraisal is an iterative process, starting at a high level and going to greater levels of detail as the project plan develops. Initially it is important to establish the high level structure of a project, with an outline business case, and then to proceed by implementing smaller sub-projects, consciously taking their benefits early into the business. Shorter project time-scales (less than 12 months) need less faith and give a better basis for comparative measurements.

However, there is no complete answer to this dilemma and in the early stages decisions have to be made with limited information by establishing boundaries (that is making assumptions) within which progress can be made. Planning and forecasting are interdependent, and forecasting is, by definition, a risky activity. The aim should be to establish the business case early and then to update and confirm it at the end of each stage of the project. Project planning can account for 2–8% of the total project expenditure and development time. It is only then that project costs and benefits will have been quantified with sufficient confidence for major resources to be committed to the project.

Good project planning is iterative; the content of the business case evolves and costs and benefits are handled differently at different stages. Three words describing costs and benefits, 'conceptualize', 'calculate' and 'control', were introduced in Chapter 1 and these are now related to project stages.

1 *Pre-phase 0 – Systems development idea and initial business case*   This will be supported by an initial business proposal. At this stage any estimates will be of a very broad nature, and possibly no more than *concepts*.

   The business justification, will assess the project's alignment with business objectives. It will answer questions likely to be asked by those who authorize the proposal, the answers at least indicating orders of magnitude. The minimum initial questions are:

   - Why is the investment being proposed?
   - What change is proposed?
   - How will it be achieved? What are the alternatives?
   - What will the net benefit be? That is, how will successful completion be measured?
   - How much will it cost to implement the change?
   - What happens if it is not implemented?

2 *Phase 0 – Feasibility planning and full business case*   By this stage, some quantification will be possible and necessary. The main costs and benefits will be *calculated*. They will be presented within a financial justification, to demonstrate (or not) the financial acceptability of the proposal. The intangible benefits will also be included.

   The previous questions will be taken to further levels of detail. Additional questions to be answered at this stage, prior to committing major resources, are:

   - Who will implement it?
   - What will they do to implement it?

- When do they start, when do they complete and when do we check on progress?
- What is the risk that it will not be successful?

The typical contents of the business case at this stage will be:

- High-level requirements
- Outline design and alternatives
- Initial estimates for cash flows
- Assumptions and constraints
- Detailed phase 1 estimates
- Cost of doing nothing

3   *Phases 1 and 2 – Requirements and design*   The allocation of major resources is imminent and purchases will be authorized within the normal management systems for *controlling* expenditure. At this stage, an assessment is normally made of financial alternatives, for example, lease or purchase, to optimize the use of funds.

For each of these three stages, procedures will be needed to guide the preparation and appraisal of the business case for the project. The procedures will set the appropriate responsibilities, tasks and expectations at each project stage.

4.1.3   *Business and investment project planning*

The purpose of a project is to drive the change from one business plan to another. Therefore, the integration of project and business plans is not only desirable, it is vital. Ultimately, the achievement of project benefits can only be assessed in the project's contribution to the implementation of the new business plan. The acceptability of a business case should depend on how well it fits with the business plan and its final success on the part it plays in the plan's achievement. However, there are problems and solutions.

Firstly, planning may only have a low priority – firefighting and getting on with the job are more fun! So often business planning does not get the attention it deserves from line management; it remains the preserve of staff groups and becomes 'bureaucracy'. This is a question of 'management style' and can be addressed as such by the Chief Executive Officer. Planning becomes a 'real' activity when performance against plan is measured and rewarded and when management controls are set up to ensure that, where plans are not being achieved, action is taken to address variations from plan. Planning must be continuous and not a once-a-year activity.

Secondly, a linkage implies that both business planning (for both the strategic and operational time frames) and project appraisal procedures exist in a company and that there are procedures within the management systems to link them. It may be that either one or the other does not really exist (except in the mind of the planners) or that neither exist, or that they are being implemented on a scale which is not compatible with the size of enterprise. What is most likely is that no strong commitment or clear procedures exist to link them.

Thirdly, selecting those projects which will most support the achievement of a new business plan has to be done on the basis of more than a simple financial case, even where one exists. Often, IT resources can seem to be allocated on the basis of which business manager is best at selling the need for and use of IT, that is, in response to 'the person who shouts loudest'.

Fourthly, although business plans and project plans both iterate down through successive levels of detail, it is unfortunate that they rarely do so in step. The timing of projects is uncertain, for both their beginning and end; they do not synchronize naturally with the business planning cycle. The alignment needed to ensure that the input from project plans meets the time-scales of the business planning cycle is shown in Fig. 4.2.

4.1.4 *Integrating business and project planning*

To bring together project business cases and business plans, the content and level of detail provided by a business case should vary for each planning stage, as follows.

1 For the strategic plan:
   - Major project investment proposals, each with an outline business case. (The costs and savings are likely to be at a *conceptual* level.)
   - Overall ITD spend, relative to other business units, supported by ITD capacity forecasts and justification.

2 For the operating plan:
   - Smaller and sub-project capital and expense proposals, with either a firm outline business cases, or full business cases for projects which have completed Phase 0. Where options exist, a full financial appraisal of each option is likely to be needed. (Costs and savings should be at the *calculate* level.)
   - IT budgets, proposed resource levels and phasing of major expenses.

3 For implementation:
   - Expenditure requests with financial sourcing and an analysis of supplier options. The full business case will have added to it a financial appraisal of the options. (Costs *and* savings will enter the *control* stage, by being incurred and reflected in current budgets.

In summary, business planning is a calendar-driven rather than event-driven activity. It is a cross-functional activity. To ensure that it achieves its objectives it needs to have the commitment of all involved, through their participation in its preparation and implementation. It is vital that business cases for large projects

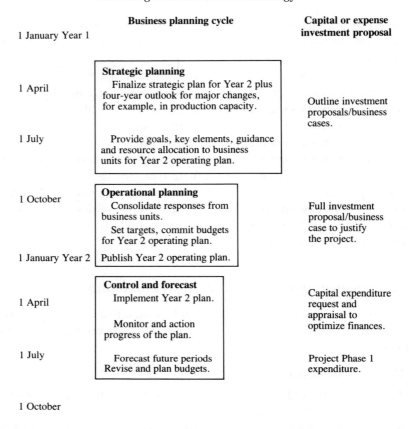

Figure 4.2.   The business planning and investment appraisal cycles together.

are available for inclusion in the strategic plan and that the planning for sub-projects, while continuing throughout the year, is aligned with operational planning activities and time-scales. Management systems and procedures will need to drive the integration of projects and business plans. Many companies are now addressing the problems, identified above, in order to integrate better business planning and project appraisal, to help align IT with business goals, to select the most beneficial projects and to ensure that the projected benefits are achieved.

4.2   Setting priorities – resource allocation

We have considered the planning and allocation of resources to the ITD within the context of business planning (Chapter 2). Now, with a clearer view of the IT project, we can return to this topic. In allocating resources to the ITD there will be constant tension with the needs of other functions. How much to spend on IT overall, both for existing operations and for new investment, is as important as measuring the direct value of individual IT investment projects.

Furthermore, 'getting the priorities right' is as important for organizations as it is for individuals. In both cases it requires a clear view of objectives and an appreciation of both internal and external constraints. Deciding on the priority involves identifying the root problem or key opportunity area which is to be addressed. An understanding of how priorities can be set is of vital importance both to the annual resource allocation and to the approval of an IT project business case (discussed in Chapter 12).

Resource planning for ITD will cover capital budgets and expense budgets. Within these the main levels of resource will be set for machines, personnel, space and real estate, software and supplies. The planning is often performed by a financial planner within the ITD or it may be done by other functions responsible for business and financial planning for the enterprise as a whole, taking input from the ITD. Approval of the strategic and operating plans, including those of the ITD, will be the responsibility of the main board. Ranking and approval of investment projects is generally delegated by the board to a smaller group of directors.

4.2.1 Strategic priorities

At the beginning of the business planning cycle decisions will be made, based on overall business priorities, regarding the level of resource which should be allocated to IT. The strategic plan will define the ITD resource levels in terms of personnel, processing capability, software costs and other expenses. Staff planning will be a key component. The strategic plan will relate the ITD resource, shown inside the double box of Fig. 4.3, to that provided for other functions. The level of resource allocated to the ITD is very relevant to project priority setting, in that it establishes a key constraint within which the relative priorities of competing projects will be established.

Those who determine IT strategic priorities will need to review the strategic business plans and then to relate them specifically to the use of information, as a key resource, within the enterprise. This is particularly necessary where the strategic plan is not fully developed, visible or agreed. Such a review can be very productive when using an executive team-based planning method, such as the process quality management approach outlined in Step 1 of our business case methodology (Chapter 8).

In considering how much to spend on IT, two points will be made. Firstly, some of the creative processes for establishing priorities (see Chapter 12) will indicate opportunities for exploiting technology, and this may lead to a justified increase in the overall level of resource allocated to IT. Indeed, it is vital that opportunities for achieving greater competitiveness through technology are not overlooked.

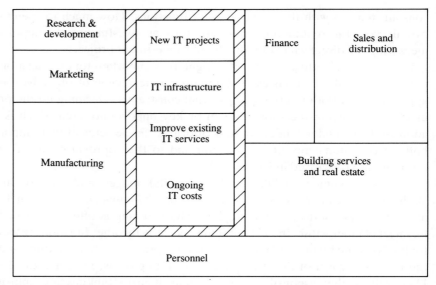

Figure 4.3.   Allocation of resources according to strategic priorities.

Secondly, the justification for making ITD resources available for systems developments will depend on meritorious business cases coming forward to take up the allocation, and this emphasizes the importance of good business cases. The constraint (provided it is not a straitjacket) of limited ITD resources and a disciplined approach to setting priorities will help to ensure that value for money is continually achieved from IT. (Contracting out is increasingly being used to ease resource and skill limitations, to contain project risks and to cap the potential escalation of project costs.)

4.2.2   *Operational priorities*

Within the context of overall IT resources, priorities need to be set between IT projects. In 'How to rank computer projects',[3] Buss has rightly concluded that, 'Without doubt, the best way to set priorities is to make them a by-product of some formal planning process at the corporate or business-unit level. Unfortunately, few organizations have planning processes so explicit and orderly that they can rely solely on them for determining information systems priorities'. And, it can be added, that the planning process has to be proven in terms of its ability to achieve consensus and action across the organization for it to be of help in setting IT priorities.

However effective the formal planning processes are, it is often valuable, in setting and reviewing operational IT priorities, to conduct an executive review of business plans and goals, as described above for strategic priorities.

Three inputs are needed to determine the priority of an IT investment project

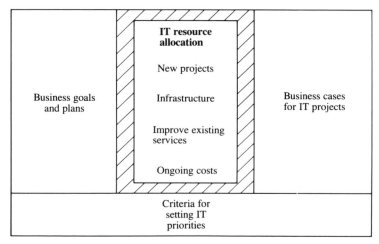

Figure 4.4. Setting operational priorities.

and they are illustrated in Fig. 4.4. The first input is the *business goals* and plans, determined during strategic and operational planning cycles. The second is the *project proposal* and the third input is the *criteria* by which the priority will be determined.

The inputs are not independent of each other. The business plans might well, indeed should, be influenced by what can be achieved with technology. The weighting given to each criterion will be determined by the business goals. As the project proceeds through its phases, a firmer definition of its scope and more detailed information of its costs and benefits will become available, so that priorities once agreed may need to be reviewed for their continuing relevance.

The activity of establishing priorities is thus bounded on the one hand by business plans and on the other by project definitions. It will involve the executive and users and IT managers. It is both a creative and an analytical activity. The processes will not be mutually exclusive and may be used in conjunction with each other, but considering them independently helps to clarify the issues involved. The process of deciding on project priorities is dealt with in more detail in Chapter 12.

The main priority-setting activity needs to take place annually and concurrently with operational planning, although amendments to priorities may have to be considered throughout the year. Negotiations will take place to determine which projects can be included in the next current plan, in view of the resource levels set by the strategic plan.

Perhaps the main problems in setting operational level IT priorities are in making available the necessary time to discuss the priorities in a structured fashion and in maintaining consistent priorities over a period of time. This naturally leads into the question of the IT strategy.

4.3   The IT strategy

The objectives of an IT corporate strategy have been described as:

> ... to plan the implementations of IT systems over a medium to long term horizon and to give guidelines on all IT related matters. Such a plan has to be written down and made available to all managers in the form of a strategic document prescribing and coordinating all activities relating to IT investments.[4]

There is evidence that key problems are reduced in severity through preparing and having a strategy (Fig. 4.5).

An IT strategy will often be formulated apart from the annual strategic and operational planning activities. It may be done by a task force or by a group of people with the job specially assigned to them. It is vital to have an IT strategy to achieve alignment of IT with the business. It is therefore necessary to have a business strategy on which to base the IT strategy.

The business strategy may not be fully understood by those needing to develop an IT strategy. The business strategy may be poorly documented or communicated. Even well-documented strategies can be out of date and not reflect current executive intentions. It is always worth validating the business strategy before creating or updating the IT strategy.

An IT strategy relates IT to the primary aims of the business in a comprehensive statement of what should be done to further these aims over a three to five year time frame; it provides a framework for the efficient and effective use of IT

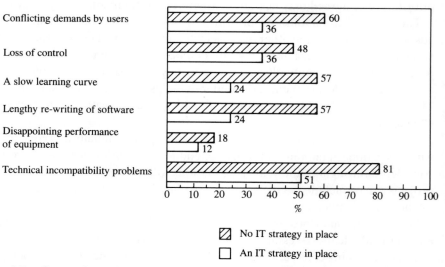

Figure 4.5.   Comparison of problem severities with and without an IT strategy.[4]

resources and it promotes an integrated approach to development, which is one prerequisite for building flexible and consistent systems. An IT strategy must contain a prioritized portfolio of IT applications, business systems or information systems. If this is all it contains, then the terms 'applications strategy' or 'information systems (IS) strategy' could be more appropriate. A comprehensive IT strategy may include many other elements, such as an overview of business process and data structures, directions for technical platforms and policies and guidelines for ITD skills and resources and for ownership and organization. Thus, the three potential elements of an IT strategy are the systems and the technical and management strategies for the use of IT. In the words of Henderson, the IT strategy will embrace systematic competencies, the scope of the use of technology and IT governance.[5] Described in too much detail it will tend to be inflexible; described in too little detail, an IT strategy will appear to be academic and conceptual.

Typical reasons for preparing an IT strategy are:

- The ITD has reached the end of a major development and future priorities need to be restated.
- There is dissatisfaction with existing systems and the value they are perceived to bring to the business.
- The business has changed, or is about to change, its direction or organization, and a major new IT development may be needed.
- Relationships between users and IT are unsatisfactory and a new 'contract' is needed between them.
- There are no agreed priorities for IT development.
- A better level of integration is needed across systems development, particularly with respect to corporate and local systems.
- There is no long-term view of business requirements on which to base technical architectures.

Many enterprises have prepared an IT strategy. However, in their survey, Hochstrasser and Griffiths[4] found that only 34% of companies have an IT strategy which sets out the involvement of IT strategically across divisions, beyond the short term. Other concerns have been articulated by M. J. Earl.[6] He found firstly that IT strategies were not always implemented and secondly that the process and the method for arriving at the strategy were not entirely satisfactory.

Earl identified five main approaches used to derive an IT strategy. These were generally a composite of activities including studies, events, daily interactions, partnerships and crises between the ITD and users. However, each approach has its own emphasis. This emphasis, and the propensity of each approach to generate applications of competitive advantage, are summarized in Table 4.2. Earl's work shows that methodologies alone will not suffice; they must be used in conjunction with visible business plans and management understanding.

As management consultants, we have produced IT strategies using a combi-

Table 4.2   Competitive advantage analysis.[6] Application frequency per firm identified

Planning approach	Emphasis of planning approach	Application frequency
Business-led	Based on existing business plans and strategies	4
Method-driven	Formal analytical method, usually by consultants	1.5
Administrative	Enterprise-wide resource planning	3.6
Technological	The search for business, application, data and application architectures	2.6
Organizational	Process to aid management learning about the contribution of IT	4.8

nation of the 'business-led', 'method-driven' and 'organizational' approaches, described by Earl, through the customized use of the application planning study. Recognizing the importance of continuing to produce and to refine IT strategies, IBM has now developed methodologies for aligning IT with the needs of the business and for developing comprehensive plans for its application. The methodologies will be used by IBM consultants on a worldwide basis through the 1990s.

The methodologies provide for IT strategy and planning and business transformation, through business process re-engineering. These lead into methodologies for information integration (which provides a tool for rapid prototyping) and application development. The IT strategy and planning methodology embodies strong diagnostic and analytical techniques while maintaining an open approach to their application in a variety of situations. The framework of the methodology is depicted in the 13 modules of Fig. 4.6.

For IBM, the initial selection of a methodology is guided by the alignment model of Henderson and Venkatraman.[5] This model, outlined in Fig. 4.7, expresses the interdependency of business strategy and IT strategy and of the business and IT infrastructures which are established to implement the strategies. The full model gives a basis for thinking about the position of an enterprise in its market, about its internal structure, about its position in the technology 'market' and about its application of IT. A consideration of these factors will indicate which three, for an enterprise at any point in time, are best addressed to achieve the alignment of IT with business needs. For example, in one case the business strategies might be stable, but a need exists to redefine the IT strategy, with a consequent restructuring of the IT infrastructure. In this case the IT strategy and planning methodology would be relevant first. Alternatively, with a stated business strategy, there might be a more pressing need to restructure the organizational and process infrastructure and then to consider the impact of this on the IT strategy or infrastructure. In this case, the business transformation methodology would be relevant first.

The Henderson and Venkatraman model is important because it offers a broader based discussion of the use of an appropriate planning-based approach to

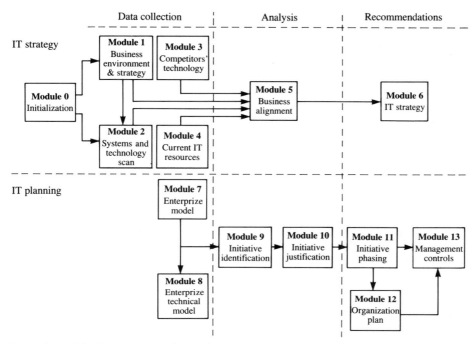

Figure 4.6. The IT strategy and planning methodology. (*Source*: IBM Consulting Group.)

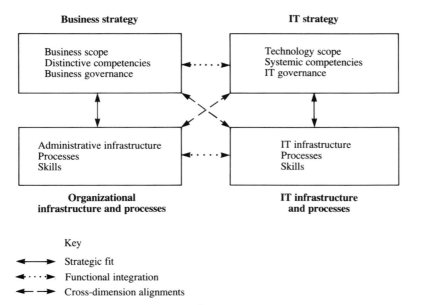

Figure 4.7. The strategic alignment model.[5] (*Source*: reprinted by permission of *Business Quarterly*, published by the Western Business School, The University of Western Ontario, London, Ontario, Canada, Winter '91 issue.)

the alignment of IT with the business. Other alignment factors are discussed in Chapter 6.

Although preparing the IT strategy is a good start, it is not the end. Implementing a strategy, whether that of the business[7] or that of IT[8] presents the more significant challenge. Ownership of the strategy needs to be established to ensure that it is implemented. Often it is owned by an IT steering group of senior managers or by the CIO. Having an IT strategy affects an organization's understanding of the business case for IT and how it is implemented will impact the value achieved from investment in IT.

References

1 *Total Project Management*, The Asset Management Group of the Institute of Management (formerly the British Institute of Management), London, 1991.
2 Leslie Willcocks and Stephanie Lester, Information Systems Investments: evaluation at the feasibility stage of projects, *Technovation*, **II**(5), 1991, pp. 283–302.
3 Martin D. J. Buss, How to rank computer projects, *Harvard Business Review*, January–February, 1983.
4 Beat Hochstrasser and Catherine Griffiths, *Controlling IT Investment: Strategy and Management*, Chapman & Hall, London, 1991.
5 John C. Henderson and N. Venkatraman, Understanding Strategic Management, *Business Quarterly*, School of Business Administration, The University of Western Ontario, Winter 1991. (*See also* John C. Henderson and N. Venkatraman, Strategic Alignment: Leveraging information technology for transforming organizations, *IBM Systems J*, **32**(1), 1993, pp. 4–16.)
6 Michael J. Earl, London Business School, Experiences in Strategic Information Systems Planning, *MIS Quarterly*, March 1993.
7 Arnold S. Judson, *Making Strategy Happen – Transforming Plans into Reality*, Basil Blackwell, Oxford, 1990.
8 Albert L. Lederer and Vijay Sethi, Meeting the Challenges of Information Systems Planning, *Long Range Planning*, **25**(2), 1992, pp. 69–80.

5
Establishing value for money from IT

Perhaps the questions in the introduction to Part 1 still haunt us. They were, 'Does my investment in IT represent value for money?', 'Can I spend my money on something else more in line with my current goals?' and 'Has my investment in IT been well managed in the past?'. We will summarize our progress in addressing the questions.

So far we have emphasized the importance of aligning the use of IT with the present and future strategic needs of the enterprise. We have discussed how IT planning contributes to this, and alignment is addressed further in Chapter 6. However, the answers to the questions will depend both on what investments are made in IT and on how the investments are subsequently managed. Relevant planning procedures will help to achieve the alignment of IT and provide a basis for benefits management. Measurement and control of ITD performance are also necessary. What techniques and measures are available to manage IT? Now we review some of the performance measures available for the effective management of IT. If these, or similar management controls, are not in place then there can be no certainty that IT is used effectively in the enterprise. This chapter concludes by describing methodologies for evaluating the effectiveness of IT investment planning and management.

5.1 Measures of performance external to the enterprise

The performance of enterprises is often compared by reference to their published financial accounts. The standards for comparing the expenditure on IT are less well defined and agreed than those for financial accounts. Therefore valid comparisons are even more difficult. Many surveys have produced comparative IT statistics, but it is hard to guarantee the quality and consistency of the base data. As overall measures they are helpful, but relevant analyses and good control require access to detailed and comparable information. Nevertheless, these limitations are no reason for not using that information which is available to help manage investment in IT.

Table 5.1   Categorized IT budget forecasts by industry,[1] 1992 (£000s per installation, totals also related to turnover; figures in parentheses are percentages of total for industry)

	Hardware	Software	Telecomms	Staff	User spend	Total (=100%)	Total (% of turnover)
Manufacturing	821 (31)	309 (12)	143 (5)	889 (34)	488 (18)	2650	0.7
Process industry	939 (25)	623 (17)	73 (2)	1504 (41)	548 (15)	3687	1.4
Retail/distribution	1064 (32)	384 (12)	279 (9)	1291 (39)	263 (8)	3281	1.6
Utilities	1435 (26)	464 (8)	240 (4)	1702 (31)	1724 (31)	5565	1.7
Finance	2270 (29)	1099 (14)	439 (6)	2930 (38)	999 (13)	7737	2.8
Education/research	400 (29)	143 (11)	30 (2)	377 (28)	407 (30)	1357	2.3
Public administration	885 (31)	291 (10)	121 (4)	985 (34)	607 (21)	2889	1.5
Computer services	840 (31)	210 (7)	210 (7)	1350 (49)	125 (5)	2735	27.4
Other	574 (33)	418 (24)	104 (6)	574 (33)	73 (4)	1743	0.9
UK average	1163 (30)	444 (11)	205 (5)	1334 (34)	802 (20)	3948	1.5

A start can be made with the relative amount spent on IT. Typical of these statistics are those published annually in the United Kingdom by Price Waterhouse. One of the tables of figures provided in their 1992/93 *Information Technology Review*[1] provides a summary of budget forecasts for major industry segments (Table 5.1). This table shows total IT spend ranging from 0.7% to 2.8% of turnover, with the exception of computer services where the spend is substantially higher. These are average figures; budgets for specific enterprises will vary, and particularly from year to year, in line with their investment cycle.

Some industry sectors and groupings of enterprises which might in other ways be in competition, collate their own statistics. Such comparisons are normal for the public sector, where commercial and competitive constraints are less, the need for public accountability is greater and the business goals and environments of operational units are often more similar. This comparative information is used by the UK National Audit Office.

IT budgets can be expressed as percentages of revenue, as above, or as IT spend per employee. These alternatives often give contradictory results when making comparisons across enterprises or between an enterprise and the average figures for its industry. This points to the need to use such comparisons with caution, to indicate trends rather than absolute measures.

Many investigators have looked for direct evidence of the value of IT. Strassman's analysis showed no correlation between shareholder returns or return on assets and the spend on IT.[2] Similarly, Hochstrasser and Griffiths found that '. . . no statistical correlation exists between the overall amount spent on IT and actual business success'.[3] However, it does not necessarily follow that there is no bottom line benefit from the use of IT; it does mean that IT is not generally the predominating influence on these measures of performance. Indeed, what one factor has been identified as having a predominating influence on the performance of an enterprise over a period of time? Findings more consistent with our own experience come from the KEW/*Computer Weekly* survey of manufacturing companies, namely, that 'Use of IT in UK manufacturing has reached a new landmark: one half of the companies in this sector now believe that IT is making a substantial contribution to their business objectives'.[4]

Shareholder returns and return on assets are coarse measures; finer parameters can be used. These will be specific to the industry or the enterprise and may be, for example, IT spend compared with stock turn, product sales, customer enquiries, and specific items of expense. Weill and Olsen conclude, in common with other investigators, that better-performing enterprises contain expenditure on IT within defined limits and use it effectively, as for all the resources they use.[5]

Most of the reported figures necessarily focus on the level of expenditure, rather than on its usefulnes to the enterprise. The next level of external information concerns a comparison of those projects and technologies in which similar enterprises are investing. The chief executive who wants to be sure that the company is spending wisely on IT, will seek to understand what the company's competitors are doing with technology and what the company might also do. In this, IT is no different from any other new or changing area of the business; it requires an informed appraisal of the marketplace, of the positioning of competing players and of their suppliers.

5.2   Measures of performance within the enterprise

If value for money from the use of IT is an issue, then it may be either because value is not delivered, or because the value is not recognized. How 'value' is to be recognized needs to be agreed by providers and users of IT at all levels. If 'value' is to be improved then measures of performance need to be established and reported. Some of these measures may be subjective and some may be numerical; both of these are quite usual in measuring the use of any resource. It is important that the ITD sets up management systems that will enable value to be seen and to be discussed. The full benefit of this will only emerge with time as procedures are refined and as trends are identified. Because the extending use of IT brings continual change to the enterprise, those who manage this resource, namely the IT Department, have a special responsibility to ensure that their contribution to the business is evaluated and recognized.

Measurement can be made at different levels. Strassman has proposed the use of Return on Management™ (the ratio of management value added to management costs), as one basis for tracking the value of IT.[2] But at this level there has been no noticable correlation between the overall performance of a firm and its investment in IT. At a lower level, Strassman recounts the practice of the Xerox Information Services Division, which '. . . charged a standard activity price for every product, such as screen transactions, reports, checks and invoices. . . . Top management judged the productivity of the Division by its ability to take down unit prices at least 15% per year while showing a profit'.

There are no established standards for measuring the value delivered by the

ITD. There is no statutory framework within which to report performance; information accounting has received much less attention than factory accounting.

However, in the early 1980s Rockhart noted that the ITDs most successful in delivering value for money paid close attention to their CSFs (critical success factors).[6] The management of IT has been compared to other technical functions. Writing in the *Sloan Management Review*, Adler and co-authors have noted that:[7]

> Three TFS (Technical Functions Strategy) characteristics show up repeatedly as indicators of sustained technical accomplishment and business success:
>
> - The technical function's overall posture and direction are clearly stated in successively more detailed versions – mission, objectives, strategic plans – and they are broadly accepted within the function and throughout the business.
> - The technical function manages technology as a 'business', with due attention to its key processes, resources, and internal and external linkages . . . .
> - The TFS can adapt as managers assess the strengths and weaknesses of their function's capabilities base and the opportunities and threats presented by the evolving market.

There are enterprises which use credible measures, and it is from the best-of-breed practice that others can select and design their own. Methods for measuring performance include:

(a) A regular executive review of ITD strategic and operational plans and policies. This might be performed by the IT steering committee.
(b) Reviews of the value of both proposed and completed IT projects, by both executive and line managers. Here round table meetings and management walk-abouts have their place. The user perception of the ITD is needed, rather than an ITD view of the user perception.
(c) A regular report from the ITD, similar to a company's annual report. The list of contents of this report is described by Amos[8] and covers:
    1 Financial position
    2 Computing capacity
    3 Support to user functions
    4 Key ITD performance indicators
    5 ITD staffing and experience
    6 User satisfaction survey results
    7 Strategic impact of IT
    8 Future directions and opportunities
(d) More frequent and direct reports on key measurable performance parameters such as:
    - The cost of IT service delivery, expressed as trends in business transaction costs, for example, for invoices.

- Service level achievement, such as response times.
- Function points (or lines of program code) produced and supported per person in the ITD.
- Recorded errors in new and old function points.
- User satisfaction surveys.

Based on IT practices within IBM UK, Jones groups these and other performance measures under the heading of Service Efficiency, Service Effectiveness and Accounting System.[8] Systems management controls are also described in IBM corporate publications.[9]

Other related approaches have been described. Keen has pointed to the value of an IT asset balance sheet which identifies enterprise-wide equipment, software, and data storage costs – the starting point for management control.[10] Carlson and McNurlin have summarized the work of Partnership for Research in Information Systems Management (PRISM), which is a research service of the Index Group and Hammer and Company.[11] Based on research with 50 companies, this work concentrated on measurements in the four areas of ITD performance, health, user satisfaction and delivered value (mainly ROI). Carlson and McNurlin conclude that there is no easy and direct answer to the question, 'What is the value of our IT investment to our business?' Any measurement programme should seek to bring users and ITD closer together, '. . . so that they are more likely to agree on what constitutes value, without requiring precise measurements'.

Also reported in 'Measuring the Value of Information Systems',[11] is an outline of the IBM Corporate Information Systems' information processing (IP) indices. These indices are collected under four focus areas, covering:

1   Contribution to the business:
    Business case results
    Users' opinion of IP importance and satisfaction with IP
2   IP resources:
    Annual IP expense by business function
    Annual IP expense by IP activity
    Year-end headcount levels of IP people by IP activity
3   IP performance:
    Service delivery process quality
    Application delivery process quality
    Installed applications and operations quality
    Operations productivity
    Installed application support productivity
    Application delivery productivity
4   IP health:
    IP–business alignment
    IP employee vitality

Ongoing support excellence
Introduction of change excellence
Auditors of IP activities

This does not appear to leave much unmeasured! In the UK, the IBM IT function
(ISL) has developed its own management systems and controls to demonstrate
year-on-year improvements in performance. ISL frequently shares details of its IT
measurement practices with other organizations and provides consultancy in ITD
productivity and service improvement. A similar service is provided by others,
such as CSC Index in their Performance Enhancement Programme.

Measures of the business contribution of IT are also discussed in 'Getting Value
from Information Technology'.[12] Here, the Butler Cox Foundation identify five
measurement approaches, no one approach giving the right answer, but together
providing a basis for an enterprise to establish its own procedures. These
measures can be summarized as follows:

- External performance measures can be easily misinterpreted, but provide a
  basis for debate and analysis.
- Internal systems performance measures, while being important management
  controls, do not indicate the business contribution of IT.
- User satisfaction surveys provide important feedback, but do not measure
  'value of IT'.
- Methods of calculating the value of IT to the business can be hard to apply on a
  consistent basis and can be unrealistic.
- The business contribution of IT should be related to key business performance
  measures, such as sales or service volumes and expenses.

The theme of balanced measurement is developed by Kaplan and Norton.[13]
Their balanced score card for measuring business performance from the perspectives of finance, customer, innovation and learning and internal business process,
is equally applicable to IT.

Martin, on the basis of his survey,[14] draws a significant conclusion:

Companies possessed detailed measures of IS resources, and of service levels.
But evidence on the effectiveness of IS performance in the central area of
applications development remains scanty. In the context of declining revenues,
and apparently inflexible IS costs, the ability to demonstrate performance in the
central area of applications development not simply through service availability
will become of major importance.

Application development is one area for improvement, but there are others.
Process analysis and ABC (Activity Based Costing) principles can be used to
investigate cost profiles and to identify cost drivers and cost sensitive areas. IT
profiling techniques and a cost model are used by the IBM Integrated Systems
Solution Corporation to achieve performance improvements and reductions in

IT costs. Such cost models may then be used to develop pricing models for IT services.

The final salutory observation is that the above refers almost entirely to that investment in IT made through the ITD. However, there is a substantial and far less monitored spend on IT in user departments. In 1991 it was expected that, for all enterprises, around 22% of the total IT budget would be by users outside the remit of IT management.[15] In larger companies the amount spent outside the ITD is likely to be 37%, which '. . . is indicative of the trend toward the new leaner and meaner IT department of the 1990s'.

ITD can and must demonstrate a continued year-on-year better price/ performance ratio through the better use of all its resources. So too must other functions which have IT resources in their budgets. Distributed performance measures are needed to match the continuing distribution of IT. The principles of IT investment decisions need to be understood by functional line managers, as well as the ITD.

The question is often asked, 'Am I getting value from my IT investment?' A more helpful question is, 'How can I know if I am getting value?' To help in answering that question, three workshops which have been run by IBM UK Management Consulting are outlined below.

5.3   Assessment of planning and management of IT

Each workshop has its own emphasis and reviews the status and effectiveness of IT planning, the management of IT and the interrelationships between ITD and other functions.

5.3.1   Planning procedures workshop

Whether an organization has developed its own planning procedures or whether it uses proprietary business planning methodologies, each organization will still have issues to resolve in connection with their planning process. Some will be in need of an overhaul, while others may simply need tuning. The planning process itself will benefit from being planned

The task requires 5 to 10 days and is promoted by an executive sponsor. It uses a team of key managers to develop a comprehensive, practical and committed planning process. The main steps of the activity are:

- Review project proposal and investment appraisal procedures.
- Review the business planning process.
- Determine the current roles of each business function in the preparation, concurrence and decision-making stages of planning.
- Identify and analyse problems.
- Determine the aims of the 'owners' of the planning process.

- Understand the constraints of the implementors.
- Draw up an action plan and propose a project to implement the proposed procedures and management systems, including the provision of the appropriate guidelines and training.

5.3.2 Information systems health assessment

This is a diagnostic workshop in which the senior ITD management team determine the ITD missions, goals, CSFs and the resulting priorities and process improvement areas. The workshop runs for two days, typically for six to eight ITD managers and is often followed by other workshops and seminars to address critical topics in more detail.

5.3.3 Constraints review

Three main groups are involved in the use of IT: the enterprise executives who ultimately foot the bill for IT; the IT group who provide the specialist skills; and the line managers who use IT to support their business systems. They all see the benefits and problems of IT from their own point of view. There is potential for confrontation.

The constraints review is an intensive one-day workshop for two senior representatives from each of the different groups. The workshop generally starts with a team briefing the evening before, in the presence of the sponsor. Concurrent syndicate sessions are run during the workshop, which concludes at the end of the day with a feedback session to the sponsor. The agreed problems which could bedevil any proposed implementation or exploitation of IT are set out and recommendations made to address them.

Aligning IT with the business and gaining value for money from IT are both affected by the quality of IT planning and control. However, there are other ways of achieving IT and business alignment, and these are discussed in the next chapter.

References

1 *Information Technology Review 1992/93*, Price Waterhouse, London, 1992.
2 Paul A. Strassman, *The Business Value of Computers*, The Information Economics Press, New Canaan, Connecticut, 1990.
3 Beat Hochstrasser and Catherine Griffiths, *Controlling IT Investment: Strategy and Management*, Chapman & Hall, London, 1991.
4 Relating IT Practice to Business Strategy, *Computer Weekly Special Report* No. 4, KEW Associates, 1990.
5 P. Weill and M. Olsen, Managing investment in information technology: Mini case examples and implications, *MIS Quarterly*, **13**(1), March 1989.
6 John F. Rockart, *The Changing Role of the Information Systems Executive: A Critical*

Success Factors Perspective, Center for Information Systems Research, Sloan School of Management, Massachusetts Institute of Technology, April 1982.

7 Paul S. Adler, D. William McDonald and Fred MacDonald, Strategic Management of Technical Functions, *Sloan Management Review*, Winter 1992.

8 Tim Lincoln (ed.), *Managing Information Systems for Profit*, Wiley Series on Information Systems, John Wiley & Sons, Chichester, 1990.

9 *A Management System for the Information Business: Volume II Service*, IBM GE 20-0749; *Volume IV Managing Information Systems Resources*, IBM GE 20-0751. Obtainable from IBM National Enquiry Centre, London.

10 Peter G. W. Keen, *Shaping the Future*, Harvard Business School Press, Harvard, 1991.

11 Walter M. Carlson and Barbara C. McNurlin, Measuring the Value of Information Systems, *I/S Analyzer Special Report*, United Communications Group, 1989.

12 Getting Value from Information Technology, *Research Report 75*, June 1990, Research Findings of CSC Index, formerly Butler Cox Foundation.

13 Robert S. Kaplan and David P. Norton, The Balanced Scorecard – Measures That Drive Performance, *Harvard Business Review*, January–February 1992.

14 Roderick Martin, *IS Resources and Effectiveness 1990*, RDP 91/5, Oxford Institute of Information Management, 1991.

15 *Information Technology Review 1990/91*, Price Waterhouse, London, 1990.

6
More value for money – aligning IT with enterprise objectives

This chapter considers three more factors, in addition to complementary planning processes, which establish the value of IT to, and alignment of IT with, the business. They are:

- Leadership of the ITD.
- Charging out the costs of IT to the user departments.
- Organization of the ITD.

Keen has claimed that, 'The key to alignment is relationships, not "strategy"'.[1] Finance is also a powerful persuader, so our three further factors include that too.

6.1   IT leadership

In some situations, where IT has been well integrated, the answer is to be found in an IT leadership which has established a good orientation towards the business. The head of IT, or the Chief Information Officer (CIO), has ensured that the business and IT strategies are linked and interdependent.

From our observations in many clients' assignments, the importance of visionary, business-based, technically balanced, people orientated leadership, in achieving the necessary synergy is beyond doubt. Although these necessary qualities are not likely to be disputed, there is less certainty regarding the appointment to the board of the head of IT. Two differing viewpoints are as follows:[2]

Peter Morgan, Director General of the (British) Institute of Directors (1990–   ) and formerly Corporate Services Director of IBM UK argues that only directors working in organizations where IT is inextricably linked to the business can expect to join the board. Where IT is subsumed by the business areas it services, such promotion is unlikely.

Steve Shirley, President of the British Computer Society (1989–1990) and Founder Director of the FI Group, argues in favour of board level responsibility . . . 'Some initiatives have started with IT. Having ideas may be hard, pushing them through is harder. That's when directors with knowledge of both business and IT are needed', argues Shirley . . . in the same way as the company secretary, usually a board member, looks after questions of legality, an IT director takes responsibility for vital tasks such as feasibility, systems compatibility and data security.

In any enterprise, it can be a Board decision as to how strongly IT is linked with the business. The KEW investigation found that organizations appointing a board member with direct responsibility for IT are more likely to perform better financially.[3] We cannot see how, in most circumstances, information resources can be properly established and directed without the involvement of the person accountable for them, the CIO, being part of the main policy and direction-setting body, particularly within large enterprises.

Applegate and Elam, in the *MIS Quarterly*, found that in the period 1986–89, of newly appointed CIOs, approximately half were hired externally, had more than five years' experience in managing a non-IT function and increasingly reported directly to the CEO. Such reporting needs to be supported by acceptance and proper evaluation of the CIO role by the senior management team.[4]

At whatever level in the hierarchy, the CIO will be concerned with contributing to strategic planning; creating the systems infrastructure; promoting IT education at all levels; and managing the bridge between the ITD and the users. Bargioni, as the Head of Information Systems for the Beecham Group of Companies within the UK (now SmithKline Beecham), has identified six major problems which, in his view, need to be addressed, for heads of IT to provide a major contribution to the competitiveness of their businesses.[5] His words are used to describe these key issues.

6.1.1   *Understand the business in which you operate*

The data processing profession has spent 20 years trying to keep up with technology. The basis of that technology is changing every ten years and, even worse, the whole approach to applying it (in terms of languages, methodologies and departmental organization) is also changing. We simply have not had the time to understand the businesses in which we operate. Likewise, we have not had the time to help the business understand us. If we do not develop a sound understanding of businesses, then we cannot perform the role of innovator and leader in applying information technology to business opportunities.

What I mean by business knowledge is not an understanding of the procedures followed in the order office, but a fundamental understanding of the business and its marketplace . . .

6.1.2   *Adopt the organization's culture*

I believe the only way that an information systems organization can innovate, lead and change a company is if its management style (culture) matches that of the parent company. Up to now, the style of most data processing organizations has been typified by a professional 'do it right' culture. This style has made it difficult for systems 'professionals' to accept a compromise. For instance, most systems departments have always insisted on using a system design approach that ensures the system is flexible and reliable, and will last for at least five years, even if the business only needs a solution for one year. We have not had an answer to that sort of need.

If the business that we serve is an entrepreneurial one, its management expects entrepreneurial, fast-moving management action, and the systems department would be wise to operate in a compatible style . . .

If we see ourselves as agents of change, then we have to be compatible with our 'marketplace' (that is, the organization in which we operate) because we have to 'sell' our ideas to the business. Any sales organization, even those selling ideas, that is not compatible with its marketplace will not succeed.

6.1.3   *Earn the stature required to enter the corridors of power*

The next subject is stature. By stature I mean the respect gained by an individual or department, and this respect is based on the recognition of, and the confidence in, the contribution being made. Stature does not come automatically – it has to be earned. In many businesses, the contribution of the information systems department has not yet been recognized as being of significance for the future success of the business. More often than not, the 'contribution' is seen in terms of additional cost, extra management hassle as a result of the changes associated with introducing new systems, and a highly dubious return on IT investments when all the follow-on costs are taken into account.

Thus, to contribute to significant business change, we first need to have earned the stature that permits us to be a member of the decision-making 'club'. Second, we have to understand the aims of the club members, so that we have a basis for our ideas. We will then be in a position to operate in the environment where intuitive judgements are made. The implication is that most of our future contributions will not be easy to justify in a purely cost-saving or financial sense.

6.1.4   *Learn how to sell ideas effectively*

If our role is to innovate, and stimulate change within a company, then we must be able to sell those ideas. Selling is not only about having a good product, but is about understanding the reactions of human beings and being good at managing interpersonal skills. Our profession has relied largely on logic to carry out its task. This is not an effective base for selling ideas to people. Selling is therefore a difficult task for us to perform, but it is absolutely critical if we are to be effective in the future . . .

6.1.5 Understand the importance of organizational maturity

However effective information systems managers are at overcoming the four major problems mentioned previously, the maturity of the organization in using, accepting and feeling comfortable with managing technology is also critical to ensuring success. The company is our marketplace, and the maturity of the market significantly influences the seller and the success of his product.

6.1.6 Continue to manage the technical strategies

. . . If technical strategies are not well managed, this can cause the systems department enormous problems in actually delivering the end result . . .

For the authors, Bargioni has articulated well the contribution to be made by the effective leadership of IT, and even in 1985 this perception was not new. Later writers have described this role as that of a 'hybrid manager', providing a union of business and technical skills.[6]

Several studies of IT leadership, which support Bargioni's analysis, are described in the *MIS Quarterly*, December 1992. Feeny, Edwards and Simpson emphasize the need for the CEO and CIO to share a 'vision to transform' through IT. They identify the 'ideal' CIO as having integrity, openness and business perspective; as being a communicator and motivator, informed on IT (and interpreting its significance); and as being a change-oriented team player.[7] Other writers identify how CIOs bridge the gap between the ITD and functional groups or external bodies. They do it through scheduled meetings; interaction outside the ITD; a focus on, and participation in, strategy formulation; and a skilled reading of situations.[8]

6.2 Charge-out

A second solution to achieving the alignment of IT with the enterprise objectives may be found in charging out the cost of IT services to users. However, many organizations have seen in 'charge-out' a panacea for achieving alignment, for establishing priorities and for ensuring value for money for IT – and they have been disappointed. The argument goes that if the users see the true cost of IT then they will apply business criteria to ensure its most appropriate use. In practice, the arguments can go on and on over what is the 'true cost' of IT. The basic questions not only remain unresolved, but political games are played with numbers and the right and proper use of IT can be missed in the resulting confusion.

Charge-out is also used to improve the accountability of ITD for IT expenditure – to help ensure that better value for money is achieved. Behind this noble aim there can exist a sense of dissatisfaction with the service provided by the ITD: a feeling that it is not really doing what the business wants, when it wants, at a price which cannot be beaten by going elsewhere for the service. There are political undercurrents. The customers are not happy.

6.2.1   The principles and practice

What is charge-out? Charge-out is a management system for recording the costs of IT and for allocating these costs to budget heads, so that the costs can be offset against the benefits. But what is a cost? Is it to be a direct expense, or to include overheads? Should different types of cost, for example those of development or of ongoing service, be treated the same or differently? Is it a price (rather than a cost), which includes a 'profit' element to reward enterprise or to provide for re-investment to enhance the service in the future?

Clearly, charge-out is not a simple panacea, especially for ill-defined political problems. It will be useful as one technique for the management toolbag, which will also need to include, among other things, IT planning processes, project benefits appraisal and management performance measures and cost controls. Frequently, the rates charged by ITD for systems usage appear to be out of line with the original investment case for the system. Thus, investment cases which are based largely on the reduction of costs charged to users may prove to be a delusion, and expectations set by project business cases are often shattered (if that is not too strong a word) by the realities of the system costs charged out. This arises because many overhead costs, such as ITD management costs, are correctly omitted from a project business case. In this way, the project evaluation is based on a marginal cost case, and includes those costs that are directly attributable to that project. This avoids an arbitrary allocation of ITD overheads to projects and provides an appropriate basis for comparing projects. Whether a particular project is accepted or not does not generally affect the ITD's overhead costs, which are therefore omitted from the evaluation. However, overhead costs do have to be recovered, and consequently the cost of the IT systems resulting from the project will attract an appropriate portion of ITD overheads, which is reflected in the system costs.

Charge-out will be an appropriate technique where the cost of a centralized IT service is a significant part of the total enterprise costs. In this case, it will be particularly important that, for individual products, the IT cost component is known, in order to be able to determine product costs and profitabilities. For management control it may be desirable to know IT costs by the main business function, or even by business process for those organizations moving into business process management. In providing this information it is intended that users will direct their priorities and set their overall demands for IT so that these are in line with their business objectives, with the overall resources at their disposal and with their ability to fund the use of IT. Also, by using appropriate charging algorithms users can be encouraged to use agreed strategic solutions.

Charge-out also aims to achieve greater visibility of IT costs. This puts increasing pressure on the ITD to be more efficient and cost-conscious and to demonstrate to users their progress in these areas. Annual reductions in the costs of IT equipment are claimed by suppliers (at least of hardware) and users would wish to see these reflected in the cost of ITD services. Investments are made by the ITD to deliver program code more cheaply; the users will want their share of the benefit too.

The aims of charge-out are worthy and the concept is straightforward. It requires a simple periodic charge, in line with forecasts, from the ITD to the users for their share of the IT service. The only problem is doing it!

The problem is shaped by three main issues: technical, financial and scope of responsibility.

1 An IT system will provide data and function to a user. Data for the system might be collected by one or more persons and used by one or more persons; the system might be used by more than one group. These groups and individuals are likely to be in different budget areas and a fair allocation of costs is difficult. Firstly, their share of the development costs will need to be identified and then their individual usage of the data and the system will need to be measured, if they are to be accurately charged. This will require a lot of detailed information. Furthermore, early users of a system may find themselves footing the development bill, which later users may be hoping to avoid.

2 Even if the cost and usage data can be provided at the finest level of detail, then accounting rules still have to be devised for the apportionment of cost across the user groups, with the attendant problems of subjective judgements and questions of consistency and fairness.

3 For charge-out to be more acceptable, or for the ITD to operate as a true profit centre, both users and the ITD must substantially be able to make their investment decisions with independence and freedom from a consideration of each other's objectives. In this case, an external service provider might well meet the users' needs. Mutual dependence for reasons of cost effectiveness, for integrated systems, for shared and secure data or for whatever reason, introduces constraints for both parties in realizing the full potential benefit of the charge-out procedures.

So much for the principles and for the problems. What can be done to make charge-out work?

6.2.2 *Implementing charge-out*

Basic requirements

Whatever objectives are set for charge-out in any enterprise, some critical success factors need to be observed. Davies of IBM UK, from his management and

Investing in information technology

Table 6.1 Critical success factors for charge-out[9]

		Nolan[10]	Allen[11]	Earl[12]	Butler Cox[13]	Olson and Ives[14]
1	Understandable and relevant to users	✓	✓	✓	✓	✓
2	Predictable results		✓			
3	Realistic in economic and resource usage		✓	✓	✓	✓
4	Fits the existing management culture/controls			✓	✓	
5	Capable of (economic) accounting and administration			✓	✓	✓
6	Users able to control consumption (and costs)	✓		✓	✓	
7	Coincidence of user cost/benefit	✓				
8	Auditable					

consultancy experience in this area, has proposed a set of CSFs (Table 6.1).[9] Based on these CSFs, management systems or procedures will be needed for three activities.

1   The costs of IT will need to be recorded and controlled as they are incurred, both development costs and operating costs.

For the purpose of charge-out, they will need to be recorded to the appropriate level of detail. Trying to achieve 'accuracy' will be self-defeating – and expensive.

Large one-off costs may need to be spread over time; the depreciation rules for capital assets will need to be determined; the lifespan of software and systems may need to be agreed.

Demand and capacity forecasting will need to be accurate to enable depreciation rates and unit costs to be calculated. To match demand, capacity will need to rise in steps at given time intervals. The interrelationship is shown in Fig. 6.1. This shows a straight line demand, with stepped capacity and depreciation charges.

2   The costs will need to be recovered from the users.

How this is done depends on the objectives of charge-out. Some typical approaches are discussed below and practical suggestions made for their application. The rules adopted for charge-out must be compatible with other IT policies.

Again, accounting rules will need to established to set rates for different services and to say what will happen for either under- or over-recovery of costs – whether these are taken by the user or by the ITD. And one or the other *will* happen. There needs to be some in-built flexibility, otherwise the 'books' of either the ITD or of the user will not balance.

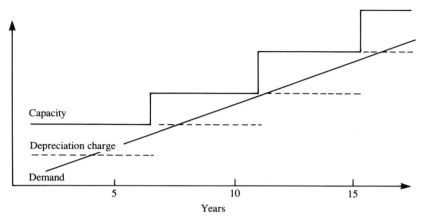

Figure 6.1. Demand and capacity forecasting.

CASE STUDY

The sales division of a large enterprise had an unexpected increase of over £500 000 in its annual IT charge. Investigation revealed that the increase had arisen when another division, previously a joint user with the sales division of a major system, had discontinued using the system. The sales division did not have any immediate alternative to using the system. The ITD, to balance its books, had put the full charge for the system on the sales division.

Above all, clear expectations need to be set for the users based on stable policies resulting in understandable, predictable and timely charges.

3   The users will need to absorb their IT charges.

This can be left to chance, or it can be planned, or it can be a mixture of the two. By 'leaving it to chance' we mean that provision is made in the budgets for IT charges, probably increasing year on year, with no directly related reduction in other budget items. 'Planning' the absorption of IT charges will provide an explanation of how increasing IT charges are to be accommodated by reductions in other areas or by increases in business activity.

Taken either way, IT charges will be visible in operational budgets and will be the subject of scrutiny by, and a factor in the decision-making of, line management.

If these are the objectives of charge-out, how might they be achieved?

Table 6.2 Rating the options for charge-out.[9] ✓ = good rating, × = poor rating

Level and type of charge-out	User understands	User control	Realism and truth	Accounting effort
1 No Charge-out				
2 Corporate overhead (based on revenue/headcount/floorspace, etc.)	✓	××	××	✓✓
3 Memo accounting ('we don't do it, but if we did . . .')	×	××	×	✓
4 'Classic' charge-out (Allocation in arrears based on CPU and development hours)	×	××	✓	✓
5 Break-even rates with year-end adjustment (estimated usage rates with YE adjustment to break even)	×	✓	✓	×
6 Budgeted rates (similar to level 5 but with adjustments as overhead)	×	✓	✓	×
7 Standard rates/negotiated prices (rates per business transaction or computer unit, based on cost plus, market prices, etc.)	✓✓	✓✓	×	××
8 Functional pricing (prices based on business transactions or computer units)	✓✓	✓✓	×	××

Main options for charge-out

Allen has identified eight ways of charging out IT expense.[11] Davis has evaluated these methods using four of his proposed CSFs, namely, user understandability, user controllability, realism and truth and, finally, the accounting effort each implies. The Allen methods and the result of Davis's evaluation are summarized in Table 6.2.

The charge-out method may vary by the type of processing employed: business transactions with on-line processing, by transaction; office systems facilities, by user; unstructured data enquiries, by computer unit; ITD program testing, by computer unit. Regardless of the options, the complexity of the system will affect what expenses are to be included in the charge-out. There is no agreed model, and individual decisions need to be made about key items, such as day and night services, central and local printing and the use of network services.

Pricing for the ITD, as for the enterprise as a whole, is a strategic tool. It can be used to encourage and to discourage the use of particular services and to support users prepared to use new and promising technologies who might otherwise be at a short-term disadvantage. The important aspect of charge-out is how well it achieves its purpose of aligning IT with the business, rather than how well it handles cost apportionment.

Ward and Ward have put IT charge-out in the following context:[15]

Rather than expend ever-increasing amounts of expertise in refining the cost recovery/charging/pricing system to accommodate the peculiarities of IS/IT, more time should be spent ensuring that the policy is more effective in measuring economic and managerial performance.

Charge-out procedures do not come free. Kept simple and used with discretion charge-out can be a useful tool to help align the use of IT with business objectives and to validate its value to the user. It should not be used as the blunt instrument that it is to 'bash' the ITD. There are wider, corporate perspectives on the value of IT which will not be apparent to the individual user – who should be shielded from their cost by an appropriate level of corporate funding. ITD must be sure that they can and do 'defend' their own improving performance and must demonstrate their ability to work to the benefit of their customers.

A project-based approach to planning and implementing charge-out procedures has been described by the IT Infrastructure Management Services, CCTA, HM Treasury.[16]

6.3   Organizing for IT

6.3.1   IT and the organization

Traditionally, the IT function or department (ITD) has been positioned within the finance function. In that the finance function has been concerned with processing much of the 'lifeblood' information for the organization, this may have been appropriate. However, information needs now are much wider than those of finance and, to reflect this, organizations have positioned IT, for example in marketing, manufacturing or operations functions. The IT needs of commercial and of technical functions are generally very different, and this often leads to the establishment of two main centres of competence, as for example, in public utilities, where two main streams of computing have coexisted, for customer service and accounting and for resource (power, water, gas, etc.) engineering. In many cases, information management has been given representation on the executive board and has been established as a specialist function in its own right. In this situation, the function is likely to include non-technology based aspects of processing information such as work study and training. The typical departmental title is then Management Information Services (MIS).

The position of the ITD is likely to be fairly stable and any potential disadvantages, or advantages, of its position can be significantly modified by other parameters, which affect its integration with the business. How it is led, its vision and mission, and how it is organized internally will be key factors. Waterman, Peters and Phillips have encapsulated this in 'Structure is Not Organization', and we will return to this theme later.[17]

Earlier in this chapter we discussed whether the CIO should be a main board

Table 6.3   Contribution to IT – percentage individual and collective views[18]

	Computer managers	Managing directors	Collective
Computer managers	22.6	24.6	22.0
Company secretary/solicitor	2.1	5.6	3.9
Accountant	18.9	21.7	20.9
Managing director	18.8	6.6	15.1
Executive director	20.0	19.8	17.6
Functional managers	19.5	21.7	20.5

director or report to such a director. The personal characteristics of the CIO are as important as the level and position of the job. It requires a so-called hybrid manager who has an understanding of the business, technical competence and people management skills. In recent years there has been a strong movement to devolve early activities of systems development, such as business analysis, to be physically located in other business functions. IBM ISL, like many others, has established IT 'business consultants' – people having a responsibility for the use and development of IT within nominated areas of the enterprise, or with external bodies. Steering committees, at the executive level, and user working groups, at lower levels, have been established.

Moreover, the effective application of IT depends on more people than just those in ITD. Assessments of the contribution made to IT opportunities by various functional managers, has been reported by Kaye in a survey commissioned by the Chartered Institute of Management Accountants.[18] The results (Table 6.3), illustrate the cross-functional nature and impact of IT.

The survey shows how equal is the perceived balance across the chosen groups. The collective result ranks the top contributors as computer managers, accountants and functional directors. There is a notable difference in the views of computer managers and managing directors regarding the role and contribution of the managing director, or CEO. This could be true for any functional manager's view of the CEO's potential input to their function; it underscores the value placed on the boss's leadership.

The role of the ITD, its organization and relationship with other functions are discussed at some length in the Butler Cox Foundation report, *Information Technology: Value for Money.*[19]

6.3.2   *Functional positioning and performance*

As mentioned earlier, the ITD has traditionally been positioned to report to the Chief Financial Officer (CFO) or Financial Director (Fig. 6.2(a)). This has changed to the ITD being its own function within the enterprise, with specialists in, or linked with, units of the enterprise (Fig. 6.2(b)). In a survey of over 650 manufacturing companies, by KEW Associates in association with the Confede-

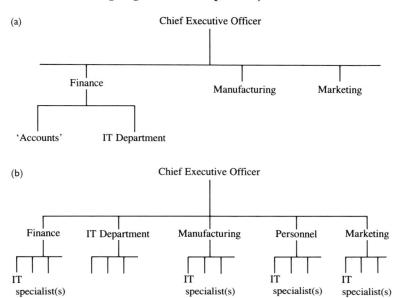

Figure 6.2. The ITD (a) within another function and (b) as a main function.

Table 6.4 Relating IT to business characteristics[3]

Position of IT	<£20m turnover		>£20m turnover		All manufacturing	
	<20% return	>20%	<20% return	>20%	<20% return	>20%
Report into another unit	39%	38%	35%	54%	37%	50%
Separate unit	12%	14%	38%	21%	26%	20%
Split off as staff unit	4%	6%	9%	11%	6%	10%
Each unit has own IT	23%	20%	11%	8%	17%	11%
Other	12%	8%	7%	4%	9%	9%
Not applicable	10%	13%	0%	2%	5%	5%

Percentage return is profit before interest as a percentage on total assets less liabilities.

ration of British Industry (CBI) and *Computer Weekly*[3] there was a trend towards organizations having IT as a separate function on the same level as other functions (for example, finance or marketing). There has also been '. . . a rise in the proportion of companies where each functional unit has its own IT'.

However, this survey also investigated the relationship between overall performance of the enterprise and the position of IT. The results are shown in Table 6.4. For smaller companies (<£20m turnover) there was a preference for IT to report to another function, as in Fig. 6.2(a), but no distinction between the higher and lower performers. Also, for larger companies (>£20m turnover) more of the higher performers, 54%, had IT reporting to another function, typically finance, as in Fig. 6.2(a); but for the lower performers more, 38%, had IT reporting directly to the executive board.

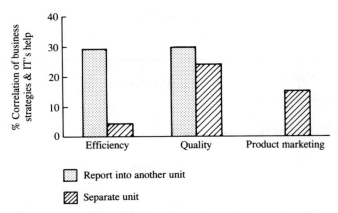

Figure 6.3. Business strategies: IT's help with business objectives.[3]

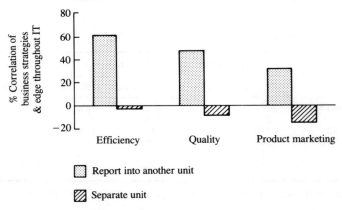

Figure 6.4. Business strategies: competitive advantage through IT.[3]

The survey also found that, for larger companies, business objectives relating both to efficiency and to quality are supported better when the ITD reports into another function (Fig. 6.3). The report concludes that, for >£20m turnover, 'Those reporting into another unit show a much closer alignment between the implementation of the key strategies and the competitive edge IT can provide'. This is illustrated in the survey results of Fig. 6.4. Only in the case of smaller companies was there evidence that, '. . . when their IT is structured as a separate unit then there is a much higher regard for IT strategies'.

On these results for larger organizations, the KEW report comments:

It seems quite ironic that the IT structural trend is away from reporting into another unit and moving more to having a separate IT functional unit since the former tend to be much better performing. Indeed half of those who are currently structured as separate units were reporting into another unit five years ago.

However, we would not have expected these results and the strength of the conclusion is surprising. There are many examples of successful enterprises in which the ITD is a separate functional unit, particularly where the CIO is a board member. The quality of people and how they are managed and the influence exerted by the 'boss' (whoever that is) on the ITD are likely to be as relevant to performance as is organizational positioning. The specifics of each situation need careful assessment in arriving at the best organizational solution for any enterprise.

There is not one answer. Positioning and organizing the IT function needs to be done consciously, to help achieve its integration with key business functions and the alignment of its objectives with enterprise goals. The issue is one of control and communication. It is about maintaining the efficiency and effectiveness of specialist personnel (the ITD), while ensuring a close working relationship with other specializations (users). IT professionals are no different from any other specialists in needing to develop and to maintain their specialized competence, except that some of their specialized knowledge tends to be obsolescent sooner on account of the rate of change of technology and its associated disciplines. Achieving good team working, with a high level of cross-functional understanding, cooperation and synergy, is vital to the health of any enterprise.

How can these high aims be achieved? Whatever structure is selected there are four key organizational issues which must be addressed to achieve the best alignment of IT with business. The first two are concerned with the governance of IT (centralization vs. decentralization and service providers) and the second two with IT skills and competencies (bridge-building and customer orientation), and they are discussed below.

6.3.3   Centralization versus decentralization

In any organization there is a cyclical swing from either a centralized control structure to decentralized or vice versa. It might be more efficient to be centralized, but it can be more effective to focus decision-making where the resources are used, particularly in periods of rapid change which demand maximum responsiveness. Low technology favours devolution: high technology and technological change thrive with high skills which need to be centrally resourced. However, devolution and empowerment are currently the predominant trend. The federal structure, of local autonomy and multi-disciplined skills with central policy making and provision of specialist skills, is commonly used for the

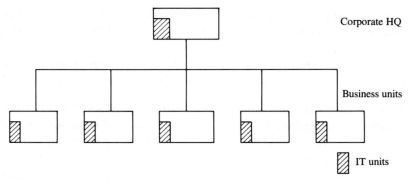

Figure 6.5.   Federal organization of IT resources.

organization of both the whole enterprise and for IT resources. It is fundamental for the organization of IT resources to reflect the enterprise culture.

A federal structure is illustrated in Fig. 6.5. Within each business unit, IT can be a separate function or, better, part of another function, headed by an executive director. The federal structure expresses the principle that responsibility for IT should be shared by line managers and by the ITD. It is not so much a question of 'Who is responsible for the use of IT?', as 'Who is responsible for what part of applying IT, and what skills do they need?'

The implementation of a federal structure means that individuals and groups responsible for the early stages of development and for the business support of IT will be located in non-ITD parts of the enterprise, reporting directly to other functional managers. It means that each major business unit has its own IT Department which works within the framework defined by the corporate ITD. Each federal IT unit will be accountable to corporate ITD management for performing their own specialized IT activities within corporate guidelines and policies. The question to be resolved is how to balance proactive control of IT strategies with a less obtrusive guidance and consultancy. The added value to the business of each IT unit needs to be defined. A decentralized approach to IT planning and delivery will not only affect the organization of human resources, but also technical and application strategies, often distributing corporate applications to a network of smaller computers.

Federal structures can work well and reflect business needs, but still have problems. Standards are more difficult to establish; business pressures can lead to compromised systems quality; and some IT tasks are unnecessarily duplicated at a particular point in time. In times of stability, vertical management, escalated decisions and an emphasis on control are rightly the predominant organizational characteristics. In times of change, horizontal management, devolved decisions, and the integrated use of skills and functions will be the order of the day.

Having the right organizational structure will help to minimize costs; it will ensure core IT responsibilities and key skills are kept at the centre; it will ensure that dispensable skills are replaced by those which are cost-effective and essential; and it will ensure that IT products are built and delivered quickly to meet changing business needs.

Boynton, Jacobs and Zmud have put it this way: 'The best way to link IT *consistently* to a firm's day-to-day core business processes is to carefully distribute IT management responsibilities to line managers'.[20] If the central ITD dominates IT management, this alignment will not occur for two reasons. Firstly, line managers are reluctant to depend for their operations or their careers on IT resources that they neither fully understand nor control. Secondly, no bridging techniques can better the unification of IT and business knowledge when these are both within the mind of one line manager.

Distribution of responsibility is necessary. But some dependence on other resources and skills is inevitable; it is why relationships are a basis of alignment.

CASE STUDY[21]

In 1986 the arrival of a new Chief Executive prefaced a fundamental review of the management and operations of the County Council. A new approach was adopted, characterized by devolution of accountabilities; a corporate framework within which service functions were required to operate; an emphasis on management, not administration; and a customer and internal market orientation.

Radical changes were made to the organization, with more departments and a flatter structure and a commitment to devolve centrally based support services, such as ISD (that is, the ITD), finance and personnel. The new approach brought two main challenges to the IS function; the need to provide suitable systems and networks to support change; and the need to undergo change to achieve departmental ownership of IS and to ensure the provision of a quality and responsive support service, within the framework of a corporate IS strategy.

The response to the challenges was to create two central departments. In support of ISD clients, the Information Systems Department was given overall strategic responsibility for IT and the provision of a range of business and systems support services. To deliver services, the Technology Services Department was given responsibility for providing a central mainframe service together with the corporate voice and data networks. Other central ISD staff were moved to major departments, with secondment arrangements in some instances, rather than permanent placements. Complementary to this, a Head of Profession role was introduced for all ISD staff, whether on central or service department payrolls. This role was concerned with functional competence, and with professional career development. All centrally based ISD support activity was targeted for full commercial operation within an internal market, and this was operated from 1989.

The changes were conducted at a time of unprecedented business change and uncertainty. This is involving a review of local government, educational reforms, pressures on services and a tough financial climate arising from the Council Tax and grant capping. There were also strong trends within the IT industry, including a renewed focus on facilities management and on IT benefits and price/performance.

6.3.4 IT service providers

Third party IT service provision comes in many guises; computer bureaux, data centres, service providers, value-added networks, facilities management, software houses. They are all based on the process of outsourcing. Information technology is not seen to be a core competency which needs to be retained within the enterprise. Cost pressures have made outsourcing attractive to commmercial enterprises. The justification is mainly financial. Sometimes there is no way in which a service requiring a large start-up investment can be provided economically in-house. Sometimes the specialized skills cannot be grown quickly enough to meet an urgent business need. Sometimes it is done to shake the computer department out of its real or imagined complacency. Often, full investigation of an initially attractive proposal shows that the financial benefits can be achieved almost as easily by other means, without the loss of control that outsourcing implies. Loss of control can mean loss of alignmnent of IT with changing business needs and objectives. To be effective, outsourcing needs to be selective in the area to which it is applied, and strategies for working in partnership with key suppliers have to be established.

6.3.5 Building the bridge

Bridge building is about closing a gap and creating a partnership. The gap in understanding between specializations is not hard to account for. The knowledge, concepts and language of each specialization are fundamental to their effectiveness. Through professional training, early job selection and experience, through ongoing personal interests and preferred working styles, the specialization is built in. These are all needed to achieve the synergy and communication within the specialization, but then immediately create a barrier with others. The barrier is reinforced by each having different performance objectives and reward structures. As a result, the IT professional is often seen to have a propensity to 'do it right', to make it complete and even to over-engineer systems. Instead of a considered and slow approach to developing systems, the user will, by contrast, be wanting a faster and more entrepreneurial response to his essential (and often parochial) requirements.

For these reasons the interface between, and cross-fertilization of, job specializations need to be continually monitored and managed, as does the level of the individual competencies within them. Action has to be taken to bridge the gap, not all of which is strictly organizational. Some of the ways in which bridges can be built are through:

1 Job responsibilities and content:

   - Ongoing participation in steering and advisory groups.
   - Temporary assignment to a project team, working party or task force.
   - Movement of personnel across functional boundaries, job rotation.
   - Personal performance objectives, related to IT.

2 Education and training, both in providing a better understanding of the business aspects of information technology and in developing skills in its use and application, for example in project management.

3 Establishing management processes which promote coordination across functions, for example, for business case preparation and IT planning.

4 Providing personal IT facilities which can be explored by users to the extent of their need and capability, for example, spreadsheets and office systems.

However the bridge is built, it will need to be crossed from both sides. Line managers, including the executive, need to get to grips with essential IT language and to understand its implications for the business. IT professionals need to treat their business colleagues with the care each customer deserves and to debate the business problems using the terminology of the business.

CASE STUDY[22]

The Hamot Medical Centre is an acute care unit of Hamot Health Systems. Physicians were involved, right from the start, in the selection and implementation of patient health care systems, through a Medical Information Systems Executive Committee. It consisted of nine physicians and eight executives. Recommendations were made to this Executive Committee by department heads and nurses who, working in a Patient Care Task Force, researched and considered IT options. Having made the selection decision, the role of the Executive Committee expanded to include a consideration of future priorities for IT investments. Including the physicians in IT selection and strategic planning procedures produced a close working relationship between medical and ITD personal. This experience was to be used as a basis for involving other medical staff in IT planning and implementation.

6.3.6   *Customer culture*

Now everybody has a customer; but it has not always been seen that way. Some IT departments have always regarded themselves as providing a 'retail' service to the individuals making up their user community. Others are changing fast to build both a commercial and a customer awareness in their people. In part, it is about where in the organization IT specialists are positioned, but it is more about their attitude as providers of a service. In many enterprises the key to successful customer relationships has been found by appointing 'account managers', or business consultants, people with an overall responsibility for the ITD services provided to a group of users (typically another major department) and for their satisfaction with those services.

However, if the users understand their own mission and have clear objectives, and if the ITD provides the information service they need to meet their objectives, IT is well aligned with the business. Of course, the ITD will still have to perform the balancing act of satisfying sometimes contending needs, economically, in the short and long terms! Many IT departments have adopted a customer awareness strategy as a means of survival, to compete with other potential sources for some of the services for which traditionally they have been the monopoly supplier.

The Butler Cox Foundation in their research report *Marketing the Systems Department*, issued a blunt warning to their members in 1988.[13] 'Computer vendors, facilities-management companies, and other organizations are after your territory. If you try to maintain the inward-looking, technology driven culture of the past, you will surely fail.'

To summarize, some of the organizational issues relevant to aligning IT with the business have been identified. The right organizational solution is often the logical solution; match the organization of the ITD to the business structure; consider the range and types of technology; and take account of corporate IT policies and their implementation.

For the concluding words on organization we return to 'Structure is Not Organization'.[17] The authors concluded that organization effectiveness has seven dimensions. These have threaded through our discussion on the alignment of IT with the business and now they can serve as a check list. The dimensions, and our applications of them, are:

- *Structure*   This has been a theme of this section.
- *Strategy*   As in earlier chapters, this provides a synergy from coordinated plans.
- *Systems*   These describe how things get done, e.g. through charge-out procedures.
- *Style*   This is set by the leaders and is expressed in how they spend their time.
- *Staff*   The factors that focus on developing managers, like the IT hybrid.
- *Skills*   From these come capability and responsiveness.

- *Superordinate goals*   These are the guiding concepts which, for example, inculcate the right attitudes to IT customers.

In likening the seven dimensions to seven magnetic compasses the authors say, 'When all seven needles are all pointed the same way, you're looking at an *organized* company'. And alignment of IT with the business will flow naturally from that organization.

References

1 Peter G. W. Keen, Shaping the Future, *Harvard Business School Press*, Harvard, 1991.
2 *Information Technology Review 1990/91*, Price Waterhouse, London, 1990.
3 Relating IT Practice to Business Strategy, *Computer Weekly Special Report* No. 4, KEW Associates, London, 1990.
4 Lynda M. Applegate and Joyce J. Elam, New Information Systems Leaders: A Changing Role in a Changing World, *MIS Quarterly*, **16**(4), December 1992, pp. 469–490.
5 Anthony Bargioni, *Computing for Competitive Edge*, Butler Cox Foundation, 1985.
6 *Business Benefits and IT – The Hybrid Skills Connection*, Business Intelligence Ltd, 1 Graham Road, London SW19 3SW, 1992.
7 David F. Feeny, Brian R. Edwards and Keppel M. Simpson, Understanding the CEO/CIO relationship, *MIS Quarterly*, **16**(4), December 1992, pp. 435–448.
8 Charlotte S. Stephens, William N. Ledbetter, Amitava Mitra and F. Nelson Ford, Executive or Functional Manager? The Nature of the CIO's Job, *MIS Quarterly*, **16**(4), December 1992, pp. 449–468.
9 S. Davis, *Proceedings of 32nd Spring Conference of IBM GUIDE*, June 1991.
10 R. Nolan, Controlling the costs of data services, *Harvard Business Review*, January–February 1977.
11 Brandt Allen, Making information services pay its way, *Harvard Business Review*, January–February 1987.
12 M. J. Earl, *Management Strategies for Information Technology*, Prentice-Hall, Englewood Cliffs NJ, 1989.
13 *Marketing the Systems Department*, Research Report 66, Butler Cox Foundation, October 1988.
14 Olson and Ives, Chargeback Systems and User Involvement in Information Systems, *MIS Quarterly*, June 1982.
15 J. M. Ward and K. R. Ward, The Transfer Pricing of Information Technology, *Management Accounting*, February 1987.
16 *Cost Management for IT Services*, IT Infrastructure Management Services, CCTA, HM Treasury, Riverwalk House, 157–161 Millbank, London SW1P 4RT.
17 Robert H. Waterman, Jr., Thomas J. Peters and Julien R. Phillips, Structure is Not Organization, *Business Horizons*, Indiana University Graduate School of Business, **23**(3), June 1980, pp. 14–26.
18 G. Roland Kaye, The Role of Management Accountants in Information Strategy, *J. Information Technol.*, **3**(4), December 1988, pp. 251–64.
19 *Information Technology: Value for Money*, Butler Cox and Partners Ltd, 1986.
20 Andrew C. Boynton, Gerry Jacobs, Robert W. Zmud, Whose Responsibility Is IT Management?, *Sloan Management Review*, Summer 1992.

21 Mike Barkway, Decentralizing I.T. Delivery – The Case of Kent County Council, *New Approaches to I.T. Organization*, Business Intelligence/Computer Weekly Conference, April 1991.
22 John F. Evans and Ronnie L. Skibicki, Physicians Play Key Role in Information Systems Planning, *Computers in Healthcare*, **12**(5), May 1991, pp. 24–32.

7
Investment decisions and competitive strategies

This chapter introduces a further method, used by the authors to align IT with the business and to produce business cases for IT applications. The more detailed principles of investment appraisal are discussed in Part 2.

7.1   Survey of application planning studies

During the period 1980 to 1987 the authors' consultancy practice in IBM UK (Applications Management Consultancy) had conducted some 300 application planning (AP) studies with clients. The study provides a financial justification for an application development and links it to business goals and strategies. The study is described further in Chapter 9; here we focus on its results.

In 1987 we reviewed the objectives which had been set for these studies and the results of the studies, as far as these were known to us at the time. We also reviewed a selection of the wide literature relating to some of the key business strategies which have been adopted to gain competitive advantage. We related the objectives of our studies to these competitive strategies to show how the intended application of IT in these projects reflected competitive edge business strategies. The linkage between the study objectives, the resulting IT applications and one or more competitive edge strategies was never hard to make, although as the studies were not set up with the intention of making this kind of analysis the conclusions were subjective. From our own understanding of business strategies and from the literature, we identified 12 key competitive strategies.

The first three strategy areas originate from Porter and his work since the early 1980s.[1] The other nine are subsets of these three, which from our own experience in AP studies and from the literature, have a particular relevance to the competitive edge. All 12 areas are listed in Table 7.1. Examples of how IT has been used to support the first seven competitive strategies are taken from the experience of our own consultancy group. The last five strategies have been illustrated with accounts from other sources. They have not all involved the use of IT.

Table 7.1 Classification of typical competitive strategies

Cost leadership
Differentiation of products and services
Focus – niche marketing
Planning and strategy
Functional policies
Customer service
Organization and change
Alliances
Quality
Innovation and creativity
People
The application of IT

7.2   Survey conclusions

1 IT and competitive edge are rarely seen as cause and effect.

Invariably, the AP studies gave a sharper perception of the contribution which IT could uniquely make to a competitive strategy. Although not directly measured, the cause and effect relationship between IT and competitive advantage was believed to exist by the client companies.

This conclusion is consistent with Michael Earl's survey of strategic information systems planning methods,[2] discussed in Chapter 4. His work shows that 'organizational approaches', of which we see the APS as a leading example, are the most likely to identify competitive advantage applications.

2 Competitive edge is not always leading edge.

Our survey also showed that the use of technology to support competitive edge strategies by no means implied the use of pioneering or leading edge technology. The use of such technology may have been proposed in a number of studies, but it was, in fact, not always necessary for the technology to be leading edge for it to produce a vital and significant support to a company's competitive position. A competitive lead obtained from the direct application of technology, even if it is leading edge, was seen to be vulnerable to 'technological leap-frog'. It was often the case that the base computer systems required further development and enhancement. The 'data' already collected simply had to be made available as 'information' to direct, manage and control the business more effectively. There was no real substitute for a firm foundation of sound base systems and it is from these, as well as from innovative uses of IT, that comes the real support for competitive strategies.

3 Competitive edge is a total package.

Finally, it was abundantly clear that IT, or any technology or system, does not of itself produce competitive advantage. That the use of information technology was only part of an overall competitive strategy did not detract from the importance given it by the enterprises concerned. It is the ability of the organization to change, to focus on customer service, to improve the quality of product and to innovate new products which gain competitive advantage; and these all depend on management and on people, rather than solely on the use of technology.

Our conclusions are consistent with those of other commentators. Clemens and Row found little evidence of direct competitive advantage from the use of IT, except in a few instances. They concluded: '. . . that benefits resulting from an innovative application of information technology can be more readily defended if the system exploits unique resources of the innovating firm so that competitors do not fully benefit from imitation. IT can change the value of key resources by reducing the cost of integrating and coordinating economic activities'.[3]

7.3   Alignment of IT with competitive strategies: case studies

The case studies are listed in Table 7.2, showing the competitive strategies which were identified in each case. One of these strategies has been highlighted to illustrate how IT was to support the competitive strategy under discussion. A résumé of each example is given below. The (a), (b) and (c) labels refer to Table 7.2.

Table 7.2   Results of Application Planning Studies: IT Contribution to competitive edge

Case study industry sector	Competitive strategy supported by IT
1 Manufacturing	(a) *Cost leadership* (b) Product differentiation
2 Process	(a) *Product differentiation* (b) Focus – niche marketing
3 Food production	(a) *Focus – niche marketing* (b) Product differentiation
4 Insurance – non-life	(a) *Planning and strategy* (b) Focus – niche marketing
5 Retail banking	(a) *Functional policy – technology* (b) Product differentiation – channel development
6 Manufacturing	(a) *Customer service* (b) Cost leadership
7 Trading	(a) *Organization and change* (b) Functional policy
Other case studies: Alliances Quality Innovation and creativity People IT	

7.3.1 *Cost leadership*

Achieving the minimum cost of production has always been an area for management focus and control. Minimum unit costs through large scale production have required investment in technology and low labour costs.

CASE STUDY

Business area: manufacturing

Study scope

The aerospace and defence industry has moved from cost-plus to fixed price contracts and competition for the business has increased dramatically.

This company believed that, within this increasingly competitive industry, the ability to gain future profitable orders would depend on a rapid response to bids, the design and delivery of products with ever shortening lead times and the productive use of engineering and manufacturing resources.

However, a substantial amount of unnecessary time and effort was expended by engineers and support staff looking for, waiting for, and transcribing engineering data. There was a lack of visibility across departments of the design data and of project progress. These difficulties were seen as significant contributors to higher costs, to delays in delivery of the products and to low productivity in the division's functions.

The main recommendation was to implement a computer-based engineering data management system that would result in one single on-line register of all engineering documentation, accessible by all authorized personnel for tracking, change control and approval purposes.

Competitive strategies

(a) Cost leadership

The IT solution proposed would reduce costs throughout the bid to design phase, design to contract phase, and the manufacturing phase. From the bid up to design the ability to handle data and access information, with a single correct version of up-to-date information made available to the right people at the right time, would considerably shorten the design cycle, reduce costs and make the bid phase shorter and more productive.

From design to award of contract, the same facilities would reduce the length and number of design iterations prior to manufacture.

Manufacturing productivity is impacted by the design process. A more complete and more accurate design definition, provided earlier to manufacturing, would result in a reduced amount of re-work and scrap.

(b) Differentiation of products and services

The solution recommended by the application planning study team would allow rapid response to bids by shortening the design cycle and allowing a good job to be done quickly and with confidence. The best corporate image would be projected by high-quality technical publications containing a complete response to the customer specifications.

7.3.2 *Differentiation of products and service*

The customer always has an alternative – or if not today, competition will see that there is one tomorrow. A clear and personal understanding of the buyer's needs and of the processes which use the product or service, is fundamental to providing a product of higher value than any alternative.

CASE STUDY

Business area: Petrochemicals

Study scope

The company in all its activities, upstream and downstream, operated in a very competitive environment with a critical emphasis on profitability within each department.

The lack of, or inability to obtain, information from the mainframe applications in the form and/or time frame required to manage the business, led many departments to introduce personal computers. This resulted in duplication of data input and storage and in the duplication of systems; 'islands of automation' were spread across the organization. There was a need to develop a company-wide communication strategy.

The solution included:

1 The implementation of communication systems across the company to reduce the 'paper chase' and to reduce the high level of manual effort currently needed in most departments.

2 The existing organization for coordinating IT was strengthened, both in authority and personnel and by adopting appropriate architectures.

3 Packaged software was used to implement the most needed applications which affected all departments, primarily purchasing, budgets and personnel.

Competitive strategies

Cost reduction featured strongly, but the strategies identified for this example are:

(a)   Differentiation of products and services
      This company had many small customers. Such small independent customers can easily switch suppliers and this means that the product has to be readily available and keenly priced. The product volumes were vast and low product availability or wrongly priced products could mean millions of pounds of business lost or under-priced. The question was how to provide a distinctive product. The answer did not always lie in product features, but in the services associated with the product.
      Implementation of the systems would distinguish the product by enhancing customer relationships, while maintaining sales at the most profitable product price.

(b)   Focus – niche marketing
      Different areas of the UK sell the products at different prices. To maximize market share, it is fundamental to know where to put aggressive pricing to achieve the highest returns against competition.

7.3.3   Focus – niche marketing

For two decades market segmentation has been in the pundit's 'good news' brochure. It has been used to revitalize tired product sales, to address unsatisfied or dormant needs and to open up entirely new areas. It is the delight of the direct marketeer. It concentrates fiercely on the precise needs of the identified segment and sets about matching the product and its delivery to those needs. It understands why and what this group of customers is really buying – as well as the visible product or the offered service.

CASE STUDY

Business area: flour mill production

Study scope

The company, although large and profitable, realized that to increase its market share and improve profitability it would have to cater for changing consumer preferences with the consequential need for flexibility in business approach and structure. The company needed to formulate a long-term strategy for the development of new computer applications, making better provision for the computing requirements of individual locations.

The proposed systems were expected to contribute considerable direct savings in maintenance and system support costs. The production and distribution facilities were located UK-wide. Installations of the systems would allow consolidation of more timely information at a regional level leading to better use of the production and distribution facilities.

There were also major business requirements for additional sales information.

Competitive strategies

(a) Focus – niche marketing
    Consumer preferences are continually changing, a recent trend being towards more healthy foods. Preferences and trends often differ by geographical area. Information on sales by product/area/customer/type would help to monitor and to exploit trends in consumer preferences and lead to the profitable exploitation of available markets.

(b) Differentiation of products and services
    The marketplace was very competitive due to other large suppliers and to the small independents. Availability of the appropriate product, at the time needed, and at the correct price is key. Introduction of the new systems would give better product availability due to UK-wide control of inventory and improved responsiveness through on-line order entry and enquiry on customer orders.

7.3.4 *Planning and strategy*

This used to be seen by many enterprises as an academic luxury, necessarily squeezed out by the priority of the moment. In recent years, as the economy has been restructured, many enterprises have found themselves in a more difficult environment and for many it has become a question of survival.

CASE STUDY

Business area: insurance – non-life business

Study scope

Several on-line management information systems had been developed in previous years, but there was a growing awareness that whole areas of vital information were not readily available, particularly in the form required. It was difficult to use and compare data across the main systems and this was necessary to achieve better coordination of business operations.

It was planned that management information applications should be further developed in the areas of performance and profit reporting, customer and marketing database and resource management.

Competitive advantage

(a) Planning and strategy
     Regular control of the whole business operation had been achieved through interactive planning and budgeting, followed through into period-end reporting. The company focused on management information systems again, to achieve even sharper planning and a faster response to market pressures.

(b) Focus – niche marketing
     Product variations need to be generated quickly in the insurance industry to address the particular requirements of market segments. The product characteristics and pricing structures need to be based on customer needs and on the risks to be covered. Well-designed products and precise information are needed to maximize profit – and the final profitability may not be known for years.

     A clear view of the market segment was seen as vital to the precise definition of products. This implies recording sales information in greater detail, careful database design and good data management techniques, particularly if flexibility was to be built in for the future.

7.3.5 *Functional policies*

In many instances a competitive strategy may be based on a key function of the enterprise and the relevant functions will depend on the industry. Three examples are manufacturing, buying and distribution.

CASE STUDY

Business area: retail banking – branch automation

Study scope

The capacity and maintainability of existing systems were serious constraints. Additional functions were required to achieve an information network capable of supporting the bank's business requirements.

For example, the collation of information from various sources, particularly with respect to customers, was at best difficult and often not possible.

New applications were to be implemented to support the operational procedures of the bank and customer and marketing related activities. Some of the applications would run on local branch processors and some would require the facilities and the capacity of the mainframe. The study proposals relied heavily on the satisfactory implementation of a comprehensive telecommunications network.

Competitive strategies

(a) Functional policy – telecommunications
As a substantial processor of information the bank depended on its ability to provide a high function data network at minimum cost. The telecommunications network had been developed and would provide the delivery mechanism for branch and head office applications.

(b) Product differentiation – channel development
The high street branches were a prime sales channel. Their ability to handle existing products and services economically was fundamental. No less so was the need to provide new products, with an increased level of customer service. Customers have less 'brand loyalty' than previously and IT had a vital role to play in maintaining the bank's product and service image.

7.3.6   Customer service

Customer service, like quality, is a matter of attitudes and relationships as much as specifics. The customer is king. Customer service is as necessary between departments within an organization as it is with the final recipient of the product or service.

CASE STUDY

Business area: manufacturing

Study scope

This company had set clear goals to improve its competitiveness through the quality of the product supplied to the customer, the level of customer service and through minimizing the costs of design and manufacture.

The application planning study team recommended the implementation of Computer-Aided Design and Manufacture (CADAM)^{TM} in order to reduce the product lead time, through fewer design iterations during the marketing and pre-manufacture stages. At the same time it was expected that better quality designs and supporting documentation would result from the systems.

Competitive strategies

(a) Customer service
     The relationship established with the customer in the marketing stage was highly dependent on the responsiveness and efficiency of the early design service. In the eyes of the customer, product lead time is a key measure of the supplier's performance. Thus, customer service would be enhanced from a shorter overall product lead time.

(b) Cost leadership
     Through the use of CADAM and associated management procedures, product cost would be reduced, due to fewer engineering changes and consequent re-work, reduced duplication of effort by the potential reuse of previous drawings and by better access to up-to-date technical information from across all functions.
     Reduced stock levels were expected, as the reuse of previous designs would require fewer duplicate parts to be retained.

7.3.7 Organization and change

The organization is an important expression of strategy. Many enterprises have changed their organization to help achieve better product differentiation or to improve their relationship with customers. Introducing a different organization changes decision and cost structures.

The introduction of technology changes jobs and offers far reaching possibilities for organizational change. Transfer-line manufacturing technology is an example from a decade ago. More recently, continuous flow manufacture has been based on the application of technology and on the reorganization of work processes. This trend has moved from the factory to the office. Now, the re-engineering of business processes, often made possible by the application of information processing technology, promises to enhance significantly the performance of an enterprise. A re-engineered business process results in new work flows and can require a redefinition of jobs and a new organizational structure. Process re-engineering is a technique which is often complementary to, and leads into, a 'quality' programme.

CASE STUDY

Business area: trading with transport and warehousing

Study scope

Recent systems developments had concentrated on handling large increases in transaction volumes economically. Profitability was becoming a key issue and margins were under increased pressures. Existing systems could not provide information at the right level for effective control.

The operating companies in the group had traditionally been fairly autonomous. A new product marketing structure had recently been introduced to emphasize product responsibilities across the group.

The study revealed that a number of management systems were not well defined enough, in terms of responsibilities and processes, to provide for a satisfactory level of control.

Additional systems would be developed to support the newly appointed product managers in monitoring the performance of product sales in all business units, and to assess the effect of haulage costs on product profitability.

Improved reports would be provided to show the content and availability of stock information and of the forward position of stocks being traded, across the group.

Competitive strategies

(a) Organization change
    The group had been formed by acquisition. Constituent companies had their own cultures and processes. Consolidated group accounts were prepared monthly and common processing systems were used for business transactions. However, greater group synergy and cohesion was needed. This was a key consideration in giving priority to the development of common planning and reporting systems for all levels within the operating companies.

(b) Functional policies
    Two important resources needed tighter management on a group-wide basis, namely cash and transport. Both played a vital role in the total service provided to customers. New group-wide management systems were needed. Their effective implementation would depend heavily on IT and could well prove to be a survival issue for the group in the less favourable business environment seen ahead.

7.3.8 Alliances

Alliances between business enterprises provide a means to share the risks and costs of new product development, to gain access to skills and technology and to reduce the overall cost of the value chain, through timely information exchange between suppliers and customers.

Richard Huber, of Continental Bank, has described how the bank startled the industry when it decided to outsource almost all of its information technology.[4] In December 1991, the bank signed a ten year multimillion dollar contract with International Systems Solutions Centre, an IBM subsidiary, and Ernst and Young for the delivery of an information technology service and development support. The decision allowed Continental to focus on its core competencies: an intimate knowledge of customers' needs and customer relationships. The bank continues to set the strategic direction for technology, while depending on its partners for information technology services. The alliance has allowed Continental to save $10 million a year and to accelerate the introduction of new applications.

American Airlines has joined with Citibank and the long distance phone company MCI to offer credits for air travel on the airline's frequent flyer program.[5] Credits are based on levels of credit card purchases and phone charges. The alliance depends on the ability of the partners to exchange large volumes of data cheaply and quickly. It has enhanced customer loyalty and allowed the partners to develop innovative incentives and to cross-market their products.

The efficiency of just-in-time (JIT) delivery systems depend on a high degree of cooperation between suppliers and customers and increasingly on electronic data interchange (EDI). Toyota links its dealers and suppliers into an electronic network which allows the rapid transmission of orders from customers and orders to suppliers.[6] It is reputedly able to deliver a car with colours and trim to the customer's specifications within five days of the order being placed.

A common theme of these partnerships is the exchange of information facilitated by databanks and electronic networks.

7.3.9 Quality

There has been widespread recognition of the competitive advantage gained by Japanese manufacturers through the systematic pursuit of quality. Honda and Toyota typify the Japanese approach. It involves continuous improvement to the manufacturing process, participation of all employees in quality circles and a legendary willingness to halt the manufacturing line to correct a problem.

Enterprises in the USA and Europe have recognized the potential benefits of quality management and have invested heavily in quality programmes. The focus has shifted from the original emphasis on manufacturing to quality as it is perceived by the customer. IBM is among the leaders of this approach, with its Market Driven Quality programme. The goal is to have delighted customers, and IBM monitors progress through regular customer satisfaction surveys.

The quality approach is characterized by incremental improvement through evolutionary change. Business process re-engineering is an exciting new approach which yields quantum leaps in performance, through revolutionary change. Michael Hammer has documented the results of business process re-engineering in the Accounts Payable department of the Ford Motor Company.[7] An initial assessment indicated an opportunity to reduce the 500 staff by 100, through automation and rationalization. A radical rethink of the accounts payable process led to a change from payment on invoice to payment for goods received. The resultant simplification resulted in a dramatic 75% staff reduction.

7.3.10 Research and development

The importance of research and development to the competitive edge in fast moving high-tech industries is widely recognized.[8] Breakthroughs such as Zantac for Glaxo and Librium and Valium for Hoffman La-Roche provide competitive advantage over a period of years.

There is a growing recognition of the need to encourage and foster innovation in even the (apparently) most slow-moving industries. Tom Peters has cited Milliken, a supplier of towels and dust mops to factories and hospitals as a model of innovation, attention to quality and staff motivation.[9] Milliken pursues new ideas through close customer relationships, develops new products quickly through teams and encourages staff to come forward with radical suggestions.

Many Japanese manufacturers have developed an alternative to the search for new technology breakthroughs, which characterize Western research and development activities. Instead they have concentrated on the combination of different existing technologies in new ways to produce innovative products. Fumio Kodama has described this approach and its exploitation by companies such as Funac, a numerical controller manufacturer.[10] Funac combined electronic, mechanical and materials handling technologies to develop an affordable computerized numerical controller. Today it is a world leader in its field and one of Japan's most successful companies.

Canon has a consistent record of new product innovation through the combination of its core competencies in precision mechanics, fine optics and micro-electronics.[11] It has recently combined its experience of personal printers and electronics to produce an integrated portable personal computer and printer. It has taken the theme of integration to a new level with the announcement of the CLC10 which combines a full colour scanner, copier and printer into a single integrated unit.

7.3.11 People

An example from the world of American football illustrates the value of carefully thought out plans for career progression.[12] Bill Walsh is credited with the turnaround of the San Francisco 49ers from a lacklustre team of also-rans to three times Superbowl winners under his leadership. Walsh, as the head coach, achieved this transformation through an assessment of each player's capabilities and potential over the life of his career. The assessment formed the basis of a training program and team strategy to build on and develop those capabilities. The success of this approach shows in the record books and made the 49ers the outstanding team of the 1980s.

Success in the National Football League is clearly dependent on investment in people. It can equally be the key to success in business. Training and education have played a key role in the transformation of British Airways (BA) from a near bankrupt nationalized industry with an indifferent reputation for service into the self-styled 'world's favourite' and most profitable airline.

A new BA management team was appointed in 1981 to prepare the company for privatization. An urgent priority for the new team was to transform staff attitudes to customer service. 'Putting People First' was an imaginative training programme for front line staff which made them aware of the need to relate to passengers as people. The programme required heavy investment in training and staff time. The success of the programme has been widely recognized. BA continues to invest in training to ensure that its reputation for service remains at the forefront of the industry.

The old nationalized BA was operations-led. The management team was weak and there was no consistent approach to management development. In contrast, the company today is market-driven. The management team is among the most successful in the world. Investment in management education, through Top Flight Academies courses for supervisors, managers and executives, has played a key role in developing the professionalism of the management team. The courses were specially designed and taught by business schools in the United Kingdom and USA and led to a Diploma of Business Administration or an MBA. Investment in training and education has been a key element in the transformation of British Airways.

7.3.12 Technology

In a sense, competitive advantage through exploitation of technology is a theme of this book. Despite some recent surveys which have questioned the value of IT investments, there are many frequently quoted examples of companies enjoying a competitive advantage through exploitation of technology.

In the United Kingdom, Michael Earl and collaborators have documented the cases, which include Thomson Holidays' TOP system for travel agents; British Steel Strip Products Division's on-line customer enquiry system; and the Frentel insurance quotation system built by Friends Provident.[13]

TOP terminals allow travel agents to book holidays directly through a videotex screen. The system eliminates much of the delay associated with looking through holiday options, checking availability and making bookings. TOP has given Thomson Holidays competitive advantage through improved distribution, decreased costs and increased sales.

British Steel Strip Products Division had a problem with surplus stock, which was in danger of deterioration. The division installed terminals in key customers' offices to allow them to enquire on the availability of a range of products. The service allows the previously surplus stock to be sold at a premium price to reflect its availability.

Friends Provident extended the Frentel on-line quotation service from its branch offices into brokers' offices providing improved service and distribution.

In the USA, American Airlines, American Express and Baxter Healthcare are frequently quoted as companies which have gained competitive advantage through technology.

American Airlines developed the SABRE airline reservation system in the sixties. It has provided enduring competitive advantage to the extent that the profits derived from SABRE exceed those of the airline.

American Express needed to speed its response to retailers for purchase approval, a competitive differentiator in the industry, and to reduce credit card abuse. American Express developed 'the Authorizer's Assistant', an expert system, to assist credit control clerks to achieve both objectives.

The American Hospital Supply Company (AHSC), now merged with Baxter Healthcare, was the first supplier to provide terminals to allow hospitals to order supplies directly on their computer system.[14] The service was extended to allow hospitals to order using their own product codes and to create standing orders of regularly used supplies. Hospitals benefitted from a reduced cost of order processing and improved materials management. Combined with a wide product range, the system was a key component in AHSC's strategy to become the 'prime vendor of choice'.

The earlier gloom of some commentators, regarding the value of IT, is beginning to lift. In 1992, productivity in the US rose nearly 3% and contributed to a surge in corporate profits. The boost to productivity is attributed to a reorganization of work, new corporate structures and to the application of information technology.[15]

References

1 M. E. Porter, *Competitive Strategy – Creating and Sustaining Superior Performance*, Collier Macmillan, New York, 1985.
2 Michael J. Earl, London Business School, Experiences in Strategic Information Systems Planning, *MIS Quarterly*, **17**(1), March 1993.
3 Eric K. Clemons and Michael C. Row, Sustaining IT Advantage: The Role of Structural Differences, *MIS Quarterly*, **15**(3), September 1991.
4 Richard L. Huber, How Continental Bank Outsourced Its 'Crown Jewels', *Harvard Business Review*, January–February 1993.

5 B. R. Konynski and F. W. McFarlan, Information Partnerships – Shared Data, Shared Scale, *Harvard Business Review*, September–October 1990.

6 L. Fried and R. Johnson, Gaining Technology Advantage, *International Systems Management*, Fall 1991.

7 Michael Hammer, Reengineering Work: Don't Automate, Obliterate, *Harvard Business Review*, July–August 1990.

8 H. A. Schneiderman, Managing R&D: A perspective from the top, *Sloan Management Review*, Summer 1991.

9 Tom J. Peters, *Thriving on Chaos*, Pan Books, London, 1989.

10 Fumio Kodama, Technology Fusion and the New R&D, *Harvard Business Review*, July–August 1991.

11 C. K. Prahalad and G. Hamel, The Core Competence of the Corporation, *Harvard Business Review*, May–June 1990.

12 R. Rapaport, To Build a Winning Team: an interview with Head Coach Bill Walsh, *Harvard Business Review*, January–February 1993.

13 M. Earl, D. Feeny, M. Lockett and D. Ruge, Competitive Advantage through Information Technology: Eight Maxims for Senior Managers, *Multinational Business* No. 2, 1988.

14 J. E. Short and N. Venkatraman, Beyond Business Process Redesign: Redefining Baxter's Business Network, *Sloan Management Review*, Fall 1992.

15 The Technology Payoff, Special Report, *International Business Week*, June 1993.

8
Investment in architectures and development methods

8.1   What is an architecture and why is it important?

Stated simply, an architecture is a structure; it is the result of a process of analysis and design which describes the boundaries of the component parts and their interfaces. It provides the basis for more detailed design.

One of the prime requirements of users is that systems be flexible and capable of accommodating change and growth. The use of an architecture helps to achieve this. 'Systems flexibility' can also, in part, be a user perception which results from the organization and attitudes of the ITD.

Architectures, describing boundaries and interfaces through standards and rules, can be developed at various levels. First, at the top level, some architectures will be briefly described; then we discuss some methods and techniques (or tools) for building information systems.

Architecture is important to the application of IT because it affects the level, timing and life of investment. Allen and Boynton have claimed that, 'Information architecture has replaced organizational design, planning, and financial controls as the key to business design'.[1] In 1991, from a survey of US enterprises, developing an information (or business) architecture was cited as the number one issue for the 1990s.[2] Therefore, the implications of such an architecture need to be understood by those concerned with IT investment, in at least the essential principles and terminology of three types of architecture, namely, business, application and technical architectures. However, there are layers below architectures which also affect the development of IT applications and, therefore, also affect the investment. In addition to architectures we also discuss and position, at these lower levels, development methods and tools, as these affect the cost of applying IT.

An architecture describes the whole in terms of the sum of its parts; it promotes consistency and gives a basis for change by providing flexibility. In order to synthesize disparate methods, for planning or for implementing IT, into an homogeneous approach, one of three conditions must be true:

1   The methods must be designed to be used together.
2   The methods must be designed to conform to a standard interface.
3   The methods must have imprecise external interfaces, so that their degree of
    fit is not critical.

The statements hold true for planning methods and for technical methods.
Different technical approaches and information systems can only be easily used
together if they are designed together, are designed to conform to standard
interfaces or have imprecise external interfaces.

The nature, value and limitations of an architected approach can be illustrated
through a familiar example.

Consider the construction of a house. A builder could be contracted to build it.
After discussion, the builder would draw up a plan and build it. For speedier
response and greater convenience a prefabricated house might even be delivered
and erected. One advantage of prefabrication lies in being able to see the product
before purchase; the disadvantage may be in having to make compromises in
personal style to live in it. As an alternative to these immediate building
approaches, an architect might be retained to design the house and to draw up
the rules under which it would be built. This could delay the start and it would be
more expensive. However, the architect would have a wider range of considerations based upon a deeper analysis of the client and the client's circumstances
and environment. Specifically, the architect would provide for any future
requirements of the purchaser and occupants (failure to do this could be unduly
expensive later); consider more carefully the cost of maintenance and the level
of security needed; provide mutually consistent specifications for building contractors.

Compared with the changing requirements for information systems, the function provided by a house is generally static. However, the design options for
systems are similar to those for houses and to those for planning methods. Systems
can be built with imprecise external and internal design rules; they can be
designed to be used together, or they can be designed to conform to a standard
interface. There are options in the use of architectures, extremes of which have
been described as The High Road (architected) and The Low Road (non-
architected) by Allen and Boynton.[1]

The advantages and disadvantages of using an architected approach to systems
development are summarized in Table 8.1. Architectural choices affect the
business case for IT. The presence or absence of architectures, their characteristics and the degree to which they are applied, all affect systems costs and
usability in the short and long terms. This chapter distinguishes between different
architectures and development methods to aid in their selection. Some enterprises
now use an architectural review board, consisting of non-ITD managers, to
understand the implications of new projects for architectural standards and to
approve proposed IT projects.

Table 8.1   The advantages and disadvantages of the architected approach

Advantages	Disadvantages
Enables data and systems functions to be more easily shared across users.	Requires a broader consideration of primary and secondary user requirements.
Reduces the cost and time-scale of extensions to systems.	Requires longer planning horizons.
Provides for future flexibility and growth in systems function.	Takes time to produce the architecture and to build the infrastructure.
Reduces duplication of data and function within different systems.	Adds the cost of architecting which has to be recovered from future systems.
Helps to eliminate errors at the design stage, where cost of correction is minimal.	Requires a more visionary and longer term approach, particularly in terms of user executive support.
Reduces the level of costly systems maintenance activities.	Specialist skills are needed within the ITD.
Facilitates management direction and control of IT.	Requires higher management skills for implementation.

8.2   Architectures

Information systems need to relate to the real world, of people and things. Today, the information technologist cannot design and build effective systems without a deep and precise understanding of the environment in which the systems will work. He needs to understand how, in the real world, information is architected.

The starting point for understanding the information architecture of an enterprise is, therefore, an understanding of the people and things within it, or associated with it. This is not the understanding of the technologist alone; it is rather an understanding by the people themselves of the information and the processes they employ. And this is the key point: if managers do not understand the architecture of their enterprise, of which they are an integral part, the technologist will misunderstand it too. Information systems, and the investment made in them, will be less than effectively used. The people who manage the enterprise, not the technologist, must provide the basic map to guide and to direct the systems development.

This map is called a business architecture. On it is built the application architecture and the technical architecture.

8.2.1   *Business architectures – data and process models*

A business map has two main elements, a data model and a process model. Data describes the people and things within, or used by, an enterprise. A data entity is an item of data relating to a physical entity. A business process is an activity, or set of related activities, performed on any physical entity or resource. A process can be a manufacturing process working on a material resource; it can be a management process working with an employee; it can be an information process working with data. Any business process, whether about the management of materials, machines, people or cash, will involve the use and generation of data about the resource and the process.

Thus data and processes are a fundamental aspect of any enterprise and what they are, for any enterprise, depends basically on the products and services offered, or to use a well known phrase, they are determined by 'what business you are in'. They depend to a lesser extent on the details of how the product or service is manufactured and delivered and even less on how the enterprise is organized to achieve its mission.

Therefore, *generalized* data and process models will be valid for similar, but discrete, enterprises. IBM has already produced several such architectures for major industry sectors, in conjunction with managers employed in those sectors.

From the data and process models, an architecture of IT applications has been determined, providing a basis for the planning and development of information systems.

8.2.2 *Application architectures*

Data entities and processes can be collected into logically related groupings. Where an IT system can be applied to support the processes of such a group, the grouping is called an application. Furthermore, how applications can be grouped and their relationship to each other are expressed in an application architecture.

Major architectures have been described by IBM, including finance applications and for the banking, insurance and retail sectors. Once customized for each enterprise, they offer the possibility of reductions in the cost of comparable systems development and they enable software suppliers to build products which, by conforming to the industry model, will be suitable for a wider range of potential purchasers. Two examples are described below.

1 Wholesale Banking Design Principles (WBDP)
   A survey was commissioned across 36 large banking institutions worldwide and, in collaboration with them, the Wholesale Banking Design Principles were developed. These describe in detail how global wholesale banking systems work. The applications cover front office systems, back office systems and include the electronic funds transfer operations of a bank. The architectures are open to suppliers of application software and they can be expected to lead to the much sought after goal of having totally integrated systems.

2 Insurance Application Architecture (IAA)
   This architecture was developed by IBM in conjuction with leading European insurance enterprises. It covers the business activities which may be undertaken by an insurance company and includes the information systems

activities that those companies would need to undertake. The architecture consists of a data model, a function or process model and an information systems model. An aim of IAA is to facilitate the move from insurance product-orientated transaction systems to systems which are integrated and orientated towards the provision of information.

It is noteworthy that these architectures are initially being developed for information based, service sector industries, rather than for manufacturing. However, many enterprises are now building their own business and application architectures to lay the basis for integrated information systems.

8.2.3 *Technical architectures*

Information systems, once designed, have to be built and to be delivered using hardware and software. How this is done and what hardware and software 'platforms' are used, are the subjects of technical architectures. These need to be established for use within an organization, but there is also considerable advantage in establishing architectures and standards across the IT industry. The cost of IT depends vitally on the development and use of technical architectures, as much as on the cost of the hardware and software components.

The use of architectures directly affects the business case for IT. Understanding and developing business architectures is fundamental; it provides the framework for technical architectures.

The principles which need to be borne in mind by senior business management, in addressing technical architectures, are discussed by Keen in his chapter 'Positioning the IT Platform'.[3] Here he marshals the arguments for extensible interconnecting platforms of architecturally compatible computer systems. He recognizes that architecture is about more than connecting systems; it is about the integration of information across applications, across functions and across locations. Keen expresses this in his concept of *reach* which 'refers to the locations a platform is capable of linking' and *range* which 'refers to the degree to which information can be *directly* and *automatically* shared across systems and services'. The degree of reach depends on whether links are only internal, whether they extend to customers and suppliers, or are even wider. The range of service to be delivered can vary from simple messages to complex transactions which involve more than one processor for their completion. Within an enterprise, the purpose of a technical architecture is to provide a valid and agreed base for all system design and use. Its contents typically include:

- A description of the architectural principles adopted by the department.
- Technical standards.
- Hardware and software options.
- Local and system-wide services, for example networking.

- Centralized and decentralized processing.
- Application development tools and techniques.
- Systems management facilities.

Many of these will call on architectures and standards (we take a standard to be a specific implementation of an architecture) originating outside the organization. There is a wide, almost bewildering, choice of both proprietary and open (not supplier-specific) technical architectures available in most areas. Some architectures cover purely technical issues, while others include both technical and application design topics. As a generalization, proprietary architectures provide a secure and proven framework for development, albeit within the limits of the vendor's chosen domain. Open architectures offer the potential for unlimited flexibility, but at present have not reached full maturity and have more ambiguously defined interfaces. A survey of large IT departments in 1990[4] revealed that a majority believed that controversies over some standards would never be settled and others would take many years to be widely adopted.

However, standards there will be, because generally they are in the IT industry's best interest. Manufacturers are responding to the requirement by offering fewer but stronger and more universal proprietary architectures and by softening the distinction and barriers between proprietary and open standards. Many business enterprises now have, or are in the process of defining, a technical strategy for IT. The IBM Corporate Technical Architectures Study provides a methodology for this.[5] Some examples of technical architectures are described in Table 8.2. However, the starting point for defining a technical architecture is the business strategy. As Gray has observed, 'When the economic and business issues that are driving users to open systems are kept in mind, it becomes easier to understand whether or not a system or product fits with an open strategy'.[6]

IBM's Systems Application Architecture (SAA), developed in the early 1980s, is one example of a technical architecture. Applications need to be interconnected and able to run on a range of software and hardware platforms, so that the investment in application programs is not tied to the investment in platforms. For ease of use, applications need to be consistent in their presentation of function and data to users, irrespective of which individual, team or supplier develops them. Overall, it is important that applications provide solutions to business requirements with maximum consistency and with minimum constraints and costs, and this is the aim of SAA.

8.2.4 *Application development architectures*

Application Development (AD) Cycle and its associated tools is an architecture and framework for the process of application development, which is currently being offered by IBM and its business partners.[7] As a true architecture, it does not describe how applications are developed, but sets a framework within which

Table 8.2   Examples of technical architectures

Architecture	Description
System Network Architecture (SNA)	A set of standards, developed in the 1970s, as a basis for interconnecting IBM machines. As an early architecture, SNA has been widely adopted within the industry.
Integrated Services Digital Network (ISDN)	This standard is being formulated by international agreement to facilitate information transmission, in any form, across digital networks. It fits within the next (OSI), more comprehensive, architecture.
Open Systems Interconnection (OSI)	Interconnecting computers and software from different suppliers is complex. The protocols of OSI are described in seven layers, namely, physical, data link, network, transport, session, presentation and application. The specification of these standards continues and is the work of the International Organization for Standardization (ISO).
Systems Application Architecture (SAA)	This aims to make computing more available through its Common User Access (with standards for screen design, keyboard conventions, etc.), to tie disparate platforms together through its Common Communications Support and to improve the productivity of programmers significantly through its Common Programming Interface.

disparate development tools can be used. It is based on the premise that software design will be preceded by the provision of a business model. It also provides a data model of the objects produced in the development process (which is theoretically the more important contribution). In doing this, AD/Cycle has overcome major obstacles to establishing a universal approach for application development and implementation.

The framework provided by AD/Cycle is illustrated in Fig. 8.1.[7] This shows that the platform chosen for application development is defined by the development tools selected and the principles followed for their selection. The tools will need to support activities in all stages of the project life cycle, from initial data and process (enterprise) modelling, through conversion of these models into computer instructions, to systems installation and handover. The architecture of AD/Cycle is open; methods and development tools may be acquired from any source provided only that they conform to the published interfaces.

The final activity in the project life cycle is system maintenance – that is correcting errors and enhancing the system to meet new, ongoing requirements of the enterprise. The cost of developing systems will depend on which business, application and technical architectures they are based, and on the development methods and tools which are used. Often (of more significance), the ability to maintain the system, the cost of doing so and its ultimate life span also have this dependency. How architectures, methods and tools are used will affect the short-term and long-term investments in IT.

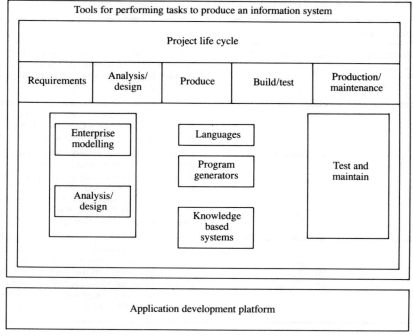

Figure 8.1. Components of AD/Cycle.

8.3   Application development methods

Earlier we noted that architectures are about structures, rules and standards. Development methods are about the processes of building – how it will be done. Two examples of application development methods are the subject of this section. What is used to build, the tools of the trade, will be described in the next section.

1   Business Systems Development Method (BSDM)[8]
BSDM provides techniques which result in the definition of data that are of prime interest to an enterprise, and the behaviour of those data. It does this by modelling the real world rather than the data records currently used by the organization. It produces a data model of an enterprise, a process model and an applications architecture. This approach differs from the more common approach of analysing information in an attempt to extract the underlying data. BSDM is also used to define the requirements of a specific information system and its external (user-orientated, rather than technical) design.

BSDM is currently only partially supported by CASE tools, described below. The successful use of BSDM has illustrated the benefit to be derived from a rigorous approach to defining business and application architectures.

However, the participation of senior management in the architecture definition is crucial.

BSDM differs from most other methods in:

- its emphasis on business modelling and applications architecture
- its early use in the development process of a specific application
- its use by both business and IT staff
- its separation of business and technical compromises

2   Structured Systems Analysis and Design Method (SSADM)[9]

SSADM is a structured set of procedural, technical and documentation standards, designed specifically for analysing business needs and undertaking software development for a specific application. It consists of a two-part framework – covering business requirements analysis and design – which is sectioned into stages. Taken together these stages provide a complete set of techniques for data modelling, requirements analysis and software design, within the development process.

Both SSADM and BSDM have their protagonists. SSADM may not have quite the intellectual breadth of BSDM, and therefore may leave some issues unresolved, but it has achieved wide acceptance by many enterprises and is well supported by CASE tools. Taken together, both methods provide a comprehensive approach to application development.

8.4   IT development tools – computer aided software engineering (CASE)

Software tools to assist IT professionals in the design and development of application systems have been evolving since the late 1970s although the acronym CASE (computer-aided software engineering) was not coined until the 1980s.

Assemblers and high-level language compilers could arguably be described as the first CASE tools. These were followed by program generators and software to support the design, as opposed to the build, phases of the development process. More recently CASE tools have been integrated into frameworks such as AD/Cycle.

Today's CASE tools claim to translate enterprise models into software, but they are not so often used in this way and more typically start from a statement of user requirements. Some examples of CASE software products are given in Table 8.3. CASE tools do not constitute a development method, but can enforce the use of, and support, a method. Properly applied, alongside a well-founded method, CASE tools may improve the productivity of IT professionals, but unsupported by a method they simply allow inappropriate systems to be developed faster. The large productivity gains anticipated by CASE technology have not been fully realized, but their use has a potentially significant impact on the business case for IT.

Table 8.3   Examples of computer-aided software engineering

DevelopMate (IBM)	Used to define, validate and refine an enterprise model through prototyping.
Information Engineering Workbench (KnowledgeWare)	Used to capture, model and analyse data about an organization and logically define application systems based on the analysis of user requirements.
Excelerator (Index Technology)	Used to develop process and data models, validate design information and generate documentation.

Even more significant improvements in development productivity than might be obtained from the use of CASE tools are likely to be realized from the greater use of 'object-orientated programming'. In this, the processes for creating and updating data, relating to an 'object' (such as any class of person or thing) of the enterprise, are held in self-contained software modules. In principle, any module can be used by any application software program, but is independent of that program. This means that the processes for maintaining data are common to all applications and provide a basis for the consistent use of data across the enterprise. Moreover, changes to the data maintenance processes can be made independently of changes to application function. This separation of the data, function and presentation provides the basis for flexibility and efficiency in meeting future user requirements and hence to the greater effectiveness of new investment in IT.

8.5   The non-architected environment

The architected environment sets the framework and the rules for the use of IT. It is likely to involve a range of platforms involving cooperative processing between central and local processors and centrally held and distributed data.

Processors, whether of mainframe, mid-range or personal computer size, will be employed depending on their performance, cost characteristics and application needs. There will be a high level of accessibility to consistent and non-redundant data across the enterprise.

However, the fully architected approach is not the only option. The power of small systems is increasing rapidly, as is the ability to interconnect them through local area and wide area networks, LANs and WANs. In the client/server approach, the needs for common systems and data administration of a community of client PCs are met by larger server processors, which may be monitored and maintained by IT professionals. The local PCs are free to provide functions wanted by the user, running applications locally. However, the widespread use of PCs within an organization can inhibit the development of corporate applications and the exploitation of corporate data, unless they are used under the provisions of an architecture, such as SAA.

Overall there is considerable scope for re-balancing the mix of central and local processing, often towards the mid-range and local mini-computer and away from the large central mainframe. The processes of downsizing (migrating from largest to smaller computers) and upsizing to achieve the optimum balance of function, usability and cost, are likely to continue. Freedom from the constraints of corporate architectures, standards and development time-scales enables the PC user quickly to acquire the function specifically needed, probably through an appropriate package. Change may be largely accommodated by discarding unwanted system components and plugging in new ones. The decision to invest and the ongoing cost is under the user's direct control and the business benefits are local and visible.

However, the utilization of the power and function of PCs is often abysmally low. Users do not always understand what function they actually require. Software packages may not be able to communicate on LANs. Many PCs are used with inadequate arrangements for physical and data security. Apparent cost advantages may prove to be short-lived. Business cases for mainframes may be few; they tend to be even scarcer for PCs.

In summary, whether and how IT architectures are implemented is becoming more crucial to the business case for IT and the issues should be spelt out in the investment cases for individual projects. Establishing value for money from IT is becoming no easier with the increasing complexity of processing and networking options. A quotation from the 1990/91 Price Waterhouse IT review,[4] attributed to a civil servant, encapsulates some of the business case issues well:

> Government procurement policy is that IT investment must be justified by benefits. But with the advent of server/workstation architecture and the core/applications systems development model, the nature of benefits is changing. Benefits come from computer applications. When it comes to the expensive business of laying down the core, however, procurement is divorced from applications. Justifying the server, the network, the shared database, what might be called the infrastructure platform, this is a whole new ball game. And any attempt to apportion the infrastructure amongst the applications is on a hiding to nothing. The fact that any apportionment is completely arbitary, although damning, is not the main problem. The fact is, as with most infra-structures, most of the subsequent applications won't have been thought of.

Above all, the right architectural choices must be made for each enterprise, for its business units and for IT applications, and in situations of complexity, instability or diversity the architectural approach might be less appropriate.

Mapping the business architecture of data and processes lays the foundation for systems flexibility. Employing an architecture for an enterprise's applications will minimize the costs of developing and maintaining them. Using an architecture to select the infrastructure platforms will minimize constraints and redundancies.

Daniels and Daniels in describing a global vision for corporations conclude,[10]

'Today, we are firmly convinced that companies attempting to go global will have to incorporate some form of global system design processes or the various pieces of the organization can never be integrated. Orchestrating this process is the major job of the CIO.' The growing global reach of many enterprizes serves to underline the message.

References

1 Brandt R. Allen and Andrew C. Boynton, Information Architecture: In Search of Efficient Flexibility, *MIS Quarterly*, University of Minnesota, December 1991.
2 Fred Niederman, James C. Brancheau and James C. Wetherbe, Information Systems Issues for the 1990s, *MIS Quarterly*, University of Minnesota, December 1991.
3 Peter G. W. Keen, *Shaping the Future*, Harvard Business School Press, Harvard, 1991.
4 *Information Technology Review 1990/91*, Price Waterhouse, 1990.
5 *Corporate Technical Architecture*, IBM GU20-1113 (obtainable from IBM National Enquiry Centre, London).
6 Pamela Gray, *Open Systems – A Business Strategy for the 1990s*, McGraw-Hill, Maidenhead, 1991.
7 *Systems Application Architecture, AD/Cycle Concepts*, IBM GC26-4531 (obtainable from IBM National Enquiry Centre, London).
8 *Business Systems Development Method (BSDM)*, IBM GE19-5387 (obtainable from IBM National Enquiry Centre, London).
9 *An Introduction to SSADM*, Information Systems Engineering Division, Central Computer and Telecommunications Agency, Gildengate House, Upper Green Lane, Norwich, NR3 1DW, 1991.
10 John L. Daniels and M. Caroline Daniels, *Global Vision – Building New Models for the Corporation of the Future*, McGraw-Hill, New York, 1993.

9
Business case planning methodology

Planning has been described as the process of deciding what to do in the future. A method is an orderly procedure for performing a process. A methodology is a system of methods or a group of methods; it can also imply the rationale behind the methods. In general we shall use the simpler word 'method', while recognizing that a planning task will often employ several methods and thus be a methodology. We have also used the word 'technique' to signify the smallest component of a method: it is the mechanics of the method.

This chapter looks at planning methods which lead to the preparation of the business case and at the principles on which their successful use is based. These methods are more structured than the methods used by most enterprises; as application planning consultants we have used them successfully for many years. Taken together these methods form a methodology for preparing the business case for an IT investment. The techniques (Chapters 10 and 11) used within these methods, are more typical of those used within many enterprises.

9.1   Planning for change

People often want to do things better. One way of doing this is to copy those who do things best. This can be seen as using the methods and techniques they use, but excellence is more than technique. Successful stage artists have more than just technique; they prepare the audience before they apparently start their act.

In making the business case for IT there are two distinct components. Firstly there is the creative idea and the proposal; then there is its implementation and realization of success. Making the business case is really about the former, but this is of no value without the latter. The idea must be converted into effective action, and that is often more difficult than proposing the idea in the first place.

Methods and techniques have to be used in the right environment to be effective. Good ideas have to be born into favourable conditions to flourish or even to survive. The 'right environment' and the 'favourable conditions' have much in common, because, whether planning (making) the business case or implementing it, we are dealing with the process of change. First comes the planning project and then comes the implementation project; and both projects are part of the change process.

Therefore, we start by considering those things which support and promote the process of change because they also help in producing a business case. These are what the successful business 'artist' gets right before using a method and techniques. They need to be observed both during project planning and also during implementation, if the project, once launched, is to stay afloat and on an even keel.

9.1.1   *The critical success factors (CSFs) of creating change*

We quote the views of other experts. Ashridge Management Consultants have identified those areas which need attention in promoting significant change within a technical context.[1] Four things need to be right:

1 The strategic environment
   The business strategy must be clear, communicated appropriately to all levels and understood; so also the IT strategy. The attitude of top management to the investment and to the potential change must be supportive during planning and, once decided upon, unequivocal in determination to implement. The culture of the organization must be able to accommodate change and risk and to integrate personal drive and skill. Shared goals promote cross-functional team working.

2 Working relationships and roles
   Senior management must set the direction but the engine that makes it move is the assignment of responsibilities to individuals; to initiate, to contribute, to audit or to approve. There must be agreed management processes on which the change will run; meetings, budgets and controls and personal performance setting.

3 Communications
   Good communications fuel the engine of change. And most engines only need one sort of fuel. For change involving IT at least two groups of people are involved, the users and the IT specialist, each with their own language of ideas and words. For most IT investments, the planning and the change will involve many functions across the organization with their own knowledge and disciplines – and their own languages. The differences can only be ironed out by constant and structured talking.

4 Success recognition
   Is any one rewarded for success, or is success taken for granted? What is success anyway? It generally means different things to different people. If success is to be recognized for an IT project, then success must be recognized for other activities of the enterprise; it must be part of the culture. It is part of realizing the benefits of IT. Success must be measured in more than financial terms: it involves personal and team glory.

Introducing IT, even on a moderate scale, as Hochstrasser and Griffiths noted,[2] introduces change in terms of new patterns of work, new working relationships, new political power and new reporting structures. They have described the four key areas for being successful with IT and effectively managing change as those of creating a proactive corporate culture; encouraging risk taking and individual responsibility; raising information and IT awareness; and redesigning the shape of an organization.

While these ideas are not new, it is their application to making the decision to invest, and to implementing it, which will make the methods and the techniques work, rather than the value of the techniques on their own. Atkinson has described how a technique may fail without also having a process for creating cultural change; he concludes, 'Eighty per cent of total quality intiatives will fail because the managers believe a simple quality system is sufficient to create change. To be a world beater, to improve your competitive edge and reduce unnecessary rework costs, you have to invest in a major cultural change and question everything you do'.[3]

Moreover, significant change is not only a one-off event, particularly at the behaviourial level. One key to Japanese industrial excellence has been in applying the principle of *Ky'zen* – conscious, continuous, incremental improvement in small steps over many years.

9.1.2 IBM planning methodology

For nearly three decades IBM has offered planning methods to assist in the application of IT. The most powerful, productive and successful methods have been consistently used within the context of the principles we have discussed above, by skilful facilitators, working with a planning team. For any particular method these principles became prerequisites or conditions, which require:

1 An *executive sponsor* who selects the team, sets the terms of reference, guides the team and receives their progress reports and recommendations.
2 *Terms of reference*, which document objectives, deliverables and time-scales.
3 A *task leader*, as the chief 'problem owner', who represents the sponsor within the team.
4 A *method leader* who advises and manages the process.
5 A *selected team*, representing the main functional interests.
6 *Structured activities* to provide an appropriate framework and a systematic approach to the task.
7 *Committed time*, which is almost the most important and is invariably the most difficult to achieve.

In addition to applying these principles, many IBM planning methods have their roots in IBM's Business Systems Planning (BSP) methodology.[4] This was a top–down approach to defining the requirements for IT, based on an analysis of business processes and of data. It used an executive team and took place over several months. Subsequent methods have been more focused in their scope and in their duration, more flexible in the application of specific techniques and more action-orientated in their deliverables. However, they retained the original emphasis on consensus and agreement within the client team and on top–down analysis.

Hochstrasser and Griffiths[2] have observed, specifically in connection with IT strategy planning, but equally applicable to business case preparation,

> To do justice to the complexity of internal and external forces involved, neither a top–down nor a bottom–up approach to planning suffices. Instead, a participatory approach is needed, combining the top level view of senior managers with bottom line perceptions and feedback from users and line managers.

This is the essence of the application planning (AP) study, which has also exploited strengths of BSP. It has been in numerous AP studies, in a wide variety of industries, that the authors have obtained their experience of building practical business cases for successful IT investments. Studies have been conducted in a wide range of industries and government organizations, covering many traditional and leading-edge computer applications.

The AP study typically ran from between four to eight weeks. An executive sponsor set the terms of reference and selected the multi-disciplinary team. The team consisted of three to eight user managers and one or two ITD managers. Direct responsibility to the sponsor for the study progress was held by the senior manager team member, working with the IBM study consultant who managed the study process. Appropriate technical and business specialists may also have been engaged either full- or part-time. At the end of the study, the team produced a report and presentation for the executive sponsor.

By 1992, the AP study had been covered by the IBM worldwide consulting practice for IT strategy and planning and the principles for building business cases, embodied in the AP study, have been reaffirmed in the IT strategy and planning methodology. These principles are expressed in our business case methodology, which is defined by ten steps. The steps and their key deliverables are shown in Fig. 9.1. The activities of each step may be highly structured and performed by a team, or less structured and performed by individuals over a longer period. The description given below for each step could enable most of them to be implemented at a basic level by a facilitator or analyst with competence in team techniques, supported by professionals with specialized skills. Some of the key facilitation techniques required will be:

- Group processes design and management
- Group task performance (project managmement)
- Charting
- Goal and objective setting

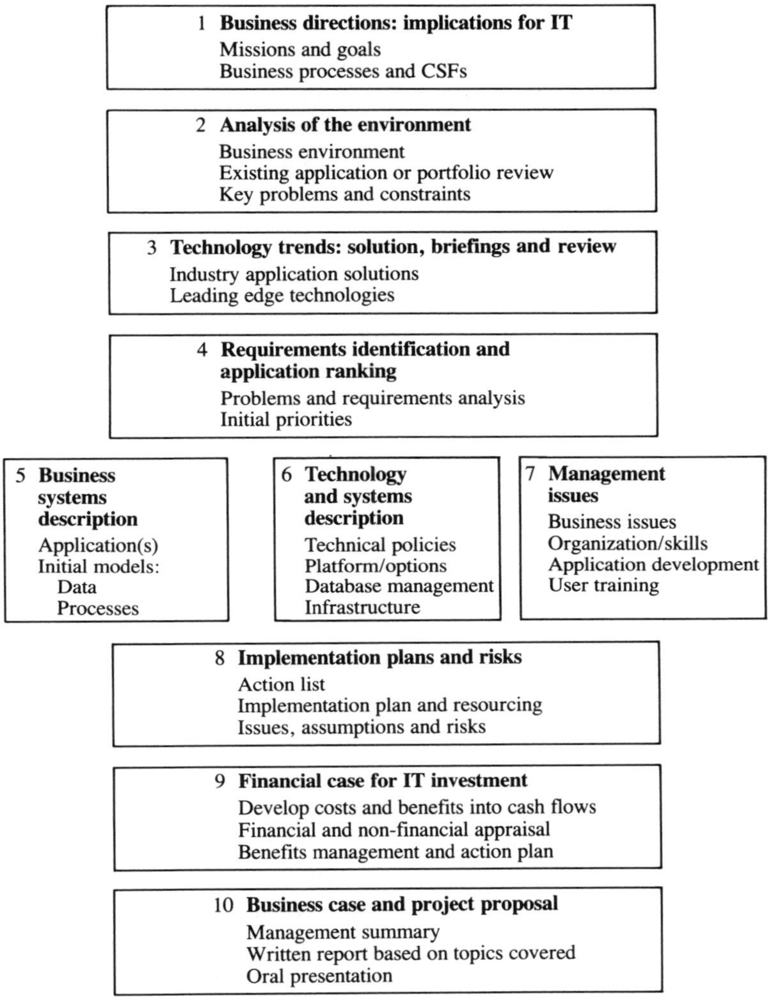

Figure 9.1.   Business case methodology.

- Vision setting
- Creativity techniques
- Brainstorming
- Metaplanning[5]
- Data collection; by interview and questionnaire
- Diagnostic techniques, for example, problem analysis
- Morphological analysis, for example, matrix construction
- Communications techniques (human)

Many of the business case activities and techniques will benefit from using IT. Word processing is fundamentally important. Enterprise-wide electronic communications will facilitate interview scheduling and speed the turn-round of questionnaire responses and interview minutes. Spreadsheet facilities will be used for activity scheduling and for data and financial analysis. CASE tools may be used to build data and process maps, where these are relevant. Desktop publishing and graphics programs are being increasingly used for the preparation of reports and other key documents.

9.2   Planning for the business case

Now we describe the ten steps. The description for each step is necessarily brief, based on our experience of what works, and includes some references to the approach of other practioners. It is assumed that the planning project will have been been properly set up. For this, agreement is needed with the sponsor regarding the terms of reference, the team members or participants, the time-scale and the arrangements for logistical support of the study. The selection of steps, and the emphasis given to each, will depend on the scope required of the business case and on information already available.

9.2.1   Step 1: business directions and IT implications

Step 1 (Fig. 9.1) starts with a definition of direction. It reviews the mission, goals and CSFs of the enterprise. It identifies the executive view of key problems of the moment and of the future. It confirms understanding of the enterprise's strategic plan and provides a foundation for the alignment of an IT investment with business needs. It often confirms and clarifies the terms of reference for the activities' subsequent steps. A specific method, Process Quality Management (PQM), has been described by IBM UK's Ward and Hardaker.[6,7] The PQM method is strongly team-based, involving the senior management team. Either in a two to three day workshop, or in a series of meetings over a period weeks, it progresses from generating a statement of mission and identifying key business processes, to defining the critical success factors for their achievement. It delivers a set of key actions agreed by all the executive.

9.2.2   Step 2: analysis of the environment

Within the AP study there are number of possible approaches to analysing the environment, to establish the current baseline from which progress must be made. Any approach will need to analyse the existing application portfolio, its potential and its problems and to review IT-related organizational constraints and problems. A high level business process model might be developed as a basis for problem analysis and requirements identification. The analysis can include any relevant aspect of the internal status of the enterprise. It might also include an analysis of the external situation and important trends, for example in a review of the competitive forces felt by the enterprise.

9.2.3 Step 3: technology trends – solution briefings and review

This step is about the art of the possible: of what is possible today and what will be possible 'tomorrow'.

It is important to generate creative thinking and to provide information on the the application of IT beyond the experience of those within the enterprise. This step aims to expand minds and to provide a seed bed for new ideas. Appropriately for such a free-wheeling requirement, the techniques used in this step are much less formalized and more varied.

This step is also important in helping to build a common language of words and ideas between users and IT specialists. It is particularly useful in this context when performed by in-house personnel. However, suppliers, such as IBM, have a role too. They can speak in more depth and with authority about their own products; they generally have industry segment specialists who research and understand the industry and its trends and experience in the application of IT.

There are two areas to be covered:

1   The uses of IT in the enterprise's industry segment. The briefing is conducted by an expert in the application area and may need to be repeated with different emphases for different groups.
2   Technology reviews and demonstrations. The latest in technology is demonstrated and that which may be available for the next generation may be indicated. Technology changes rapidly and it is important that users can make their own first-hand assessment of the applicability of technology to their processes.

   The session can be expected to include information on subjects beyond hardware and software, like those of architectures, open systems and business modelling.

9.2.4 Step 4: requirements identification and application ranking

Benefits assessment is often inhibited by an inadequate understanding or statement of business requirements. Therefore this step is critical to the whole business case.

Requirements will have been identified in the previous activities. However, more now need to be collected, sifted, related to the scope of the investigation, and then grouped into application areas, so that an initial view can be taken of priorities. This will indicate those areas needing closer attention in subsequent steps.

The main technique in this step is normally that of interviewing. However, structured workshops are applicable where it is desirable to take a broader view which is more orientated towards the external environment and the competitive world in which the enterprise operates. It is sometimes necessary to stimulate a creative response to emerging threats.

A method relevant to this step has been developed by Enid Mumford of Manchester University. Called Effective Technical and Human Information and Communication Systems (ETHICS),[8] it is simple and well-documented and depends on participation and discussion.

In ETHICS a team of about nine users from a small unit of the enterprise are assembled for two and a half days. In addition, two facilitators are appointed, and these are likely to be managers or senior professionals from the unit. The work activities are performed in subgroups by team members who have similar job profiles, using a questionnaire. The subgroups review their findings with the main group during and at the end of the first two days. After this, the facilitators summarize the group's work into an overall statement of requirements.

9.2.5   Step 5: business systems description

This builds on Step 4 by structuring the requirements into business systems or IT applications and by adding more detailed descriptions. The overall process needs a more structured and technically orientated approach. The evaluation of software packages begins in this step. Evaluation is made against checklists and necessarily covers functional comparisons and demonstrations. Data structures and technical platforms (Step 6) will feature in the assessment, as will supplier stability and competences.

Based on these descriptions, assessments and estimates are made of the savings and benefits which can potentially be realized from meeting the requirements. In some circumstances, parts of the Benefits Assessment Workshop (stages 4 and 5) described later in this chapter, can be used for the benefits assessment activities of this step.

Components of the IBM Business Systems Development Method (BSDM) (Chapter 8) may be used in this step.[9]

9.2.6   Step 6: technology and systems description

For many project proposals, the description of 'how to implement' will be clearer and better defined than the description of requirements. It is not unusual for more creative thought to be given to the solution than to the problem. This is one reason why the costs of projects seem to be easier to estimate than are their benefits.

This being so, we might expect to find some effective methods for developing initial systems solutions. But the process is not so easy to formalize, particularly in the early stages of the proposal. There are dangers in producing 'instant' systems designs; and yet some systems hypothesis must be proposed as a basis on which to build the business case.

If any set of business requirements for IT can be met at all, it is likely that there will be several options available. For software, an early classification of system solutions is likely to be into 'help', 'make' or 'buy'. For the hardware, there will be a possible classification into using centralized or distributed mainframe or personal computers, perhaps connected on a local area network (LAN). To avoid premature selection of the 'best' solution; the options must be described, selection criteria determined and then the advantages and disadvantages of each option carefully evaluated. The optimum solution may represent a compromise made from two or more options.

Apart from the business requirements, there will be technical requirements, coming from technical policies and architectures. These will act as constraints on the available options. The IBM Corporate Technical Architecture Study[11] provides a fuller methodology and a more rigorous approach to designing the technical structure of a specific business system is provided in the IBM End-to-End Systems Design Method.[10]

9.2.7 Step 7: management issues

For the successful implementation of any project, a number of issues will need to be addressed by management, some of which will be concerned with IT and some of a more general nature. Many of these will emerge as a result of the methods used during earlier steps. In this step these issues need to be identified, documented and appropriate actions recommended to address them. To help to identify such issues, a short constraints review workshop can be run, as described in Chapter 5.

9.2.8 Step 8: implementation plans

This step structures and describes the sub-projects which are needed to deliver the proposed solution. The tasks identified will include both the ITD and user activities as well as tasks performed by specialist functions, such as education and training. For an initial project proposal, this planning will only be done in broad terms and estimates of resources required will often need to be confirmed as the sub-projects are planned in more detail. However, the implementation plan is the key to preparing the business case. It determines what resources are used and when. It provides a forecast of when the benefits of the project can be expected to materialize. The project risks need to be identified and action taken to contain them.

Most organizations have adopted some standards for project definition and management. Some of IBM UK's are described within the Managing Information Technology Projects (MITP) procedures.[12]

The Central Computer and Telecommunication Agency (CCTA) has developed PRINCE (Projects in Controlled Environments).[13] This is described as '. . . a structured set of procedures designed specifically for managing projects in IS/IT environments. It offers a framework within which projects can be correctly designed and implemented'.

9.2.9   Step 9: financial case for IT investment

This is the climax of the investment planning process. This step collects together the financial output from the earlier steps and expresses it in a form suitable for financial evaluation. It also evaluates the intangible benefits and reviews the financial implications of the project risk assessments made in the previous step. The techniques available are described in Chapter 11 and components of IS/IS are relevant (see below).

9.2.10 Step 10: project proposal and business case

Good communication of the results of previous steps is essential. How this is done is bound up with the culture of the organization; some will emphasize the written word, others the spoken word. Pictures, graphics and exhibits have their place in adding clarity and emphasis. There is a need for immediate impact to gain attention and to precipitate action. There is a need for a more permanent record which will not fade, like memory, with time. And the adage 'What isn't written down, isn't said' is well worth remembering. No one method on its own will be sufficient to carry out this important task.

Most organizations have a nomenclature and standards for the format and content of project proposals at different stages of planning. We discuss the content of the business case throughout Chapters 10, 11 and 12. The business case can be presented either as a written report or an oral presentation – both have their place as a communication medium.

9.3   Alternative methodologies

In the two examples given below, the first provides an alternative approach to the business case methodology discussed earlier and the second method focuses on the traditionally difficult task of benefits assessment.

9.3.1   The total business case

The IBM Information System Investment Strategies (IS/IS) methodology is based on methods and techniques recommended and used by leading consultants, business schools and major corporations.[14] The methodology consists of five stages.

Firstly, it reviews an organization's expenditure on IT and compares it with industry statistics, where they are available. Then it models a company's published profit and loss account and balance sheet for the base year and extends it into the future for different business scenarios. IS/IS assesses the 'quality' of existing applications. It then investigates and compares the potential effects (on the profit and loss accounts, the balance sheets and on key ratios) of developing significant new IT applications. It provides for a sensitivity analysis of costs and benefits and for an assessment of project risks. This enables a comprehensive financial view of priorities to be made.

IS/IS is particularly strong in providing a technique for our Step 2, in which the main relevant activities are:

- Identify and age the existing portfolio of major applications.
- Evaluate each application (user view) against a 'best-of-breed' (expert view), based on:
  - state-of-the-art technology
  - meeting business needs
  - support for future business strategy
- Produce an evaluation of the portfolio as part of the planning baseline.
- Identify existing applications in need of renovation or replacement.

Generally, the use of proprietary methodologies, such as IS/IS, requires a level of expertise in their use not readily available in most enterprises.

9.3.2 Benefits assessment workshop

This workshop is based on the application planning study (discussed earlier), in which the groundwork for the actual estimation is done at a greater level of detail.

The workshop procedures

The workshop takes from one to five days depending on the size of the project, the numbers of people involved and the level of detail available in the inputs and required in the outputs. In some situations, using the powerful impact matrix, one day may be sufficient to analyse the key benefit areas. As well as quantifying benefits, the process will make a significant contribution in helping to define the objectives of the applications, to set priorities across them and also to identify some of the constraints and risks in implementing them. The process can also be applied to mature project proposals for which no business case has previously been prepared.

To be effective, the process must be set up carefully, by appointing a sponsor, a workshop team and clear terms of reference. The process consists of six steps.

1   Preparation
    Identify an executive sponsor who should:
    - Set the objectives of the task.
    - Nominate the group members (four to eight), including a task leader and a process leader, or facilitator.
    - Set the dates for the task and its completion.
    - Initiate the task, by attending a setup meeting and receive the workgroup's report in a feedback meeting.

    The time spent in the workshop is then apportioned in roughly equal parts across the following activities. If the group does not need to collect further information by interview, then this will shorten the workshop.

2   Initiate and prepare for interviews
    - Review the objectives, activities and key dates.
    - Review, by presentations, the work to date and particularly the statement of requirements.
    - Identify additional information needed, to be provided through interviews by members of the group, briefings for the group or through documents.
    - Prepare for the interviews, as for further discussion of requirements.

3   Interviews and briefings
    Members of the group, working in pairs, interview five to ten key managers. The questions for interview fall into four main areas, namely their job reponsibilities, the key problems which they meet and their critical success factors, their main information requirements, and the quantified benefits they expect as a result of receiving additional information.

4   Consolidate and analyse
    - Review the interviews and group requirements by application.
    - Analyse proposed applications using an impact matrix (see below).
    - Identify and document assumptions.
    - Develop quantified benefits estimates for applications or agree guidelines and an action list to do this in the next step.
    - Develop an outline solution.

5   Complete estimates
    - Individuals or subgroups are assigned to applications, to document details of benefits and assumptions and to obtain appropriate validation from colleagues through, for example, interviews.
    - Make initial estimates of orders of magnitude of costs.

6   Consolidate into presentation and report
    - Review the output from previous steps.
    - Agree the structure of any report and assemble draft.
    - Agree the structure of the presentation and assign preparation tasks.
    - 'Dry run' presentation prior to subsequent meeting with sponsor.

Table 9.1 (a) The 'impact' matrix

IT application	Positive impacts									Negative impacts					
	1	2	3	4	5	6	7	8	9	10	11	12	13	14	15
A	H	—	M	M	L	—	L	H	H	M	M	H	M	M	L
B	—	M	L	—	—	—	H	L	L	L	—	M	L	L	L
C	—	—	H	L	H	L	H	—	M	M	L	H	H	L	H
D	L	L	L	—	—	L	M	L	—	M	L	H	M	L	M
E	H	L	H	M	M	M	H	H	L	H	M	M	M	M	H

Impact rating: H = high; M = medium; L = low

(b) Examples of business criteria

Positive impacts	Negative impacts
1 Revenue – sales	10 Equipment costs
2 Income – interest	11 Network needs
3 Direct costs – people	12 IT development cost
4 Direct costs – materials	13 Users involved
5 Direct costs – space	14 Level of technology
6 Indirect costs	15 Dependencies
7 Management control	
8 Customer service	
9 Employee morale	

The impact matrix

The impact matrix (Table 9.1) is a key technique for analysing the benefits of applications. Two lists need to be agreed to construct the matrix. The first is a list of the applications to be analysed. The second is a list of the criteria by which they are to be analysed.

The criteria may be for positive and negative impacts of the applications on the business. Examples of positive and negative impacts are given in Table 9.1. The positive impact criteria can often be taken from major items in the management accounts and from key intangible benefits. Examples of negative impacts are size, technical complexity, number of users and the level of downside risk. The negative impacts are not strictly necessary for benefits assessment, but the process can readily include a high-level view of them, and is greatly enhanced by doing so. The impact criteria are best determined finally by the workshop participants, to ensure their understanding of them.

The first list is now made into the rows of the matrix and the second list provides the columns. The group, by discussion, assigns ratings of high, medium or low impact to each cell of the matrix. Initially, these perceived ratings are not quantified further, but numerical examples should be noted as the process procedes. The use of the impact matrix is discussed further in Chapter 11. In some cases, a more detailed analysis might be required of the impact of an IT application, and in other cases it might not be realistic to reduce the benefits to numeric values. However, in our experience this focused workshop contains the essential ingredients to enable benefits to be quantified in most situations.

References

1 *Bringing about change in a technical environment*, Workshop by Ashridge Consulting Group Ltd, Ashridge Management College, Berkhamsted, Hertfordshire HP4 1NS, UK.
2 Beat Hochstrasser and Catherine Griffiths, *Controlling IT Investment: Strategy and Management*, Chapman Hall, London, 1991.
3 Philip E. Atkinson, Creating Cultural Change, *Management Services*, November 1988.
4 *Business Systems Planning*, IBM GE20-0527, obtainable from IBM National Enquiry Centre, London.
5 Eberhard Schnelle, *The Metaplan-Method*, Metaplan GmbH, 2085 Quickborn, Goethestrasse 16, Germany.
6 Bryan Ward and Maurice Hardaker, Getting Things Done, *Harvard Business Review*, November–December 1987.
7 Tim Lincoln (ed.), *Managing Information Systems for Profit*, John Wiley & Sons, Chichester, 1990.
8 Enid Mumford, *Designing Human Systems for New Technology (The ETHICS Method)*, Manchester Business School, 1983 and 1990.
9 *Business Systems Development Method (BSDM)*, IBM GE19-5387, obtainable from IBM National Enquiry Centre, London.
10 *End-to-End Systems Design*, IBM GU20-1121, obtainable from IBM National Enquiry Centre, London.
11 *Corporate Technical Architecture*, IBM GU20-1113, obtainable from IBM National Enquiry Centre, London.
12 *Managing Information Technology Projects (MITP)*, IBM GU20-9076, obtainable from IBM National Enquiry Centre, London.
13 *PRINCE OVERVIEW, The PRINCE Project Management Method*, Information Systems Engineering Division, Central Computer and Telecommunications Agency, Riverwalk House, Millbank, London SW1P 4RT, UK.
14 *IS Investment Strategies (IS/IS)*, IBM G520 6497, obtainable from IBM National Enquiry Centre, London.

Part 2
The decision-making process

The five stages of making the business case

At the beginning of this book three questions were posed: 'Does this investment potentially represent value for money'?, 'Is this investment what I really want'?, and 'Has this investment been managed well'? Some answers to these questions have been discussed and many fundamental issues addressed. The first few bites have been taken, but the core requirement of how to decide, on the basis of a business case, whether an investment in IT is warranted at a particular time, still remains.

Figure P1 gave a pictorial view of the book. The topics of Part 2 now discuss the five stages of the decision-making process, from its inception to its achievement and feedback. The topics of Part 1 have taken a wider view of the context in which investment decisions can, and should, be made. Chapters 2, 3 and 4 considered the relationship between, and implementation of, business and IT plans. It is there that managing the benefits and value of IT finally comes to rest. Measuring the performance of the total resources allocated to IT, rather than just new investments, was discussed in Chapter 5. Planning is important in aligning the activities of the IT department with the objectives of the business, but there are other approaches, and these were covered in Chapter 6. In an analysis of our own consultancy assignments we showed how links are established between competitive strategies and the application of IT (Chapter 7).

Investment is about building for the future, and for this the subject of architecture is relevant; its impact on the business case for IT was explored in Chapter 8. Investment is also about change; that is why it is made – to do things differently and better in future. In Chapter 9 we considered those factors which are vital to realizing successful change, before reviewing a practical and proven method for preparing a business case for an investment and for change.

Part 2 of the book concludes by describing how to manage benefits and to measure them after the investment has been made. But first we describe how to build and evaluate a business case for an investment project, prior to making the decision. We are concerned with the difficulty of doing it at all, as much as with how to do it 'properly'. While keeping within the boundaries of our own successful experience, we describe our view of current best practices. We do not seek to give a counsel of perfection or to prescribe how it should or could be done. We shall let others help to set the stage for the scenes of this act.

Aspects of the task and recent investigations

'However, their [Western-trained managers'] unwillingness to take risks is less a consequence of differences in national cultures and risk preferences than of a flawed institutional process for capital investment decision making'. Sharp,[1] writing in the *Sloan Management Review*, spotted a key problem – a flawed process. Solutions are less easy to formulate because decision-making is necessarily a complex activity. In his article, Sharp gives some help: he 'adds a stage to the appraisal process in which managers identify, analyse, and approximately value the options embedded in high-risk investments, without recourse to complex option valuation formulas'.

Although this is a useful addition, which we shall explore further, it does not give a broad enough account of 'the process for capital investment decision-making'. The decision-making process needs to start with a clear statement of objectives. It proceeds by assembling the information on which to base the decision and an appraisal process to arrive at the decision. It then continues with the implementation of the decision, measurement of its success and feedback of the results. These will form part of the information presented for the next similar decision and this feedback completes a necessary cycle of events.

Part 2 discusses key aspects of this process in some detail. A 'process' is a sequence of activities undertaken to produce, in this instance, a business case and an investment decision. It is the business process for the business case. (In Chapter 1 the term business case is defined as the rationale for making an investment and it is positioned relative to the financial case and to the project proposal.) Many 'quality' programmes are based on process improvement. Investigating the process of 'making the business case for IT' is, therefore, likely to be a good starting point for improving the quality of the investment decision.

Besides Professor Sharp, others have considered the evaluation process and cycle. Willcocks and Lester have looked at the evaluation of IT projects at the project feasibility stage.[2] They proposed an evaluation framework consisting of five stages, as shown earlier in Fig. 4.1. This can be compared with our own process framework in Fig. P2. We have more stages associated with the proposal and feasibility evaluation and provide for iterations through finer levels of detail, while they provide for more stages during and after implementation.

In their investigation, Willcocks and Lester asked the respondents of 50 questionnaires to assess the success of the evaluation procedures that they used at the five stages of their evaluation cycle. Only 66% of the respondent organizations completed an evaluation at all five stages. Some organizations completed evalu-

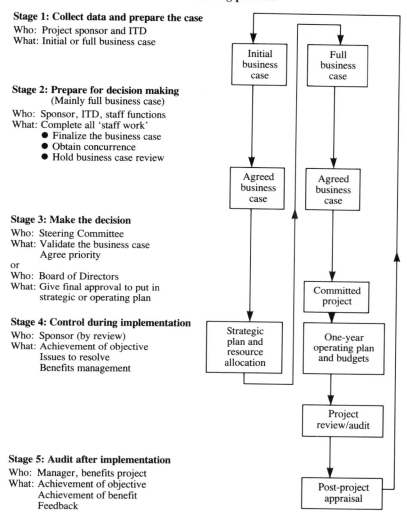

Stage 1: Collect data and prepare the case
Who: Project sponsor and ITD
What: Initial or full business case

Stage 2: Prepare for decision making
       (Mainly full business case)
Who: Sponsor, ITD, staff functions
What: Complete all 'staff work'
       ● Finalize the business case
       ● Obtain concurrence
       ● Hold business case review

Stage 3: Make the decision
Who: Steering Committee
What: Validate the business case
       Agree priority
or
Who: Board of Directors
What: Give final approval to put in
       strategic or operating plan

Stage 4: Control during implementation
Who: Sponsor (by review)
What: Achievement of objective
       Issues to resolve
       Benefits management

Stage 5: Audit after implementation
Who: Manager, benefits project
What: Achievement of objective
       Achievement of benefit
       Feedback

Figure P2.   The decision process – a framework for making the business case.

ations at other stages. In our experience, many organizations will have procedures which cover all five of these stages but, subjectively, we would consider a figure as high as 66% to be somewhat optimistic, if taken to reflect consistent practice. (Farbey, Land and Targett[3] found that 12 out of 16 projects had *ad hoc* or 'no justification' procedures.) Nevertheless, the results of the survey are worth repeating and are shown in Table P1. They show a good level of satisfaction, at least by the survey respondents, with evaluation procedures across all stages of IT development.

However, the procedures do appear to have problems. As one of their conclusions, Willcocks and Lester draw attention to the growing concern over the inadequacy of present cost–benefit analysis methods, in assessing the true worth

Table P1   Types of evaluation and levels of satisfaction[2]

Type of evaluation		Satisfaction level*					
		A	B	B/C	C	D	V
Feasibility	(50)	7	36	3	—	—	4
Development	(44)	5	31	1	3	—	4
Implementation	(42)	2	33	2	1	—	4
Post-implementation	(40)	3	30	2	1	2	2
Routine operation	(41)	9	27	1	—	1	3
Other (not specified)	(7)						

*A = very satisfied
 B   = satisfied
 B/C = not satisfied
 C   = obstructive
 D   = pointless
 V   = varies

of IT. They restated that, '. . . many organizations could not justify their future investments in IT because their calculations for investment in IT were not as rigorous as those for other capital investments'.

In our view cost–benefit methods alone have never been a satisfactory way of evaluating IT investments and, in practice, when the decision to invest is made, other criteria also figure large. This view is shared by other writers, including Willcocks and Lester. Before proceeding to discuss in Part 2 the principles and techniques which can be applied to analyse and quantify the potential benefits of IT investment, we take a closer look at the decision-making process.

A framework for the investment decision

The purpose of preparing and evaluating the business case is:

1 To assure top management that the input to the investment proposal and concurrence with it is complete across all functions.
2 To quantify its value and priority with respect to other investments.
3 To provide an informed basis for authorizing the inclusion of the investment proposal in the business plan.
4 To provide a basis for monitoring and control within the business plan and to establish value for money from the investment.

The framework used to describe the process of making the business case is given, in five stages, in Fig. P2. Where does it all start? Sometimes it is hard to say where the germ of an idea originates. It might come from a creative activity in which attention is focused on 'What *should* we be doing that has not yet been proposed?' It might come from an imaginative individual who links a business opportunity to a new IT capability. It might come from watching competitors or industry developments. Sometimes it needs no imagination to see that IT is the only practical answer to the need, the only questions to answer are 'How?' and

'When?' Our assumption at this stage is that someone, somewhere in the enterprise, believes that a beneficial change can be brought about or supported by IT. The decision to investigate the idea further is the first decision to be made.

The process shows (Fig. P2), how both the initial and the full business cases (and particularly the latter) are likely to go through each of the first three stages:

- Prepare the business case: collect data.
- Evaluate the business case: prepare to make the decision.
- Make the decision.

Initial proposals are needed as input to the strategic plan, and the full business case is needed for the one-year operating plan, as described in Chapter 4. Each stage will involve different activities, requiring different techniques. The stages will not necessarily be clear cut; in practice they will merge smoothly into each other.

Within the first two stages various methods and techniques will be used to build the business case, and some of these have been described as a 10-step methodology in Chapter 9.

The process of committing to investments in IT needs to be iterative. It needs to proceed through stages of growing confidence, involving first concepts, then calculations and finally controls. This approach was introduced in Chapter 4 and is taken further in Chapter 10.

It is increasingly common for project sponsors to initiate project proposals. They will depend heavily on the skills of the Information Technology Department (ITD, Chapter 2) for their preparation and look to other functions (for example, other business units, finance, premises and personnel) for further input or for validation. Each stage of the process will involve people with different job roles and responsibilities (and hence skills). For an effective process, these must be defined and communicated clearly to all involved (Chapter 11).

How the decision is made is discussed in Chapter 12. At the end of it all, benefits, like justice, need to be seen to be done. Therefore, the fourth and fifth stages, described in Chapters 13 and 14, will provide for:

- Control during implementation.
- Audit after implementation.

The basis for any business case lies in collecting sound data in Stage 1. What these data are, and how they may be collected, is next addressed in Chapter 10.

References

1 David J. Sharp, Uncovering the hidden value in high risk investments, *Sloan Management Review*, **69**, Summer 1991.
2 Leslie Willcocks and Stephanie Lester, Information systems investments: evaluation at the feasibility stage of projects, *Technovation*, Winter 1991.
3 Barbara Farbey, Frank Land and David Targett, Evaluating investments in IT, *J. Information Technol.*, **7**(2), June 1992, pp. 109–122.

10
Stage 1: collect data and prepare the basic case

10.1 Types of data needed

At the heart of the wide range of information which is needed for the business case is that which relates to costs and benefits and to the price and the value of change. Benefits generally appear to be more difficult to quantify than costs. Therefore, while this chapter gives a broad overview of collecting data it concentrates on identifying and estimating benefits.

Data collection activities will often be defined and carried out in accordance with an organization's systems development standards and checklists. However expressed, a project's business case will need data in three main areas:

- Requirements and business objectives, describing the desired changes. The specification of these forms the basis for generating other data.
- Systems solutions and options, including resource estimates for internal systems development work, prices and specifications for purchase items with technical constraints and assumptions.
- Estimates of the benefits which will result from satisfying and meeting the requirements.

As quantified benefits are needed for most business cases, before discussing other types of data the factors critical to quantifying benefits must be considered. Techniques for estimating benefits will only be fully effective when applied within a supportive environment. There are four critical success factors (CSFs) for identifying and quantifying benefits.

10.1.1 The critical success factors of collecting benefit data

It is vital to:

1 *Describe the changes that are required and which the proposed system will achieve*
Initial statements will be factual, describing the changes needed. Follow-on

124

statements need to concentrate on the potential effect of meeting the requirements and to quantify the change in numerical or financial terms. The effect of the expected change needs to be thought through and developed until it is expressed in terms that can be first measured and then managed. It is important to search for a measurable basis for making comparisons between the situation now and that which is proposed. Frequently the question 'What is the alternative?' helps to focus on the value of the proposed change.

2 *Find a person with the relevant accountability and authority to make (or to accept) an estimate of this change*
   For any one benefit area this may be a different person at successive stages of the project, generally moving down the organization hierarchy for more specific items and finer levels of detail. Ultimately, all the business benefits will need to be endorsed and accepted by the project sponsor.

3 *State the assumptions and levels of accountability within which the estimates are made*
   The boundaries within which the estimates are being made must be established. Costs and benefit estimates should be viewed, at any given stage, as equally difficult to make and roughly equivalent in their levels of confidence; both will be based on assumptions and will imply risks.

4 *Use a group of people and a structured process to facilitate making the estimates*
   This provides the necessary cross-functional, multi-disciplinary synergy, the lack of which often leaves benefit estimation beyond the capability of one or two individuals. It implies an appropriate level of sponsorship for this task.

These CSFs show that benefits estimation is not a mechanical process to be applied as an afterthought, but rather a culmination of successful planning. Willcocks and Lester,[1] in investigating the evaluation of IT projects at the feasibility stage, found that only 56% of the organizations surveyed admitted to including users in the evaluation process. One problem encountered in identifying and quantifying benefits begins to take shape.

The next part of this chapter will look further at the first two types of data needed for the business case, and this will lead into a fuller discussion of estimating benefits. But first we introduce a simple, real-life (but disguised) situation to illustrate how aspects of this and later chapters may be applied.

CASE STUDY

Al Luchini is Store Manager of a family-owned and run food supermarket, situated in a local community. The turnover of the store in 1992 was $4.25 million and it stocked some 6000 products.

This business is linked to a wholesale and distribution enterprise, Superfood, under which name the family business operates its franchise.

Superfood provides bulk purchases for branded goods and its own-label products, as well as systems facilities and support for its business associates.

In 1990 the supermarket's Executive Board were considering an investment of $150 000 to refit the store. Al Luchini was convinced that any expansion of facilities should include electronic point of sale (EPOS) checkouts, and computer systems for stock control and reordering, to be available from Superfood. These new systems would involve installing new weighing scales, bar coding all products, a stock audit and the replacement of five manually operated tills with three EPOS checkouts.

The store refit had originally been planned for early 1991, but was delayed to mesh with the availability of stable software and systems from Superfood. In 1991 Al Luchini was co-opted on to a Superfood Steering Committee, to advise on store requirements for IT and to achieve his and other store managers' buy-in to Superfood systems.

The new computer systems, including the purchase of EPOS checkouts and software and the stock audit, represented an investment of $45 000. Benefits were identified by Al Luchini as the reduction of checkout staff, tighter stock control and better weekly sales information on margins and profits by line of business. Subsequent system modules from Superfood were to provide its independent associates with direct order facilities to suppliers, through EDI.

Al Luchini worked with his accountant to estimate costs and benefits and to prepare the business case for the store refit.

This case study will be referred to in later chapters as we move through the five stages of the decision-making process. This chapter discusses costs and benefits, who can estimate them and how. It provides ideas, checklists and a pro-forma which Al Luchini could have used for his business case.

10.1.2 Requirements and business objectives

The importance of having a clear statement of requirements can hardly be over-emphasized as a basis for estimating benefits. The business requirements for an information system describe the changes that are expected by the system users. However, developing a statement of the full requirements of a system is not straightforward. The real requirements can be hard to visualize without practical experience of using the system. The additional, and often contending, requirements of secondary users can be easily overlooked. Systems requirements should be created by users and not simply be the functional specifications of a software package, although this may be used to suggest and to modify requirements. Even in the early stages of a project, requirements can often be described by users in sufficient detail to give a basis for initial estimates for both costs and benefits, albeit with some carefully stated assumptions.

Angell and Straub sound warning notes against the expectation of easily achieving quality requirements in a 'Manifesto for information systems', published in the Price Waterhouse *Information Technology Review 1991/92.*[2] Their five point summary is:

1 It is no good complaining that users do not know what they want. Nobody does.
2 Even if they did, events would prove them wrong.
3 An IT management style that insists on complete statements of requirements encourages the construction of massive, monolithic systems, which are an immediate security risk, become increasingly inappropriate, and yet are incapable of change.
4 The situation demands a method of systems development that produces admittedly wrong systems faster rather than spuriously accurate systems slowly.
5 It demands a style of IT management that concentrates more on the consequences of information systems than on their construction.

Overriding requirements, often given by users, are for systems to provide for growth and for flexibility: the manifesto amply illustrates an awareness of this issue. Enterprises are organic and dynamic (some more than others) and constantly in a state of change, from internal or from external pressures. Sometimes the requirements for an IT project change so dramatically that the original project has to be abandoned. Flexibility and a process to manage changing requirements are always needed.

In spite of the difficulties, change, and its net benefit to the organization, must be predicted. In specifying requirements and predicting benefits, the right balance must be struck between seeking impossible perfection and settling for a myopic pragmatism.

Although line managers are owners of requirements and responsible for their formulation, as individuals they do not have the time or the skills to define them. Consequently, requirements definition is typically a joint activity between the user, who has the knowledge, and the ITD business or systems analyst, who has the skill. Even then, experience and the passage of events brings changes into the requirements definition.

Nevertheless, a correctly owned, clearly understood, comprehensive statement of requirements describes the changes to be achieved and the impact that these will have on the business, and these are needed to assess the value of a proposed IT investment.

There are a number of sources from which requirements can be culled.

Goals, trends and competition

What the enterprise is trying to achieve, as described in strategic and operational plans, the environment in which it is operating, and the competition it is facing will all suggest some important high-level requirements for IT. But, of more significance, an understanding of these requirements leads to an appreciation of the priority to be given to other, more detailed, requirements.

Business processes to be supported

A business process lists the activities needed to manage a resource, such as materials, plant, real estate, product, sales channels, people or cash. The main activites in managing any resource are its requirements planning, its acquisition, its use or stewardship and its disposal. Business processes can also be determined for activities such as strategic planning, keeping financial records or monitoring customer service. With inter-enterprise electronic communications it is frequently necessary to consider the business processes of suppliers and customers. Initially, as an aid to determining IT requirements, it is the act of making the analysis which is of value, as much as the precise contents of each business process description.

A business process can be defined at many levels, and a format suitable as a basis for initial requirements identification is given in Fig. 10.1. A full process model is not required for the initial, or even for the full, business case. A description of 10 to 20 business processes provides a starting point for identifying the requirements for IT support. It describes what the enterprise does within a framework that transcends any present organizational structure. A set of business processes will help to pinpoint high transaction volumes, time-dependent activities, key communications as process inputs and outputs, and critical performance parameters.

However, new systems should not simply support existing business processes. The implementation of the processes may need to be redesigned; only when this is done may the full benefit be achieved and the most complete transformation of the business take place.

Requirements for IT support can also be identified by 'functional decomposition'. In this approach, the activities performed by a specialist discipline, such as marketing, are listed and analysed. The approach is similar to that of using business processes, but is more orientated towards the organization.

Information systems to be renewed

Even new information systems can fail to meet all of the expectations of all of its users. Older systems will have many deficiencies. Often the problems are more to do with unrealistic expectations of the life of systems. If information systems were visible, as are other assets, such as buildings and plant, then the problems that can

---

Business Process Title: Manage People

Objectives

1   To maintain the skills and numbers of people required by the operating plan.
2   To establish management programmes which maintain the motivation and morale of company employees.

Activities

1   Plan staffing requirements in line with operating plan.
2   Recruit and train.
3   Prepare and maintain industrial relations policy.
4   Prepare and update personnel procedures manuals.
5   Administer remuneration and benefits.
6   Prepare job specifications.
7   Set objectives and monitor employee performance.
8   Develop employees skills.
9   Maintain statutory records.
10 Initiate retirement.

Critical success factors

1   It is vital to have efficient human resources administrative systems.
2   Human resource policies must be fairly and consistently applied.

Process performance indicators

Staff turnover.
Salary drift.
Training performance.

Key decisions

Levels of remuneration.
Hire and fire decisions.

Note   This business process will be owned by the Director of Human Resources and performed mainly, but not entirely, by the Human Resources function. Line managers will perform some activities in the process.

Figure 10.1.   Example of business process format and contents.

arise from extensions and patches applied throughout their life would be more readily understood. Not suprisingly, most reviews of existing systems will lead to a considerable list of enhancements to the functions currently provided.

Problems to be overcome

A problem is a negative requirement. Therefore a list of problems, whether from present systems or from other other areas of the enterprise, will provide a potential source of requirements for IT. Such a list can be produced from a problem brainstorming session, but the list requires further treatment. Problem statements do more than simply furnish requirements.

Each brainstormed problem, or group of problems, must be carefully articulated and properly structured to give root problem statements. For each root problem, the cause of the problem, and its effect, need to be identified. Generally, there will be multiple causes and effects. The causes will indicate the nature of the solutions needed to solve the problem and the effects the potential benefits of implementing the solutions.

Next, the root problems, or their causes, must be regrouped into common solution areas, together with their associated effect or benefit statements. The problem cause statements can now be converted into requirements, for the solutions to meet.

Further analysis indicates priorities for solving the problems. This analysis can be made by using the impact matrix described in Chapter 9. Now, either the root problems or groupings of the root problems form the rows of the matrix. Similarly, the effects are grouped to form the impact criteria in the columns of the matrix. This problem impact matrix is completed by rating each root problem statement against the list of potential effects. A final analysis can then be made of the solutions proposed to address the problems, by rating each against the same impact criteria on the matrix.

Sources external to the enterprise

While it is important that systems address known requirements, it is also vital that this does not constrain more creative thinking. Simply to automate known processes and to solve today's problems is likely to be poor use of an investment. Business process redesign will shake up current thinking, but there are also external sources which can be of value in generating requirements statements:

1 Literature reviews and external consultants, such as IBM industry specialists, are a source of state-of-the-art IT application descriptions.
2 Developments and trends in technology are a vital source of information: requirements are a function of what is possible.
3 A software package's functional specification can provide an excellent check-list and can also suggest requirements that might otherwise be missed. Supplier demonstrations are normally available for packages.
4 Industry segment conferences and associations will generate an awareness of developments in IT and prompt consideration of new potential requirements.

Having identified requirements, the costs and benefits of meeting them may be estimated.

10.1.3 Systems solutions and cost estimates

The costs of an IT project are often perceived to be easier to estimate than the benefits. This is rarely the case, although cost estimates do become a reality before savings. The cost estimates of a system solution appear to be more tangible because the assumptions and dependencies on which they are based are often not acknowleged or are poorly understood. Furthermore, costs seem easier to estimate because the task of making estimates is normally within the job specification of individuals who have the necessary skills and experience. Consequently, cost estimation is generally better understood. However, as a rule of thumb it is prudent to view both costs and benefits, as far as they are quantifiable, with equal confidence, especially in early project planning activities. It is equally wise to take upper estimates for costs and lower estimates for benefits, and to note those items not yet quantified.

Our discussion of costs is brief, not because cost estimation is easy, but because our present focus is on benefits. Typical cost areas, for which data must be collected are:

- Hardware and its installation
- Software provision and its customization
- Maintenance of hardware and software
- Running and operating
- Networking
- Supplies
- Staff, for development and management (IT and users)
- Training
- Consultancy
- Supplier support services
- Security and legal
- Risk and benefit management

A contingency factor of 10–25% will typically be added to the identified costs, particularly in the initial business case, depending on the types of costs included, the level of detail supporting the estimates and the associated assumptions. A further 10–15% will be added for project management.

Hardware costs are frequently only 20–30% of the total cost, and are often the easiest to identify. However, the combined performance of hardware and software will depend crucially on having unequivocal specifications of systems function and volumes. Software and organizational costs are significant and rising. Unless a software package is used, human resources is generally the highest and most continuous cost. Costs (and benefits) must be revisited as development proceeds.

It is easy to see how costs can be underestimated and 'hidden'. Generally this happens, not from a deliberate attempt to mislead, but rather because there are many interdependencies between different cost items; and sometimes costs are omitted through woolly thinking. (As a compensating factor, complete benefits are equally difficult to forecast.) To minimize misunderstandings, assumptions on which the estimates depend and unquantified costs should be documented.

Estimates will depend on:

- The performance required of hardware and software to process types and volumes of transactions.
- The development work content needed to provide a given set of functions.
- Shared processing facilities, for example terminals and networks.
- Function which is extra to a given user's immediate requirements, for example in 'mandatory' security facilities.
- System design factors which might protect performance in the long term but which have a short-term development cost. Operating costs can be hard to manage down, other than by redesign.
- The balance of development cost against eventual maintenance cost.

In addition, there will be matters of principle to be decided. For example, should the proper cost of processing include both direct and indirect costs? For a new system, which can use available processing capacity, the cost can be calculated as the marginal cost of the processing power needed to run this extra application, or a full processing cost, which includes operating and management expenses. The marginal cost may be acceptable for one new system, but will lead to an understatement of the total costs for all systems.

Apportioning the full cost of the IT infrastructure is even more difficult. It is often omitted from the estimation of system operating costs. There are parallels in deciding how to charge for transport facilities. For the highway infrastructure, it is by national tax or highway toll, or a mixture of the two. For air transport, the full cost is more directly borne by the user. A satisfactory road transport infrastucture is vital for national economic growth; air transport is more specialized. Some IT systems should be supported by a corporate investment in the IT infrastructure, and some should pay their way. The policy established for this will change over time and with system maturity. Whatever the policy, the initial decision to invest will also be a decision to incur, for the life of the system, the management, operating and maintenance costs of the supporting IT infrastructure, which may be some four times the original investment, taken over a period of five years.[3]

Alternative solutions need to be considered. Most of the options will relate to the platforms on which the system might be delivered. Some financial appraisal can be so concerned with the evaluation of options, technical or financial, that it can fail to address the basic justification for proceeding anyway, with any of the options identified. Two main options will be to buy a program package or to develop new systems in house.

Packages can generally be installed more quickly and lead to an earlier realization of benefits, but they can restrict the user in terms of the function they provide, both in the short term and in the long term. In fact, to gain maximum advantage from the use of packaged software it is generally necessary to modify some business procedures in line with the packages' function. Of most importance is how the package structures and manages data and how well this fits with the business use of data.

Even if a package solution is envisaged it is still fundamental that the users produce a carefully thought through statement of requirements, rather than simply using the specification of function in the package as a checklist. The evaluation should include an assessment of the supplier's ability to provide support for ongoing use of the package, in the buyer's business environment, in the longer term. Finally, the existence of software provides an excellent opportunity for users to evaluate key parts of the package with their own data before finally committing to that option. Given an acceptable supplier and a package which runs on acceptable platforms, then a 60–80% functional fit is likely to make the package approach an attractive alternative to in-house development.

The main costs associated with a software package are its purchase price, its maintenance cost, the cost of customizing it and the cost to the business of implementing it.

Estimating the work content of systems development depends on key skills; some claim it to be an art as much as a science. Nevertheless, the quality of estimating can be enhanced and made more consistent by use of appropriate tools and techniques. The IBM Development Estimating Workbench, using an IBM PS/2, supports three main tasks, namely estimates of project effort, assessments of risk and function point calculations. Function point analysis recognizes five functions that a system might need to support. These are external inputs, outputs, enquiries and files and internal files. Each function is classified for its level of complexity and given a numeric weighting. The total of the function points for the application is then adjusted for the overall characteristics of the application. This total can then be used to determine the number of lines of program code, the length of time to develop the application and to provide measures of development productivity.

Many of the hidden or extra costs that occur with an IT project are associated with systems testing and handover. Often the resources needed for this, including user training, are sadly underestimated. The potential for loss of effectiveness during early systems familiarization is well known, but rarely admitted.

The collection of requirements and business objectives and of systems solution and costs has now been covered. The third main type of data needed for the business case relates to the benefits of the project.

10.2 Benefits

By what criteria should the value of an IT investment be judged? Any quantifiable measure, however attractive, taken alone will be inadequate. IT investments are not peculiar in this respect; it is the same for any capital investment project; it fits with our everyday experience.

For example, a survey of independent schools has ranked the top 200 performers (*The Daily Telegraph*, 24th August 1992). The ranking was applied on the basis of measured academic performance in national examinations – how else?

But what is measured? The original pupil selection procedure? Or a school's ability to enhance an individual's performance? Many other criteria of excellence will be claimed by schools. To most of us, the objectivity of percentages is persuasive, but intangible benefits, such as with whom our child best mixes (if our own prejudice is any guide!), are often equally powerful. Considerations of cash flow and geographic location may override all others.

There is little doubt that IT projects are now harder to justify with only quantified benefits and that intangibles are being more highly rated in the overall assessment of the value of an IT investment. Some clients with whom we have worked have declined to produce or accept quantified benefits. Others will not entertain a project without acceptable financial figures and evaluation. Between these extremes lies the right balance for the majority. The rest of this chapter lays the groundwork for reaching that balance.

10.2.1 Sources of benefits

As the requirements for IT are met, so benefits can be expected, otherwise there is no point in satisfying requirements. Therefore, the sources of requirements described above provide a checklist for identifying benefits.

However, potential benefits of IT can additionally be provided by:

1 *Post-project appraisals*   When these are conducted, they will provide a ready source of benefits examples (Chapter 14).
2 *Objectives and performance measures*   Even if benefits cannot be identified and estimated, they can be set as targets. These may be based on business or systems parameters. It is important, anyway, to set measurable objectives for a project and to establish a measurable baseline against which to monitor achievement.
3 *Business parameters*   These are likely to be existing management performance indicators, such as inventory levels and turn, debtor days, customer service or response levels, production volumes, raw materials and supplies usage, financial risk and exposure, waiting list length, etc. Every enterprise has its own measures of performance (and some more than others!) and the aim is to select or to establish that indicator which is most directly related to the proposed system.

     To be useful, the parameter must be numerical, with its meaning and content defined. A time period must be set for the required or predicted incremental change in the parameter. Most important of all, the owner of the parameter, with responsibility for managing the change, must be named.

     There is plenty of scope for setting performance objectives that do not form part of the normal management system. For example, an important objective might be to achieve an organizational change as the result of a major redesign of business processes. The extent and timing of the change becomes a performance objective.

Table 10.1   System performance parameters

• Function	The provision of additional or more complex functions, such as those providing a higher level of security.
• Service level	A faster or more relevant service for ITD 'customers', whether internal or external, probably set out in a service level agreement.
• Volume growth	The ability to handle additional transaction volumes, particularly at peak periods.

For replacing earlier computer systems, other parameters can be used, such as:

• Systems maintenance	The amount of maintenance or skill level required to perform it.
• Obsolescence risks	Upgrades to hardware or software will reduce or remove the risks which can arise from relying on potentially obsolete technology.

4   *System parameters*   There are a number of systems-related changes which may be used as a basis for making measurable comparisons of the status before and after implementation. Examples, for which objectives can be set, are system performance parameters, such as in Table 10.1.

5   *Other investigations and surveys*   Many investigations have been made of potential productivity benefits, particularly in the area of office systems, by IBM internal studies and by other consultancies. Not all enterprises surveyed have achieved tangible savings, but many claim to have done so. In this and other areas, and across many investigations, there is evidence of savings that have been, and can be, achieved.

Hochstrasser and Griffiths[4] found that, 'The exploitation of IT to extend the economies of scale by enabling companies to speed up the business cycle (56%) and to take on more work with the same level of resources (52%) has become a widespread benefit for the majority of managers'. There are many anecdotal accounts (some more supported than others) of savings achieved by individual companies. They are regularly published in the press and given at conferences; examples are the accounts from the Trustee Savings Bank[5] (Chapter 13) or the Woolwich Building Society.[6]

At a strategic level, the Butler Cox report, *Information Technology: Value for Money*,[7] provides an extensive list of case histories of organizations using information technology to achieve competitive advantage. Management consultants Touche Ross and the Institute of Administrative Management (IAM)[8] report that, for office systems, the users' experience of productivity exceeds that of the non-users' perception of productivity; both groups accept productivity gains are achievable.

The benefits of IT achieved and reported provide a useful guide; they do not replace the need for an organization to think through what benefits it can reasonably expect to achieve, in its own circumstances, and the need for objectives and controls to be set which reflect those estimates.

10.2.2 Types of benefits

In Chapter 4 we reviewed the life cycle of a project. We showed that as the project is planned in greater levels of detail the nature of its costs and benefits change, they are first conceptualized, then calculated and finally controlled. This chapter is about the stages of 'conceptualize' and 'calculate'. Chapters 13 and 14 relate to 'control'. Benefits, which are rightly presented in conceptual terms in the early planning stages, must be re-expressed, as far as possible, in controllable terms before implementation.

In building the business case, the most important stage is that of 'calculate'. Tangible quantified benefits may give the impression of being calculated. In most cases this will only be partially true, because even quantified benefits depend on large amounts of personal judgement, regarding the effect and the certainty of achieving the change. (Some people refer to all meaningful benefits as tangible, some of which can be quantified and some not. We shall continue to use tangible and intangible to equate with quantified and unquantified.)

Within the category of tangible benefits, some further useful classifications can be made. They can be:

● Cost or expense reduction.
● Cost or expense replacement.
● Cost or expense avoidance.
● Revenue or income, expressed as a profit contribution.

The classification of intangible benefits is less easy, at present there being no standard definitions to follow. Some important types of intangible benefit are discussed later in this chapter.

Sometimes benefits are classified as those which improve *efficiency* (enable tasks to be performed more quickly), improve *effectiveness* (enable tasks to be performed better) or those which assist *innovation* (enable new things to be done). However, benefits in these categories still need quantifying.

10.2.3 Tangible benefits

The three stages through which tangible benefits progress, conceptualize, calculation and control, are now considered further.

Stage I: Benefits in concept

From the viewpoint of the chief executive there are some business principles and technology trends that suggest that there will be benefits from investing in IT. Typical of these are:

- Income must rise faster than expense. The trends must be wedged open to increase profitability.
- Key business ratios need to be maintained or improved. These will include ratios for expense, profitability, working capital and return on assets.
- The cost of people is rising and that of technology falling.
- The functions delivered by technology are increasing.
- For office workers, the per capita investment in technology is increasing.
- Speed of access to information and faster communications gives rise to new business opportunities and helps to raise the productivity of people.
- Action-orientated enterprises with good cross-functional coordination are characteristically strong. Local autonomy needs to be combined with central control.
- National governments have actively promoted IT.
- Further significant cost restructuring will only be achieved by redesigning business processes, and this will need IT support.

Any of these trends can point towards the general need for information systems. It is not likely that any of these alone will precipitate a greater investment in IT, although it is not unknown for funds to have been made available for the purchase of PCs simply to enable staff to become familiar with their business and leisure use. The trends imply that there is benefit to be gained from IT.

However, for any enterprise there will be more specific conceptual benefits. Three terms are sometimes used to describe key benefits potential, namely automation, information provision and business transformation. Information provision provides a good example. Many executive boards have, over the last few years, had a strong feeling that the provision of better management information would be of strategic benefit. Individual executives may have had specific benefits in mind, but overall the full and far-reaching benefit of management information will have remained a concept until the second stage of detailed planning has been entered. Then the concept has had to be tied down and quantified through specific examples.

The next stage depends on clearly understanding the total change which a project will bring about in the business.

Stage II: Benefits calculated

In this stage, the 'top–down' view of Stage I benefits concepts has to be underpinned by a 'bottom–up', Stage II evaluation. The middle and senior managers are those who can contribute most to this stage.

Because some new applications for IT appear to be unavoidable this might seem to provide an *a priori* justification for them. Meeting new legal or regulatory requirements and replacing or maintaining systems may all be viewed as mandatory. However, to avoid a justification myopia, the full business need must be established. Mandatory requirements may precipitate systems development, but other business requirements will, and can, be met at the same time and the benefits of doing this must be spelt out. It is not good enough to carry infrastructure developments on the back of 'mandatory' requirements; identifiable benefit generally accrues from infrastructure developments. Many business developments may be held to be unavoidable in the long term but they can still be evaluated with and without the application of technology or with different technological solutions.

In IT research and development projects, benefits are hard to estimate and, of more importance, are of uncertain achievement. However, financial evaluations can be made of the level of investment against the downside risk of a subsequent project being aborted. More often, the objectives of such projects are set to resolve technical issues rather than being expressed in terms which describe the value of the investment. It is unfortunate that some pilot projects slip into this area for want of a more purposeful approach to the validation of potential benefits.

Change is not alone in having a cost; zero change may also prove to be expensive. The cost of no change can often be foreseen, and that becomes a benefit of change.

For most, if not all, applications of IT, quantified benefits can be developed on the basis of potential people-related savings, other cost savings and additional income generated.

1 *Expense reduction: productivity and headcount*
   In many situations, direct estimates can be made of the potential headcount savings when a system is implemented. These are often expressed as units of labour such as 'full-time equivalents' (FTEs) or 'headcount', rather than actual people. Otherwise, the approach is to estimate potential productivity improvements, a technique that is often used for office systems.

   For this, employees are first grouped into suitable categories. These may be by function or department or more usually by job type, such as managers, professionals, secretarial and clerical, or by a combination of both function and job type.

   Estimates are made of time spent on 'office' activities, e.g. document processing, oral communication (meetings and telephone), filing, data retrieval and processing, general administration and travel. It is effective to collect estimates from individuals by means of questionnaires. Although the approach is very simple, and more rigorous measurement techniques can be used, studies have shown that the average activity times for similar employee groups are comparable. Based on a good knowledge of current procedures, and on an understanding of the proposed applications, further estimates can be made of the potential percentage productivity gains by employee category. These are weighted by the numbers of employees and their total costs in each category in order to calculate the productivity savings.

2 *Other expense reductions*

The nature of these depends very much on the enterprise. As for people-related savings, estimates are sometimes calculated as percentages and sometimes more directly. Examples are of savings in the costs of materials, documents, communications, printing and copying, inventory and storage, transport and distribution, rates and rents, space and buildings and in the utilization of plant and equipment, cash or lending limits. The list is almost endless. The savings are best first estimated in operational measures of performance and then financially.

Wherever a resource of the business is to be utilized more efficiently, there will be a potential tangible saving. To optimize the use of any one resource across an enterprise requires information about that resource to be collected and reported consistently. This leads to two main requirements. Firstly, integrated systems, with agreed definitions of data, are needed as a basis for good management information systems. Secondly, responsibility for managing a resource across the enterprise and for the quality of the business processes used to manage it, are best assigned to an individual. Typical traditional applications of this principle are in the management of personnel, cash and inventories. However, other key resources and performance parameters, such as enterprise-wide office accommodation and financial risk, are used.

3 *Expense avoidance*

IT will often be required to support new functions of the business, for example, in the need to supply information to meet new government legislation. In other situations, a new office or factory might have been proposed; or a new product or marketplace might be in plan; or business volumes might be expanding fast. In all of these cases it will be possible to develop scenarios with different levels of IT involvement and with different investment profiles.

Better usage of resources, resulting from IT, can often delay the need for further major investments in fixed or current assets. More productive staff will postpone the need for additional recruitment and office space. Lower inventory will reduce warehouse needs. Distributing computer power into PCs and employing cooperative processing techniques may take away the need for mainframe upgrades. Delaying a large increment in a major asset by smaller investments elsewhere can be a valuable benefit.

4 *Revenue-related savings*

One of the more important areas of benefit, and one of the harder to quantify, relates to the marketing position of the enterprise and its income. Applications which improve the level of service to clients and customers or support new products and services may lead to an increase in revenue. Applications which reduce the exposure of the enterprise to areas of business risk or to adverse competitive and environmental influences will be given a high priority. Percentage calculations and estimates of credible levels of

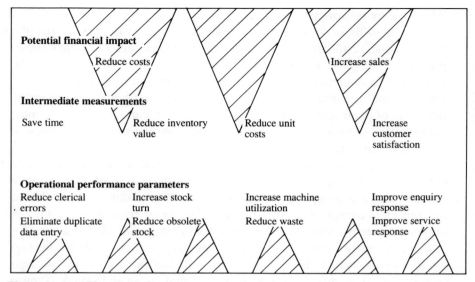

Figure 10.2.   Where benefits concepts and calculations meet.

increased revenue or of reduced risk are normally used in this area. Estimates of sales increase can sometimes be made by reference to the effect of previous projects, where, for example, some action has been taken to improve customer service and increased sales have resulted. Here, making an estimate is not the difficulty. Rather, it is being sure that the effect is reproducible, under management control and not unduly influenced by external factors. Revenue income from sales has to be converted into a net cash inflow by multiplying the income by an appropriate profit contribution factor.

Where concepts and calculations meet

Reference was made earlier to top–down and bottom–up estimates, and the situation is illustrated in Fig. 10.2. The diagram can be interpreted in two ways.

The first interpretation emphasizes the integration of many small savings and of cross-functional linkages. When developing the justification for an application, individual managers can often identify specific savings which they estimate could be achieved. Such an item is represented by a 'stalagmite' at the bottom of the diagram. It is unlikely that, taken individually, these estimates of benefits will fairly represent the full potential benefit. These 'personal' estimates need to be generalized to other users of the application. For example, a manager may state that the provision of one consolidated weekly performance report will obviate the need for staff to combine several others manually, saving one personday per month. But this is one manager and one report, making a 5% saving in time.

Other groups using other functions of the application will also make savings, and overall it might be estimated that 20 staff will be, say, 8% more productive. This is represented by a 'stalactite' at the top of the diagram. Moreover, better linkages across groups can result in significant productivity savings.

This paradigm helps to ensure that the overall benefit to the enterprise is properly assessed and supported by specific examples. Benefits then can be expressed as overall percentage improvements with a higher level of confidence.

The second interpretation of Fig. 10.2 is illustrated by the text. It emphasizes the migration from numerical to financial performance criteria; from cause to effect.

Figure 10.3 gives another view of the relationship between 'conceptual' and 'calculated' views of benefits. At the top level, profit is derived from income and costs. These are built up from intermediate groupings and from the lowest levels of cost savings or of potential revenue increases.

Thus, there is a linkage between benefits at different levels, and they will often be developed at successively lower levels as project planning proceeds. Curley and Henderson[9] have considered the evaluation of investments at the four levels of:

- National economy/industrial segment
- Strategic business unit
- Department, project or group
- Individual or personal.

From their investigation they conclude that,

> While it is important to refine both the models and the data gathering techniques used at each level of analysis, we believe that there is a greater need to focus on the *linkages* between levels of analysis. Thus, we need to better understand how changes in the productivity of individual workers could enable restructuring of a function or department. Similarly, how better integration of functions enables more effective strategies for gaining competitive advantage.

This has emphasized linkages between levels. Benefits from linkages across functions, either performance or time related, are neatly described by the 'value linking' and 'value acceleration' concepts of Information Economics, covered in Chapter 11. Both linkages, between levels and across functions, need to be considered in 'calculating' benefits.

Stage III: Benefits controlled

However, there is still a need to show how the improvement will be achieved, which leads to the third stage. How can time saved through an overall productivity improvement be used? Unless an enterprise has plans and programmes for

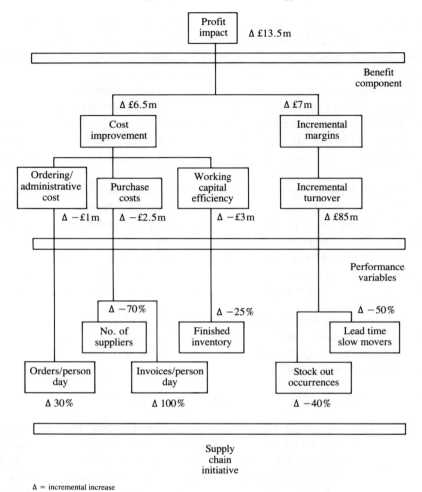

Δ = incremental increase

Figure 10.3. A chart of benefits: linking detail and summary statements of benefits. (Source: Glen Peters, Beyond strategy – benefits identification and management of specific IT investments, *J. Information Technol.* (1990), **5**(4), pp. 205–214.)

improving productivity through people it is not so likely that any substantial improvements will be realized through technology; but given that middle management and supervisors are motivated to control the business tightly, then technology will play its part. In fact, individual managers can often point to specific ways in which time saved in mundane tasks can be more profitably spent.

Non-people costs must be treated similarly. For example, an overall percentage saving on raw materials for a production process will not be achieved unless, within specified production units, material wastage is reduced by management action and control.

Hence the third stage is concerned with implementation and closes the loop of cost justification. An organization needs to have experience of, and a process for, cost justification of applications at all three stages, and to get progressively better at doing it.

If budgets are set and controlled, savings can be expected to accrue. The process of estimating benefits in the planning stages ought to highlight the need for appropriate management action during the implementation stages. This topic is expanded in Chapter 13.

10.2.4 *Intangible benefits*

Many of the most significant benefits cannot be reduced to credible, quantifiable amounts and are referred to as 'intangible' or 'soft' benefits. Sound business reasons may exist for a project that are not easily or credibly quantified. As we have emphasized earlier, if measurable financial results are the only, or even the main, criterion for accepting a project, then a vital project may be missed or rejected. Even financial professionals are encouraged to take a broader view than just that of a financial evaluation; and in fairness most do. As management accountants Littler and Sweeting[10] concluded,

> The competitive positioning of business in world markets requires that accountants in management teams adopt a strategic perspective. The primary significance of their work may be that it should influence people to achieve strategic objectives . . . . In doing so, it may be that the inherent inaccuracies in the data which they use and limitations of analyses are of secondary importance.

The issue really is not whether intangible savings can be expressed in potentially measurable parameters (although often they can), but whether this can be done with a worthwhile degree of certainty. It is the directness of connection between the function provided and the effect that it has on the performance parameter which is the limiting factor.

Tangible benefits, measured in quantifiable terms, give the more absolute measures of value. The value of intangible benefits can only be expressed in relative terms, and sizing them is discussed in the next chapter. Now we describe some examples of intangible benefits; we seek to demonstrate that intangible benefits are real benefits.

It is hard to produce a mutually exclusive set of definitions for intangible benefits; frequent interactions appear between them. Intangibles may be, by their very nature, undefinable. The main categories we use are:

- Management and organization
- External
- Internal

- Strategic
- High downside risk

It will be noted that 'assists competitive advantage' and 'improves profit' have been omitted, as all other benefits should lead to these.

Management and organization

1 *Improved planning and forecasting*
Planning can be improved by having better information and by better planning tools. These will often lead to quantifiable savings in planning time and effort. However, there is also a value in having plans which have been taken through more iterations with a wider investigation of options, as well as to greater levels of detail. The future will be more certain and the enterprise's response to the unexpected more measured.

2 *Improved levels of management control*
Comparison of plans with actuals gives a basis for control. Much of the benefit derived from this will be measurable, particularly at a high level. Often the provision of information will initiate many smaller management actions, each of which taken individually will be of no great significance, but which taken together will raise the enterprise's performance. There needs to be an ability to 'drill down' through levels of information to achieve control in this way.

3 *The time value of information*
Good control demands a short response time. To the human mind there is a value in maintaining a continuity of thought, which requires a timely presentation of relevant information. For all its shortcomings in completeness, there is a value in 'hot news'. How to use such news and information requires discernment, and hence its value tends to be relative rather than absolute. (Note also that there is value in being able to review complete information, collected over a longer time span and in a broader context.) Specifically, earlier information may lead to reduced inventories and improved service levels.

4 *Improved quality of decisions*
Arguably, this benefit is an end effect, like profit and competitive advantage. The benefit can always be explored by asking, 'What decisions and what effects do they have?' For an insurance company, an expert system can lower the risk of poor underwriting decisions, or enable less experienced staff to make the decision. However, in the early stages of planning a project the general benefit statement of 'improved decisions' is entirely appropriate.

5 *Organizational excellence and flexibility*
Ideally, systems should not be designed around an organization, but aligned with the more permanent structures of data and processes. This demands well-designed systems. Removing information restraints to reorganization, can be

of incalculable value to management. In IBM UK, the National Office Support Service has facilitated the strategic movement of people and jobs. In the findings from the Butler Cox 1991 Foundation Conference,[11] a survey by the Management Consultancies Association showed that the medium-term issue for chief executives will be maximizing profits through organizational effectiveness. Touche Ross and the IAM have noted that in 10% of their surveyed sample, concerns about disruption of the business were given as the reason for *not* implementing office systems.[8] For the 10% that might have been right; for many, the opportunity to reorganize and to re-train is a major benefit. The opportunity for reorganization is often linked to business process re-design.

External

1 *Customer service*
   This is important to both profit- and non-profit-making organizations. Serving other people is fundamental to good human relationships; people will also pay for good service. Long-lasting customer service recognizes both factors. Customer service is multi-faceted and is represented by what an individual customer actually wants, in addition to provision of the basic product or service. In the profit-making organization, providing customer service will result, more or less directly, in increased sales. In the non-profit-making organization, which is often in a non-competitive environment, the level of service (and cost) is set without the same recourse to market forces.

2 *Enterprise image*
   It is important for an enterprise to present a 'good' image to all its stake-holders: shareholders, employees, customers, suppliers and the community. Image builds confidence in the enterprise as a reputable supplier of products and services; the demonstrable use of IT for the good of stakeholders, is an intangible benefit. However, the image of an enterprise can depend much more directly on the use of IT, for example, where publicly available documents are produced to a higher standard or when the organization is more responsive in its communications.

3 *Better market development and market share*
   Customer databases and information systems are needed in retail organizations. Their development is normally expensive, not least of all in cleaning up old data. Provision of the new database is often phased over a year or more. Linking increased sales and market share to its completion is uncertain; there are too many other dependencies. But marketing professionals will declare that it is fundamental to market segmentation and to initiating effective marketing and pricing strategies; so why shouldn't they 'pay' for it in their performance objectives? Whether this remains an intangible depends on who wins the debate.

Internal

1 *Employee morale*
   IT brings change, and change can arouse feelings of insecurity and occasion-
   ally cause job losses. There can be a downside to using IT, but surveys
   generally show that IT is a welcome support for most jobs. In fact, most jobs
   are expanded through the use of IT. Even if a task is deskilled through the use
   of IT, the chances are that a less skilled person then has access to further
   training and a more challenging job. We all find satisfaction in doing a job well,
   and quality work needs quality tools. Attention to human factors delivers
   benefit. Happy people work harder and stay in their jobs. Some IT investments will have a calculated benefit based on reduced labour turnover.
   Customers and profits matter; so do employees.

2 *Product development*
   The time taken to specify, design and develop a new product is often of crucial
   competitive importance. IT will have a part to play in reducing product
   development time-scales. For manufactured products the design work can
   depend on it; for financial services their cost-effective delivery may not be
   possible without information systems. Whatever absolute contribution IT can
   make, the relevance of the time-scale may not be evident until it is too late, and
   the competition have got there first. For some enterprises the investment in IT
   might be the insurance premium against being last to the market.

3 *Manufacturing/processing responsiveness*
   Being responsive to customer demands and meeting market fashions
   requires flexibility upstream of the customer interface. Some of the benefit of
   just-in-time responsiveness will be measurable in inventory levels. Some of the
   benefit will accrue from the second-order effect of better customer acceptance
   of the product or service. Many enterprises are looking for major improvements in the performance of business (not just manufacturing) processes.
   Quality programmes have a vital part to play, but business process re-
   engineering, with its radical re-examination of both process components and
   assumptions, is more likely to deliver the tangible level of improvement
   required, both in the productive use of resources and in customer satisfaction.
   However, the techniques are complementary, although IT has a more central
   role in process re-engineering

Strategic

1 *Support for business policies and strategies*
   How far an IT investment supports a key business strategy can only be a matter
   of judgement. This is a true intangible: of great importance but not measurable. The management assessment of this benefit will depend on how directly
   the proposal for IT is seen to affect the business strategy.

2   *Fit with technical policies and architectures*
The relevance of architectures to IT investment was discussed in Chapter 8. Whether a systems solution is consistent with architectures and policies can be determined; whether it matters, in a particular instance, can be a more subjective assessment. In some cases, the costs or benefits of inconsistency in the short term can be calculated.

3   *Availability of future options*
Sharp has written,[12] 'an option . . . is the ability, but not the obligation, to take advantage of opportunities available at a later date that would not have been possible without an earlier investment'. His analysis is helpful for a key intangible benefit. He identifies incremental options and flexibility options. What premium should we pay for a more expensive software package which has interfaces for future extensions, compared with a cheaper, simpler program? How far will systems developed on rigorous data mapping now enable unforeseen user requirements to be easily incorporated in the future? Sharp says, 'My framework rests on two notions: that well-informed experienced managerial judgement is an excellent, practical substitute for exact option valuation; and that managerial judgements must be embedded in a formal decision-making process'. And that managerial judgement will be shared by users and IT professionals.

IT can also open up opportunities now, as well as options in the future. 'What-if' calculations, made during planning, could be done by an army of clerks. That is not a realistic option; the use of IT for this task is.

High downside risk

1   *Legal and government*
Although, to directors faced with legal responsibilities, some demands for IT seem irresistible, there are nearly always options; most legally required information could be provided manually, at a cost. It is a combination of the alternative cost and the risk of failing to comply that lifts the benefits of this requirement for IT above the status of intangible benefit to mandatory.

2   *Security*
The security, safety and continuity of data, equipment, programs, people and buildings is continuously at risk. In commenting on loss of security from fraud and espionage, the Price Waterhouse *Information Technology Review 1990/91* makes sobering reading: 'In total, assuming these figures to be representative, 65% of UK installations have suffered financially'.[13] The report reflects that, 'Beset with the problem of . . . meeting deadlines, few IT managers are going to aggravate the situation by insisting on some fancy security routines'. However rare the big disaster might be, security is an important intangible to identify and to evaluate – and some savings might well be quantifiable.

3   *Relative loss of position – what if we don't invest?*
    Sir Denys Henderson, as Chairman, ICI, has been quoted as saying:[13]

> I still worry enormously, both about the amount we spend on IT and the
> increasing difficulty of justifying that expense in terms of the bottom line. In
> the end, I think that this will work to the disadvantage of the suppliers of
> hardware, software and systems because simply to say, 'Can you afford not
> to spend when you look at your competitors?' or alternatively, 'There is
> hidden commercial advantage that is unquantifiable', will quite frankly not
> be enough in future.

We have been warned! But, if your competitor backs an IT horse which wins
– and this does happen – the benefits are no longer hidden. This intangible
benefit must be seriously identified and evaluated, but not taken for granted.
The UK government guidance for IT investment requires evaluation of the 'do
nothing' option.[14] The possible impact of delay or prevarication must be
realistically assessed.

10.2.5 *Further considerations for benefits estimation*

Benefits in non-profit-making organizations

Profit is sometimes seen as the ultimate benefit; but this is not so for all
organizations. Some enterprises, typically charitable bodies and public services,
provide no-charge services. They may generate some incidental revenue, but their
main measure of financial performance will be the cost of the service. In 1980,
Ryan, writing on 'Profitability in the non-profit environment',[15] noted that
financial control systems are essential in any business or service organization, and
that managers in a non-profit environment cannot be primarily motivated by
profit-related measures.

However, the benefits of cost reduction, or of providing more service for the
same level of resource, are the same for any organization. Difficulties arise when
increasing the level of service and at the same time increasing its cost. Typically,
the non-profit-making client will not expect to pay extra for the better service,
whereas the profit-making customer is open to persuasion. Thus, although service
is what the client wants, its greater provision has no price tag, and often has no
tangible value as a benefit. Neither, historically, have there been any competitors
to the non-profit-making organization. Many UK government initiatives, such as
the Citizens' Charter, are likely to bring a greater sense of realism into our
perception of the priorities and value of public service.

Meanwhile, in non-profit-making organizations the trickle of being more
customer service orientated has a stronger flow and the straight financial criteria
for project acceptance are no longer so tightly drawn.

Dis-benefits

A dis-benefit should be costed and included in the costs, on the negative side of the equation. Hidden costs are often feared; they arise from lazy planning, inexperience and the unexpected. A contingency provision, based on experience, normally covers the unexpected.

However, there will be some intangible costs that may be foreseen but not quantified. Management attention during system implementation, possibly involving overtime, is not likely to be costed; neither is the initial loss of productivity by those using the system normally calculated. If a potential dis-benefit is a real concern, then it must be taken into account. However, many dis-benefits are short term compared with longer-term, unquantified, spin-off benefits, which most projects also experience.

Benefits of 'unstructured' computing

'Unstructured' computing presents a special challenge in terms of assessing its benefit to the organization. By 'unstructured' computing we mean the provision of shared IT facilities that are not designed to provide the same function to all users; it is sometimes referred to as 'end-user' computing. Examples of unstructured, or end-user, computing are:

- *Office automation*   Electronic mail, diary management, document creation and distribution, filing and retrieving information.
- *Management information*   Including enquiry into enterprise data held centrally with local manipulation of data extracts and information reported periodically as part of normal management controls.
- *Personal computing*   Processing data under local initiative and control, but with communicatons links to other users on LANs and WANs.

These application areas will be used to illustrate some of the problems met in assessing IT benefits.

In many enterprises, unstructured computing is becoming a major component of the decision support system. Users are expected to be substantially independent of the IT department, looking to them (typically through an Information Centre or Help Desk) for advice and guidance or for help in tasks requiring specialized skills. Office automation requires specialized skills, but mainly in installing packaged software, rather than developing new systems. Across the organization, unstructured computing often represents a considerable usage of computer power, and for this reason setting priorities and justifying costs is important.

By its very nature, the estimation of costs and savings for unstructured computing is demanding. Techniques based on multi-disciplinary teams are more likely to yield quantitative results than other approaches. The techniques have to be capable of:

- Bringing together benefits and costs which are spread widely, and perhaps thinly, across the organization, for example, in better communications.
- Relating disparate areas of cost and benefit; for example, the cost of data entry may be repaid in the value of management information.
- Relating short-term costs to long-term benefits.
- Maintaining a balance between financial controls and local autonomy.
- Viewing unstructured computing as 'retail' computing and as a business in a business, which requires an appropriate basis for pricing its services.
- Combining and quantifying the value judgements of people at all levels in the business.

This last requirement is most important. For example, electronic transmission of documents at a clerical level can imply less document handling and fewer delays. To sales management it might imply an improved service to customers with potentially more sales. For other senior management it would mean better communications leading to more timely control and improved decision-making. In this environment, some benefits can be readily quantified; others are more difficult, but all are important. At one level, senior managers can assess what information system costs are acceptable for given levels of support; at another level, work measurement may help to identify some of the areas of potential saving.

All the techniques described later in this chapter can be used to collect data on which to base benefits estimates for unstructured computing. The technique of critical success factor analysis is particularly helpful in focusing on the value of management information. Questionnaires which elicit overall profiles of office activities are often used for office systems justification. Frequently, the three areas of unstructured computing are not easily separated and depend on, and interlink with, traditional database applications.

Benefits of infrastructure projects

The IT infrastructure consists primarily of hardware and software platforms, of databases and communications networks. It necessarily includes the associated management and operational staff and their supporting 'infrastructure'. These are set up to support both existing applications and to provide a sound base for future developments. There are two problems: firstly, when trying to justify management information, business communications and other cross-functional systems, it is often difficult to apportion infrastructure costs. Secondly, without a direct connection to the benefits of individual applications the infrastructure appears to lack business justification. Moreover, infrastructures are needed for any widespread use of IT, be they based on mainframe or on client/server platforms.

Benefit type	Potential achievement levels		
	Pessimistic	Realistic	Optimistic
Cost reduction	1	2	4
Cost avoidance	3	5	7
Revenue/income	6	8	9

Figure 10.4. Benefits sensitivity matrix.

There are two answers. Firstly, some infrastructure investment projects will deliver benefits within the ITD, for example in helping to contain application maintenance and operating costs. This will result in unit cost reductions, particularly as volumes increase over time. Secondly, infrastructure requirements can reasonably be linked to major application developments, or to the combined effects of several smaller applications, and to the benefits to be derived from them. The fixed costs of IT will be increased, but variable costs elsewhere in the enterprise will be reduced. The justification of infrastructure projects is best made within the context of overall IT strategy, rather than being attempted on a piecemeal basis.

Although some infrastructure costs can be reclaimed in this way, not all will be recoverable. IT facilitates change and enables innovation. Like education and research and development, the benefits of IT infrastructure may be unprovable, but within limits they are undeniable. In discussing the metrics of benefits management, Keen writes, 'Business logic, not financial evidence, will determine whether the infrastructures that create a firm's technical platform are essential capital investments'.[3]

Sensitivity analysis of tangible benefits

Some benefits are not within direct management control, or may be subject to external influences, as for example, estimates of increases in sales volumes. These are less certain of achievement. Sensitivity analysis, using financial models and 'what-if' techniques, may be used to assess the effect of including such benefits in the overall business case. Senior management will accept, to a varying degree, benefits that are intangible and beyond their direct control. (Indeed, not all benefit estimates *within* their control may be acceptable!)

In any one of the three areas of cost displacement, cost avoidance or revenue increase, three different levels of benefit can be projected. These correspond to pessimistic, realistic and optimistic estimates (Fig. 10.4). The justification of an application can then be assessed by progressively including savings from the most certain level, namely pessimistic estimates of displaced cost (cell 1), through to the least certain level, that of optimistic estimates of increased revenue (cell 9). For more risky projects, only lower levels of saving would be included. The benefits included for any project will then depend on an assessment of the risks affecting the success of the project and on the achievability of the benefits, for example:

High risk: Include benefits in cells 1 to 3
Medium risk: Include benefits in cells 1 to 5
Low risk: Include benefits in cells 1 to 9

This analysis can also help to determine the level of benefit which needs to be realized, or to be set as an objective, in order to meet financial acceptance criteria for the project.

The further evaluation of tangible and intangible benefits is dealt with in Chapter 11, but this section is concluded with an example of tangible and intangible benefits in the following account, from *Getting Value from Information Technology*.[16] It illustrates how strategies for customer service and for product differentiation can be combined and delivered through IT.

CASE STUDY

One of the most spectacular success stories in using IT to improve competitive position is that of Thomson Holidays, a packaged-holiday company. Thomson Holidays' share of its market in the late 1970s was 8 or 9 per cent. Its management decided to embark on a strategy to increase that share significantly – not just by a few percentage points. It considered four possible strategic options: reducing the cost of holidays, increasing expenditure on advertising, increasing the commission incentives to travel agents, and using IT to provide information on availability and instant confirmation of bookings.

A mixture of the third and fourth strategies was chosen. It introduced a videotex system that enabled travel agents who were equipped with terminals to provide a much improved service to their customers, leading to more sales for Thomson. As a consequence, Thomson Holidays' share of the market had increased to well over 30 per cent by the end of the 1980s.

10.3   How to collect data and assemble the business case

10.3.1 A typical set of activities

The principle sources and types of costs and benefits required to build the business case have been described earlier in this chapter. The sequence of activities in

Table 10.2   Activities for building the business case

Activities	Main responsibility	
	User function	Technical function
1 Determine objectives and requirements	●	
2 Estimate potential benefits	●	
3 Propose system solution and options		●
4 Estimate the realizable benefits	●	
5 Estimate project resources and their costs	●	●
6 Derive net benefits with time-scales	●	●
7 Collect all information into business case	●	●
8 After implementation conduct an audit	●	●

which data will be collected for the project business case is listed in Table 10.2. More than one pass through these activities may be needed to compile the full business case and to gain approval for a project proposal.

10.3.2 *Techniques for collecting data*

There are several techniques that can be used to collect and analyse the data. Those discussed here are particularly appropriate for the initial definition of requirements and cost and benefit estimates, rather than for detailed analysis and definition of this data. A mixture of approaches is needed including structured, semi-structured and unstructured techniques, appropriate to the level of data being collected, to achieve comparable and complete data. Whatever technique is used, the information will need to be collated and recorded.

Two formats for recording requirements are illustrated in Figs 10.5(a) and (b). They are intended to help *users* express their requirements in a structured way and to provide a basis for discussing how the requirements will be met by IT systems. The first format, the input/process/output statement, is aimed at recording the processes now performed, or needing to be performed, which are to be considered as candidates for IT applications. Not all processes now performed will necessarily need to be performed in future; they should all be carefully scrutinized for the contribution they actually make to achieving the desired objective. The format of Fig. 10.5(b) is more descriptive and provides for an initial description of how the requirements will be met. However this information is presented, the formats indicate what is required as a basis for subsequent estimates of costs and benefits.

Some techniques that can be used to collect these data are:

1   *The interview*

     This is probably the most powerful technique, on account of being an effective communication medium. A structured interview with an informed

(a)

Application name:	Date:

Input

Existing system files

Process

Output

Users

Performance criteria

(b)

1   *Application title*

2   *Objective(s)*

3   *Requirements*

Outline requirements, as a list or narrative
Key users and performance considerations

Input: Transactions, documents, input via keyboards
             System files: fields or data input
Process: Automated process steps as input, update or output data
             Associated clerical procedures
Output: Reports, contents, frequency, systems files updated

4   *System description*

Narrative and diagrams
How the system will meet requirements: how the user will see it
Limitations/assumptions
Hardware/software
Alternative solutions

5   *Initial cost estimates*

6   *Initial benefits estimates*

Figure 10.5.   (a) Input/process/output form for application requirements. (b) Format for documenting application requirements.

and responsible individual can be expected to provide a statement of requirements and the benefits of meeting them. There are typically four main areas of discussion, which will lead towards identifying the benefits of an IT project:

● Interviewee's job objectives and responsibilities.
● Critical success factors and key problems of the job.
● Requirements for information or information processing facilities.
● The value of having the information or the 'facility'.

Within the interview, a number of questioning techniques can be used. Assuming that some requirement for information processing has been stated, then these questions can be asked to help estimate benefits:

- What will be the benefit of providing that? How could that benefit lead to a cost saving or to an increase in income? Can you make an estimate of what costs will be saved or of what increased income will result? Could someone else make that estimate?
- Within what range would you expect the benefit to be – £1000–£10 000, £10 000–£50 000 or over £50 000?
- Would you be prepared to pay £5000, £50 000 or £100 000 for that?
- Are there any comparable situations which might provide a basis for making an estimate of the benefits in this case?
- What further analysis is required to improve the estimate? If your requirement is not met, what will be the result?
- If your requirement is not met by IT, what else would meet it? What would that cost?

2   *The questionnaire*

A larger population can be covered than with an interview. It is good for collecting personal estimates and responses on specific questions, but it does have limitations in achieving a good level of understanding between the parties involved.

The content of questionnaires must be simple and kept to the necessary minimum. Typical areas included in a questionnaire might be:

- Job profile of respondent.
- Analysis of time spent on key work activities, using a checklist.
- Assessment of problems areas, against a checklist.
- Main reports or information received.
- Main reports or information produced.
- Other people/departments mainly in communication with.
- Service hours and levels desired from the ITD.
- Checklist of potentially useful information processing facilities.

3   *Business process analysis*

A business process often runs across organizational boundaries, reflecting the cross-functional use of a resource, such as people or cash. Identifying and describing business processes often shows how to improve business operations, both with and without the use of IT. Process analysis can provide a good basis for establishing measurable comparisons of operations before and after systems implementation.

4   *Work measurement*

This is more specific than process analysis in establishing the baseline of what is done now. It provides no direct indication of the future, unless combined with work planning, or with subjective views collected in interviews.

5   *The pilot and prototype*
    These are often established to test proposed solutions and, provided their
    objectives are correctly set, to assist in making more detailed estimates of costs
    and benefits. Users are rarely able to define precisely and finally what their
    requirements are. Once the system is in use, other requirements are inevitably
    seen, and late unplanned additions may be very costly. Prototyping has proved
    to be particularly cost effective when core functions and their associated
    benefits have been delivered quickly, with further cost-justified functions
    being added later as experience with the system grows.
       Prototyping is also used to speed application delivery. In one enterprise, six
    ITD professionals and six line managers are dedicated to work for 120 days to
    produce the core of an IT solution. Similar protoyping activities are conducted
    by IBM consultants and others, using interactive and iterative development
    methods.

10.3.3 A process for estimating benefits

This chapter earlier described four critical success factors for estimating benefits,
and several ways of collecting data to facilitate the estimating.

The fourth critical success factor identified the importance of using a group of
people and a structured process. Indeed, this is often of more importance than the
use of any specific analytical technique.

Ways of using a group in the benefits assessment workshop, and in the fuller
application planning study, have been described in Chapter 9. These use an
impact matrix, but there are other group-based techniques that can be used to
help quantify benefits. One of these is the quality improvement and problem-
solving methodology of problem, cause and effect analysis. In this approach, the
application objective is taken as the 'problem' statement and the requirements are
developed as 'causes' on a fishbone diagram. The benefits are then similarly
developed as 'effects', being decomposed until, as far as possible, they are
expressed in terms which enable them to be measured and managed. However,
whether any methodology can identify achievable quantified benefits depends on
the nature of the investment project, the stage of the project, the experience of the
organization in previous attempts and, to some extent, on the management
culture.

Moreover, methods alone cannot deliver benefits. The second critical success
factor for estimating benefits focuses on involvement of the right people. Benefits
must be owned by functional line managers, both in their initial estimation and in
their achievement. The mind-set must be that of a commitment to demonstrably
improving the enterprise, using an investment in IT to help do it, not to install a
system.

Workshops help to achieve commitment to results, but finally the benefits
estimated by line managers must be signed off and managed by them to ensure

that they are achieved. This is discusssed further in Chapter 13. The preparedness of line managers to accept responsibility for the estimation and achievement of benefits depends on organizational factors, and these are identified as decision constraints in Chapter 12.

10.4   Assembling the draft business case

10.4.1 *The business case contents*

Through the activities and processes described above, much of the information needed for the core business case will now be available. Although preparation of the business case is the responsibility of the sponsoring function, it is likely to have been drawn together by a limited group, centred on the IT department, with recourse to other functions as required. The contents of the business case at this stage will depend on whether it is an initial or full case and on the type of IT investment project under consideration. The document containing this proposal for investment can have a variety of names in practice, such as the Project Objectives Document, the Initial Systems Proposal or the Feasibility Report. The content of each of these is likely to vary, depending on the perceived main purpose of the document and its stage in the preparation of the full business case. In most organizations there are in-house standards for its contents, but the main sections need to be:

Project objectives
Requirements
Systems solution and alternatives
Constraints and risks
Costs
Tangible and intangible benefits
Financial assessment

A draft pro-forma for the typical contents of the business case at the end of this stage is given in Fig. 10.6.

10.4.2 *Building and presenting costs, savings and cash flows*

In preparing the business case, whatever the document in which it is contained is called, the data will have to be drawn together from a number of sources. Quantified costs and benefits now need to be presented in a consistent and usable format. Some costs will arise from the development project and others will be ongoing as a result of a continuing provision of the IT service. Some of the benefits will be one-offs; others will continue for the life of the system, making, in effect, a permanent change to the structure of the business plan.

In evaluating the project and in deciding to proceed with the investment

Project title: Project sponsor: Project manager:
System objectives
Scope of the system
Estimated expenditure – capital and revenue
Estimated benefits (tangible and intangible)
Project plan key dates
Financial evaluation   (Stage 2, Chapter 11) Intangible evaluation (Stage 2, Chapter 11) Risk evaluation   (Stage 2, Chapter 11)

Signatures: Sponsoring manager:
                     Project manager:
                     Concurring managers:
                     Authorizing managers:

Figure 10.6.   Business case pro-forma.

(Chapter 11), it is vital to understand how the costs and benefits, whether one-off or ongoing, will be incurred and realized with respect to the passage of time. This will be determined by the project plan, and the project schedule is normally presented on a Gantt chart. The structure of projects and phasing of sub-projects can affect project affordability in the short term and cost and benefit streams need to be optimized through careful project phasing.

Where it is possible and intended to take the benefits by building them into the relevant business plan, then it is the project schedule which determines into which period or periods they are planned. Some enterprises will take benefits in the same month or quarter as that planned for system roll-out; others will plan to implement them some months or quarters later; others never devise a plan to take the benefits, and consequently have poor control in their realization.

In addition to considering the timing of costs, there may be two or three alternative systems solutions. Costs and benefits may have been estimated within ranges and on the basis of assumptions, many of which will be tested and refined during further planning. All of these factors mean that the optimum business and financial case will only be attained after several iterations and investigations of the alternatives. Consequently, it is important to prepare costs and benefits from the bottom up, retaining the finest level of detail practicable for individual items, so that these items can be assembled in different 'packages' and spread over different time periods. Many of these data will be retained in the project working papers and on computer-based spreadsheets, with a summary in the draft business case (Fig. 10.6). The process steps are similar for costs and benefits.

Cost development

Any development project is likely to be broken into a number of sub-projects and the costs of each sub-project need to be itemized. The sub-projects will be scheduled by time periods, which are likely to be monthly or quarterly. Costs are then built up from the bottom level of detail in the following steps:

1   Obtain the unit costs for the main items, such as:

Hardware (including mainframes, mid-range PCs, communications, etc.)
Software (for all the above)
Maintenance
Personnel (as 'salary-plus', for ITD development, for training and for user resources)

2   Establish the numbers of units of machines/people/programs required by each sub-project.
3   Establish the schedule for the sub-projects, by time periods.
4   Calculate the cost for each *sub-project*:

unit costs (step 1) × numbers of units (step 2)

5   Determine the time period/s for each sub-project and assign costs by *time period*:

unit costs (step 1) × numbers of units in the period (step 3)

6   Document costs by *cost category*, such as hardware, software, maintenance, people, etc.:

list of items within each category × unit costs

Benefits development

This follows a similar pattern to that described above for costs.

1   Obtain *unit* benefit values, that is existing or projected costs, for people, machines, materials, buildings, interest rates, etc.

2 Estimate *numbers* and hence the value saved by *sub-project*.
3 From the project schedule estimate the numbers and thus the value saved by *year* or *period*.
4 Summarize by benefit *category*, for example, by staff, space, sales or stock.

Once the data have been assembled and manipulated into these formats the project evaluations described in the next chapter can be readily performed and the investment case finally prepared for making the decision to proceed.

References

1 Leslie Willcocks and Stephanie Lester, Information Systems Investments: evaluation at the feasibility stage of projects, *Technovation*, **II**(5) (1991) 283–302.
2 *Information Technology Review 1991/92*, Price Waterhouse, London, 1991.
3 Peter G. W. Keen, Shaping the Future, *Harvard Business School Press*, Harvard, 1991.
4 Beat Hochstrasser and Catherine Griffiths, *Controlling IT Investment: Strategy and Management*, Chapman & Hall, London, 1991.
5 Des Glover, Cost justifying very large, strategic IT projects, in *Managing IT Investment Conference Proceedings*, British Intelligence in association with *Computer Weekly*, May 1991.
6 Stephen Quigley, A. British savings and loan profits by 'counter attacking' customers, *IBM Think Magazine*, Number 1, 1991.
7 *Information Technology: Value for Money*, Butler Cox and Partners Ltd, 1986.
8 *Office Automation, The Barriers and Opportunities*, Touche Ross and Institute of Administrative Management, London, May 1991.
9 K. F. Curley and J. C. Henderson, *Valuing and managing investments in information technology*, working paper, Sloan School of Management, MIT, July 1989.
10 D. A. Littler and R. C. Sweeting, Cases for Change in Management Accounting Practice, *Management Accounting*, November 1989.
11 *Information Systems: The New Economics, Findings from the 1991 UK Foundation Conference*, Butler Cox Foundation, 1991.
12 David J. Sharp, Uncovering the hidden value in high risk investments, *Sloan Management Review*, **69**, Summer 1991.
13 *Information Technology Review 1990/91*, Price Waterhouse, London, 1990.
14 *Investment Appraisal in the Public Sector: A Management Guide for Government Departments*, HM Treasury 1983.
15 Joseph E. Ryan, Profitability in the non-profit environment, *J. Systems Management*, August 1980.
16 *Getting Value from Information Technology*, Research Report 75, Butler Cox Foundation, June 1990.

11
Stage 2: develop business case – prepare to make decision

11.1 Completing the business case

The plan by a small supermarket to install EPOS checkouts and stock and reorder systems was outlined at the beginning of Chapter 10. The account is expanded here to illustrate some of the topics covered in this chapter.

CASE STUDY

The Store Manager, Al Luchini, championed the IT investment proposal. He was convinced that business expansion was only achievable when coupled with stock control and just-in-time ordering, based on EPOS-generated sales information.

Al Luchini worked with the Superfood Steering Committee to ensure that the systems met his requirements, with his accountant to make the financial evaluation and with his Executive Board to gain their agreement to the investment.

His accountant recommended a three year minimum payback on the investment, and Al reckoned that this would be achieved from savings in staff time, faster stock turn and increased sales, although the benefits were not formally quantified. The guidelines of Chapter 10 might have helped Al here, and this chapter discusses the further evaluation of tangible and intangible benefits.

However, Al needed more help in risk assessment. Bar codes can be read by horizontal or vertical scanners. Initially, one vertical and two horizontal EPOS bar code scanners were installed. The horizontal scanners proved to be unsatisfactory, and for two months, only three EPOS checkouts were available as replacements for the five cash tills, and these checkouts were only usable as cash tills. Initial installation was made in the relatively quiet month of August, but had it been nearer Christmas the impact could have been disastrous.

'Had I understood this risk better', said Al, 'I would still have proceeded with the installation, but with far greater caution and with more consideration of backup arrangements'.

11.1.1 Summary of inputs to the business case

Stage 2 of making the decision to invest (Fig. P2) aims to establish the net worth of the project to the enterprise.

The key data required for the business case were described in Chapter 10. Some ways of collecting and presenting data were suggested, mainly for costs and benefits. Moreover, we concentrated on obtaining benefits data, as this is generally perceived to be the most difficult area in which to make quantified estimates. Although, as noted earlier, there will be considerable variations in the data depending on the type of investment project and on its stage of planning, in summary it will consist of the following main areas:

- Requirements and business objectives.
- Systems solutions.
- Project resource estimates and activity schedules.
- Costs and benefits.

In addition to these data, Stage 2 needs the financial parameters and procedures on which the case will be built. For example:

- People, space and money costs.
- Acceptability of benefit types.
- Financial and business planning timetable and procedures.
- Accounting principles for tax, inflation, depreciation and cash flow evaluation, for example, by discounting.
- Sources of finance and acquisition options, for example, leasing.

Finally, criteria will be needed against which to estimate the business case, in terms of its financial implications, the value of intangible benefits and the potential project risks.

11.1.2 Doing the work

Often the business case is not prepared well, or even prepared at all, because responsibilities and procedures for doing it are poorly defined and misunderstood. There are two main issues that need to be addressed: firstly, how different functions are to be involved in completing the staff work needed to prepare the case for the decision-makers, and secondly, how and on what basis the financial and non-financial analysis and evaluation of the project will be made. The 'staff work' involves the collation of base data and their assembly into an agreed business case and project proposal. This will need the professional advice and concurrence of specialist groups and individuals, and of other parties involved in implementing the project. This work is vital to gain commitment and concurrence across the organization, particularly from those owning resources required by the project.

Several functions or specializations have roles and responsibilities in this stage. The functions primarily involved are those of the project sponsor, finance and the ITD. Other functions, such as personnel and building services, may also be affected by the proposals. Guidelines are needed for the way in which, and the stage at which, people in different functions are to communicate in meetings and through documents and for identifying, escalating and resolving issues which threaten to prevent agreement. Typically the stage will conclude with a meeting of the proposers, concurrers and implementers in a project or business case review meeting (Fig. P2) before the project is submitted to the steering committee for approval. In this meeting the sponsor will need to endorse the benefits, the ITD will need to commit to delivering the systems on time and in budget, and business and financial planning will need to agree that the proposal is compatible with and included in current plans.

The purpose of Stage 2 is not to promote an administrative bureaucracy, but rather to facilitate the construction and approval of the business case. A clear understanding of roles and procedures is fundamental to any methodology for producing the case and typical responsibilities are outlined in the following paragraphs.

11.2   Functional responsibilities

11.2.1 *Proposal or project sponsor*

The project sponsor is the person whose business area will potentially benefit by introduction of the proposed change. Experience has shown the value of identifying a sponsor at the right level and, for major projects, this will mean an executive director. Most projects need to be seen as a business project which involves IT. Resources, other than just those from ITD, will need to be coordinated; the system users will need to prepare for implementation and for changes in working patterns. Indeed, the user community increasingly needs to provide project management skills as well as hands-on sponsorship.

The sponsor is not always the primary initiator of a project. It often starts from the vision, initiative and determination of its champion – and that person can be in the ITD or in the business. However, management responsibilities of the sponsor will include:

1   Initiating and guiding the preparation of the project proposal, with an appropriate supporting business case.

2   Ensuring the availability of skills and resources from other functions, for
    example from the ITD, to assist in preparing the proposal.
3   Ensuring concurrence and approval from other groups affected by the pro-
    posal. Communications during this process should be both written, in the
    proposal documentation, and oral, in meetings.
4   Personally signing off and making the proposal available to Business Planning
    by published deadlines, for inclusion in the business and IT plans and for
    approval by the Board of Directors or the IT Steering Committee.

The sponsor typically delegates these responsibilities, and the management of
project work by business resources, to a business project manager. This role is
sometimes referred to as a project administrator, to distinguish it from the
technical project manager having responsibility for the larger ITD resource.

11.2.2 The finance function

As the outcome of any project inevitably affects financial results, measurably or
unmeasurably, a role exists for the finance function in project planning. A sound
financial evaluation cannot be made without financial skills. It is remarkable that
Kaye's survey[1] of management accountants did not identify a clear role for them
in the financial assessment or auditing of IT capital projects or in some of the
complex issues relating to computer cost recovery. The non-involvement of
financial specialists often arises from the difficulties of making financial estimates
and of putting together a quantified business case; accountants do not always find
it easy to apply their expertise to IT investment cases.

Nevertheless, a role exists for the finance function to:

1   Provide advice and guidance to other groups in their preparation of outline
    and full investment proposals.
2   Have guidelines established to determine types and amounts of discretionary
    spending for budget holders of controllable and fixed costs.
3   Confirm that the investment is in line with enterprise goals and strategies and is
    affordable within the proposed time frame (this will also involve the business
    planning group).

Some projects may be included in the annual development plan without a
previous business case; in this event, financial approval confirms their inclusion.
Other projects may not be included until signed off by the finance function.

11.2.3 The Information Technology Department

For IT projects, significant resources will be required from the IT function, in
addition to those required from the sponsor's function for requirements definition.

In contributing to the project proposal, the job of the ITD will typically be to:

1 Conduct feasibility and design studies, and investigate systems options with recommendations.
2 Assist in the definition of functional and service level requirements.
3 Estimate the resources needed to implement and operate the proposed system and draw up a project plan acceptable to the sponsor.
4 Provide project management.
5 Provide quality assurance of both planning and implementation activities.

The ITD will also need to provide an overall planning function which will typically be the responsibility of an 'IT requirements and strategy' planning group. The role of such a group will include activities to:

1 Develop IT project appraisal procedures (in conjunction with the finance function) and oversee the preparation of IT investment cases.
2 Develop the IT strategic plan to ensure that it balances both short- and long-term considerations and that it is aligned with corporate business plans.
3 Coordinate technical architectures.
4 Obtain funding for year one of a rolling five year plan.

11.2.4 The Business Planning Group

Those in corporate business planning often find it hard to link with other functions; business planning can be seen as of less than immediate relevance. Sometimes the finance function has some responsibility for business planning. Nevertheless, in preparing major investment cases, it is important that those responsible for business planning:

1 Advise other functions of the procedures and deadlines for the business plan (strategic and operating) and monitor submission of major investment proposals.
2 Arrange investment project and business plan review meetings.
3 Validate proposals for completeness and collate them in support of business plan figures, thus enabling both the costs and benefits of all major projects to be built into the business plan.

11.2.5 The Information Technology Steering Committee

This group may have a variety of titles and responsibilities. In principle, the IT Steering Committee consists of all the potential executive sponsors, as heads of the main functions of the organization. At a lower level of representation it will simply be a project review board. Typical responsibilities of the committee, particularly with respect to investment appraisal, are to:

1   Gain an understanding of competitors' use of IT.
2   Understand alternative technical scenarios, determine the overall levels of investment in IT and monitor IT strategies and plans.
3   Approve guidelines and policies for the management of IT across the enterprise, including investment level authorities and technical architectures.
4   Approve R&D expenditures in IT.
5   Agree the priorities for major new IT-related projects (this will involve determining the criteria and the process for priority assessment).
6   Ensure that there is effective cooperation between functions in planning and implementing IT projects.
7   Make decisions to:
    ● Submit proposals to the main Board or an executive committee for inclusion in the strategic and operating plan.
    ● Authorize the start of and expenditure on, projects committed in the operating plan.
    ● Authorize investments not previously included in the plan but falling within business unit budgets.
8   Review the progress and completion of major projects with respect to their function, cost and timeliness and to the realization of the projected benefits.

11.2.6 The main Board and Chief Executive

The main Board's connection with IT, as a Board, is not likely to be more than a few times a year and then mainly within the context of business planning. However, major IT projects and expenditure normally need Board approval and, therefore, the Board role in making the decision to invest is to:

1   Determine the business strategy as a framework within which new investments will be proposed. Approve the IT strategy.
2   Approve business plans, with supporting investment proposals. Approve major IT projects.
3   Finally resolve any non-concurrence issues.

Having covered the roles and responsibilities of individuals and groups involved in preparing and evaluating the final business case, the techniques of evaluation can now be described.

11.3   Financial evaluation and capital budgeting

The financial case is a key component of the business case for a project proposal. Financial evaluation is an area for which elegant financial techniques can be proposed, without recognizing either the quality of the estimates on which the evaluation depends or the increasing importance of non-financial factors in the decision-making equation. For these reasons, there has been a decreasing emphasis over recent years on quantitative financial appraisal. The fact is that considerable investments continue to be made in IT without their financial cases strictly satisfying company standards for investment projects. For most projects, the financial case remains a viable and necessary component of the overall evaluation, particularly in the later and more detailed planning stages of a project. The following paragraphs outline the essential principles which need to be grasped by non-financial managers. They have been prepared by David Hankin, IBM UK, and are based on the text of an IBM internal publication – the *Financial Decision Process*.

11.3.1 *Capital budgeting and capital structure*

Some of the most important questions that will be asked by executive management about any project are: 'Will the capital we invest in this system bring us more return than other alternatives?', 'Are there better opportunities for investing our assets?', 'How much better?', 'When?' and 'How sure are we?' These questions have to do with long-term financial planning, of which capital budgeting is an important part.

Capital budgeting deals with how a company should invest its cash. It is a predictive process, with a mixture of some science and much financial judgement. Capital budgeting involves:

- The development of alternative investment proposals.
- The estimation of cash flows from proposed investments.
- Selection of the most promising investment alternatives.
- Ongoing review of investments to evaluate the degree to which each performs according to expectations.

Since the opportunities for investment are virtually unlimited and the cash the company has to invest is limited, the chief financial officer must pick that combination of investments which is likely to bring the greatest profit. This is an investment decision.

11.3.2 *Capital budgeting decisions*

Capital budgeting decisions are usually based on four considerations.

1 *Cash sources*
- Where will the cash come from?
- What will it cost us to get the capital?

2 *Cash amounts*
- How large an investment is necessary?
- How much return can we expect?

3 *Timing*
- When will the cash to be invested be required?
- How soon will we realize a return?

4 *Degree of risk*
  - How sure can we be that the money we invest will not be lost?
  - How certain is it that the predicted return will accrue in the expected time frame?
  - How good is the past track record of the proposer of the investment?

IT is usually a significant investment. However, it is only one of many investment alternatives a business has to consider and it is in direct competition with those other alternatives.

It should be noted that the meaning attributed to financial terms may vary both across and within organizations. Therefore, the terminology being used needs to be defined and understood by all involved. For example, the term 'return on investment' might be used to refer to any one of the measures described below.

11.3.3 *Financial ranking of investment proposals*

There are three main methods of evaluating investments. All three measure the cash outflow versus the potential cash inflow of an investment, and they are:

  - Payback period.
  - Average rate of return (ARR).
  - Discounted cash flow (DCF) techniques, of which we will examine two:
    — net present value (NPV)
    — internal rate of return (IRR).

All three of these methods measure the cash outflow versus the potential cash inflow of an investment. In the payback method, cash flows are considered up to the time of payback. The average rate of return additionally considers cash inflows and outflows after payback for a specified period. The discounted cash flow method allows for the reducing value of money with time. All three are best computed using 'after-tax' pounds because these are the only pounds the chief financial officer has to invest. Thus, a project which returns 6.5% after tax is equivalent to 10% before tax. Therefore, when discussing methods of evaluating investments it can be important to differentiate between before-tax or after-tax pounds.

Payback period

This measures how long it will take to get back the money invested. It is the length of time required for the net cash inflow to equal the initial cash outflow. Prior to completing any calculation, it will be necessary to specify the maximum time limit within which the project must generate sufficient cash flows to pay back the required outlay.

On this basis, a project would be accepted where it had generated sufficient cash flows to pay back the initial outlay within a maximum specified period. Where

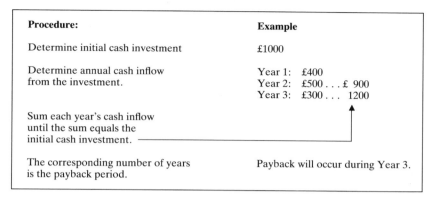

Procedure:	Example
Determine initial cash investment	£1000
Determine annual cash inflow from the investment.	Year 1: £400 Year 2: £500 . . . £ 900 Year 3: £300 . . . 1200
Sum each year's cash inflow until the sum equals the initial cash investment.	
The corresponding number of years is the payback period.	Payback will occur during Year 3.

Figure 11.1. Procedure for computing payback period.

Table 11.1 Advantages and disadvantages of payback period investment evaluation

Advantages	Disadvantages
Easy to compute and understand.	No rule for determining the maximum payback period criterion.
Emphasis on a project's 'speed of return' which may be important where liquidity considerations exist.	Definition problem of 'outlay' and where payback time period starts from.
One of the most commonly used methods of project appraisal.	Fails to consider cash flow past the payback period.
	Ignores the timing of cash inflows and outflows.
	Ignores the time value of money.

there are competing projects, the one which pays back its initial outlay the quickest and within the specified maximum time period, is accepted. The procedure for computing payback period is illustrated in Fig. 11.1.

Computing the payback period is easy, and the concept is simple. It comes down to 'How soon will I get my money back?' Because it is easy to calculate, payback period is a widely accepted and used method of ranking investments.

The advantages and disadvantages of evaluating an investment according to its payback period are summarized in Table 11.1.

Average rate of return

Average rate of return (ARR) is sometimes referred to as 'accounting rate of return'. It takes into consideration cash flow both during and after the payback period. It is the ratio of the average annual return from the investment, compared to the total investment over the project's life; typically for an IT project this life is five to eight years. Alternatively, the average (instead of the total) capital or investment employed may be used in the calculation.

Procedure	Example		
Assume an original investment of £1000.			
Over the life of the project, compute the total cash inflows from the investment.		*Project A*	*Project B*
	Year 1 –	£ 400	£ 400
	Year 2 –	300	300
	Year 3 –	300	300
	Year 4 –	100	1000
		£1100	£2000
Subtract the total investment to determine the net profit of the total project.		−1000	−1000
		£ 100	£1000
Divide the result by the total number of years to determine the average annual profit.		$\dfrac{100}{4} = £25$	$\dfrac{1000}{4} = £250$
Divide the annual profit by the investment to obtain the average rate of return.		$\dfrac{£ \ 25}{£1000} = 2.5\%$	$\dfrac{£ \ 250}{£1000} = 25\%$

Figure 11.2.   Procedure for computing average rate of return (ARR).

Table 11.2   Advantages and disadvantages of ARR method

Advantages	Disadvantages
Easy to compute and understand.	Does not consider the timing of cash inflows and outflows.
Considers the cash flows over the entire project life.	Does not consider the time value of money.
	No set rules for setting the minimum acceptable ARR criterion.
	Definitions of capital employed and profit unclear.
	In the case of competing projects, a percentage figure means that a 10% return on £10 000 is more favourable than an 8% return on £100 000.

A project would be accepted where it generated an ARR greater than or equal to some minimum acceptable ARR. Where there are competing projects, the project accepted would be that which yields the largest ARR and meets the minimum ARR criterion. The average rate of return method for evaluating a capital investment is illustrated in Fig. 11.2 and the merits of the method are summarized in Table 11.2.

Return on capital employed (ROCE) is a variation of ARR. Here, the distinction is made between capital expenditure, typically for plant and equip-

Table 11.3   Present value factors for discounted cash flow calculations

	8%	9%	10%	11%	12%	13%	14%	15%
1	0.9259	0.9174	0.9091	0.9009	0.8929	0.8850	0.8772	0.8696
2	0.8573	0.8417	0.8264	0.8116	0.7972	0.7831	0.7695	0.7561
3	0.7938	0.7722	0.7513	0.7312	0.7118	0.6931	0.6750	0.6575
4	0.7350	0.7084	0.6380	0.6507	0.6355	0.6133	0.5921	0.5718
5	0.6806	0.6499	0.6209	0.5935	0.5674	0.5428	0.5194	0.4972
6	0.6302	0.5963	0.5645	0.5346	0.5066	0.4803	0.4556	0.4323
7	0.5835	0.5470	0.5132	0.4187	0.4523	0.4251	0.3996	0.3759
8	0.5403	0.5019	0.4665	0.4339	0.4039	0.3762	0.3506	0.3269
9	0.5002	0.4604	0.3241	0.3909	0.3606	0.3329	0.3075	0.2843
10	0.4632	0.4224	0.3855	0.3522	0.3220	0.2946	0.2697	0.2472

The cash flow anticipated for each year is discounted by the factor appropriate to the rate of interest selected and the number of the years n (reckoning from the start of the project being considered) in which the cash flow will occur. Example: The present value, discounting at 8% per annum, of 300 due 10 years hence is 300 × 0.463 = 138.90p.

The factors are calculated from the formula $1/(1 + r)^n$ where r is the rate of interest expressed as a decimal and n the number of years. Strictly, these factors apply to money passing on the last day of each year, but for most practical purposes they can be used when money passes more or less evenly throughout each year.

ment, and revenue expenditure, typically for operations and maintenance. To calculate ROCE, the net inflow (benefit) of non-capital cash flows is expressed as the percentage of the capital items taken over the life of the investment.

Discounting principles

Before describing two discounting techniques for appraising financial investments, two key concepts need to be discussed.

1 *The time value of money*
  This is the key to understanding more sophisticated investment ranking techniques involving discounted cash flows. The idea behind the time value of money is that a pound today is worth more than a pound at some future time. The reason for this is that a pound available today has a potential value to the business as a generator of interest during the intervening period.
  Assuming an arbitrary interest rate of 10%, 91 pence invested today will be worth a pound in a year.
  Conversely, a pound returned one year from now is worth only £0.91 today, because £0.91 + (£0.91 × 10%) = £1.00.
  A formula may be used to calculate discount factors, but a quicker and easier method is to consult a discount table from a standard (present value table) financial reference book. An example is shown in Table 11.3.

2 *Discount factor and cost of capital*
  What discount factor or rate does a business use in real life? A business's discount factor must be at least as great as its cost of capital.
  The cost of capital is the *average weighted cost* of the capital provided by

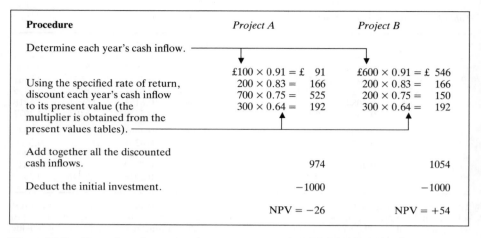

Procedure	Project A	Project B
Determine each year's cash inflow.		
	£100 × 0.91 = £ 91	£600 × 0.91 = £ 546
Using the specified rate of return,	200 × 0.83 = 166	200 × 0.83 = 166
discount each year's cash inflow	700 × 0.75 = 525	200 × 0.75 = 150
to its present value (the	300 × 0.64 = 192	300 × 0.64 = 192
multiplier is obtained from the		
present values tables).		
Add together all the discounted cash inflows.	974	1054
Deduct the initial investment.	−1000	−1000
	NPV = −26	NPV = +54

Figure 11.3. Procedure for computing net present value (NPV) of an investment.

long-term borrowing and by shareholders. The projects in which the business invests must pay at least this much, or else the business will lose money. A company acquires its capital from a number of sources and it must average out how much it gets from each source and at what cost. The discount factor used should be at least as great as the cost of capital.

Some companies use a risk-adjusted rate for the different levels of risk for different projects. Hence the riskier the project, the higher the discount factor used.

Two of the more advanced methods a business may use to rank investment proposals are net present value (NPV) and internal rate of return (IRR). These are illustrated below.

Discounting: net present value

Net present value attempts to adjust the cash flows of an investment proposal to account for the time over which they occur. It discounts future cash inflows to their present value and compares them with the present value of the outflows. The business's *specified rate of return* is used as the discounting factor.

For example, a business is comparing two projects A and B. They use the same discounting factor of 10%. The initial investment for both is £1000 and the cash inflow for each project is illustrated in Fig. 11.3.

A positive NPV indicates a favourable project, while a negative NPV indicates an undesirable project. The project yielding the highest positive NPV should be accepted. A positive NPV indicates that over the period of evaluation:

1 The capital will be repaid.
2 Interest on the amount outstanding will be paid.
3 Additional benefits equal to the NPV will accrue.

Table 11.4   Advantages and disadvantages of net present value (NPV) evaluation of investments

Advantages	Disadvantages
Takes into consideration the timing of cash flows. Includes all cash flows over the life of the project. Takes into account the time value of money.	Difficult to compute manually. Cannot be used until the appropriate discount rate has been determined, after considering the cost of capital and risk involved.

Table 11.5   Procedure for computing the internal rate of return (IRR) of a capital investment

	0	1	2	3	4	5	Total	
				Year				
Original investment	£2033						£2033	
Expected cash savings		£616	£634	£642	£659	£669	£3220	
Discounted @ 12%		550	505	457	419	379	2310	(Too high)
Discounted @ 15%		535	479	422	377	332	2145	(Close)
Discounted @ 18%		522	455	391	340	292	2000	(Very close)

Thus, in this example; Project B would be the better investment. The advantages and disadvantages of NPV evaluation of investments are summarized in Table 11.4.

Discounting: internal rate of return (IRR)

Sometimes called yield, this is the final method of ranking investments to be considered. It allows an assessment of the overall profitability of a project, while at the same time considering the size of the investment and the length of the project.

When using the internal rate of return, a business is, in effect, comparing the actual rate of return of a project with the rate of return it wants to achieve. This is the discount rate at which a given project's NPV equals the original investment and is called the project's internal rate of return. That is, the discounted cash outflows equal the discounted cash inflows. In effect, IRR is the cost the company can pay for capital and still break even.

To calculate the actual discounted rate of return to the company it is necessary to discount all cash savings to equal the original investment. The discount rate that equates the present value of cash savings to the original investment is called the internal rate of return. It can be found by trial and error, manually or by using a computer model.

Table 11.5 illustrates the trial and error method and produces an IRR of

Table 11.6 The advantages and disadvantages of the internal rate of return (IRR) method for evaluating a capital investment

Advantages	Disadvantages
Reflects the impact of timing of cash flows in the same manner as NPV.	Assumes that all cash inflows are reinvested at the *internal rate of return*. This would be an unrealistic assumption where similar high yields are not available or not anticipated.
Includes all cash flows over the life of the project.	
Provides a discounted rate of return on investment rather than absolute values.	Difficult to compute manually.
Can be used where the business's discount rate is unknown.	

approximately 17.9%. The advantages and disadvantages of the IRR method are summarized in Table 11.6.

Over the past 30 years or so there has been a growth in the application of discounted cash flow methods and in particular the use of the IRR. Nevertheless, there have also been growing signs of dissatisfaction with discounted cash flow methods and many businesses employ appraisal methods that are simpler but theoretically less satisfactory. Furthermore, the decision criteria may shift as business conditions change. A company in a 'cash bind' for example, would probably place heavy reliance on payback.

Most companies employ some combination of appraisal methods, in which payback is usually featured. For many businesses, payback satisfies the requirements of ease of understanding and communication. It is also popular with financial managers because it provides the right intuitive 'feel' about a project.

Profit and loss account or profit flows

A less widely used technique for the appraisal of capital investment projects is to measure the effect that the project will have on the business's profit and loss account over the life of the project.

It differs from cash flow evaluations in that:

1 The cost of capital expenditure would be spread over a number of years by charging depreciation in line with the company's policy for writing off capital expenditure.
2 The 'accruals' concept would be applied so that costs and benefits would appear in those periods in which they arose and not when cash was actually paid or received.
3 Interest charges on the money invested would be included.
4 The effect of taxation would be included. However, taxation may also be included in cash flow calculations.
5 No account is taken of the time value of money.

Items		Time periods – by year (or quarter)					
		1	2	3	4	5	Total
Investment costs (one-off)		a					
Investment costs (recurring)		b					
Running costs (recurring)		c					
	Total costs	$a+b+c=d$					
Benefits	(one-off)	e					
Benefits	(recurring)	f					
	Total benefits	$e+f=g$					
Net cash flow (NCF)		$d-g=h$					
Cumulative NCF							
Example discount factors (i)		1.000	0.8696	0.7561	0.6575	0.5718	
Discounted NCF		$h \times i$					
Cumulative discounted NCF							
Net present value (NPV) of the investment = Total discounted NCF							

Figure 11.4. Sample layout for cash flow calculation, with discounting.

In summary, for capital budgeting, the method or methods to be used to evaluate an investment, the period of the evaluation and the discount rate, where appropriate, must be selected.

The key financial considerations for project acceptance will be for the project which has:

1 The best after-tax cash flows, compared with other capital projects.
2 Cash flow patterns fitting within budget requirements and within the funds currently available for investment, that is, it is affordable.
3 No adverse impact on the profit and loss account.
4 No better alternative system or project structure.

Sample layout for cash flow calculation, with discounting

Organizations normally have their own standards for structuring the cash flows and for evaluating projects. A typical layout for a cash flow analysis is shown in Fig. 11.4. Typically, the major costs will be be incurred only once, that is they will be 'one-off', even if they are spread over several time periods. Most benefits will continue for the period of the appraisal and beyond, but starting in a later period than the costs.

The 15% discount factors over five years (shown at (i) in Fig. 11.4) are available from tables of discount factors. The annual cumulative net cash flow figures are multiplied by the discount factor to give the cumulative discounted net cash flow

(NCF). The five-year cumulative figure then gives the NPV of the investment, when discounted at 15% over the five years.

When the discount rate (for example 15%, as above) is set at a value to give an NPV of zero, then the discount rate equals the IRR.

Break-even can be determined from either discounted or non-discounted cumulative NCF. A return on investment is achieved in the period when cumulative investments become less than cumulative benefits less costs.

Note that, on account of the approximate estimates of costs and benefits, in the early planning stages of a project, discounting may not be a relevant technique. In this case the break-even period for non-discounted cash flows (cumulative NCF) is likely to be most appropriate, giving a measure of the return on the capital and revenue investments. With or without discounting, provision can also be made for the effect of inflation or deflation on the costs and benefits, year on year, at appropriate rates.

In summary, for many IT projects, the most appropriate evaluation will be to demonstrate an acceptable payback time-scale on the basis of non-discounted cash flows that are affordable period by period.

11.3.4 *Financing considerations*

Leasing

The decision on whether to acquire capital equipment by leasing is a financing decision, not an investment decision. It is viewed as a convenient way of borrowing to pay for assets outside the company's usual lines of credit. The leasing industry grew rapidly at the beginning of the last decade and this growth has been attributed to the following factors:

- A favourable taxation environment.
- It is easier and quicker to lease an asset rather than to arrange a loan to finance its purchase.
- For many years all payments under leases were treated as expenses in the profit and loss account rather than sources of finance in the balance sheet. Some businesses felt that this was a valuable source of 'off balance sheet' financing. The fewer assets there are on a company's balance sheet, the healthier some of its key ratios look.

Leasing may be attractive where the following considerations apply:

- Cash flow requirements.
- Budgeting constraints.
- Borrowing capacity and needs.
- Impact on balance sheet.
- Financial risks and resource demands of ownership and later sale or disposal.

Leases may be categorized as either full payout (finance leases) or as operating leases.

Full payout or 'finance' leases are those where the lessee has the 'full economic ownership' of the asset and bears the full cost in the primary period.

Operating leases are those where the lessee bears a partial cost in the primary period (the balance is the residual value). At the end of the primary period the lessee usually has the right to renew at a substantially reduced rental or to hand the asset back to the lessor.

Off balance sheet financing

Before 1987, in the UK, all leases were off balance sheet and all lease payments were charged directly to the profit and loss account. Since 1987, leased assets must be capitalized and included in the balance sheet if the lease transfers to the lessee substantially all the risks and rewards of ownership. The rules for this are set out in Statement of Standard Accounting Practice 21 (SSAP 21), which in summary requires:

> If the present value of minimum lease payments is 90% or more of the fair value of the asset then the lease is a finance lease and must appear on the balance sheet. Any other lease is an operating lease and is not included in the balance sheet and lease payments are charged direct to the profit and loss account.

The importance of taxation

It is essential to take taxation into account when calculating incremental cash flows. In considering the tax implications of capital expenditure analysis, the following points are relevant currently in the UK:

1   Sales revenue and other income less allowable business expenses is taxable.
2   Depreciation of capital assets is not an allowable expense for tax purposes and must be added back to arrive at a taxable profits figure.
3   Capital allowances are given on eligible plant and equipment, and are deducted in calculating the taxable profits figure.

The present system of granting capital allowances is by way of annual writing-down allowances for expenditure incurred on plant and machinery at the rate of 25 per cent, calculated on the reduced balance of expenditure after subtracting allowances for earlier years. The 25 per cent on the unrelieved balance will be claimed until the machinery is sold or scrapped. At this stage any unrelieved expenditure is relieved and any excess of relief is added to taxable profits.

Thus the effect of capital allowances is to grant tax relief on the difference between the cost of the asset and any sale proceeds, spread over the life of the

Table 11.7 Checklist of information required to build a capital investment appraisal

---

1   What is the financial structure of the business and are there any capital limits or constraints?
2   Are there any short- or medium-term cash flow or budget constraints?
3   Will purchase and leasing be considered?
4   When is the financial year-end?
5   Is tax paid? If so at what rate and when is it payable?
6   Does VAT have any effect on the proposal?
7   What is the policy for depreciating fixed assets?
8   Where fixed assets are being replaced, what impact, if any, will written-down values, loss or profit on sale have on the current financial justification?
9   What effect will the proposal have on the profit and loss account and balance sheet and is this relevant?
10 What methods of financial evaluation are to be used?
11 What investment criteria must be met?
12 What is the capital planning and budgeting process?
13 How is the business case to be prepared and what are the key ingredients that may influence the investment decision?

---

asset. However, the benefit of capital allowances is only available where a business is in a tax-paying situation.

Checklist of financial information

In order to prepare a financial case, a great deal of information is required. In Chapter 10 we discussed how to quantify the benefits which might arise from a project and we recognized the need to make similar estimates of the costs. These are the basic data required before any further financial analysis can be made and any analysis will depend on the reliability of these estimates.

Given that these data are available, then to make any worthwhile evaluation requires them to be put into the context of the enterprise to which they relate. More information has to be collected to complete the procedures outlined earlier in this chapter, and some of the questions that will need to be answered to build a capital investment appraisal are listed in Table 11.7.

11.3.5 The use of computer-based models in evaluation

For projects in the early planning stages, with a lower level of confidence in the estimates and less complete data, there may be little advantage in using a computer. Indeed, in some cases, it can be quite unrealistic to have to work within the necessary disciplines.

However, the preparation of some financial cases can involve substantial computation. For a large project with alternative implementation approaches and methods of financing, in an advanced stage of planning, there is great value in using a computer to assist in the evaluation. It is not that the arithmetic, even for discounted cash flow evaluations, need be that complex, but rather that there is inevitably a need for many iterations and 'what if?' investigations of the financial scenarios. For smaller projects, while the volume of data is less, repeated iterations with new estimates and financial parameters make some form of computer-based financial modelling of benefit. For evaluations involving the use of discounting techniques, such as IRR, which in themselves involve iterative techniques, there is a clear benefit in using a computer-based evaluation model.

Guidance in the collection of data and the calculations to be performed can be provided by a simple pro-forma. An example was shown in Fig. 10.6, to which can now be added the analysis of Fig. 11.4. These pro-formas also help to ensure consistency of method, of presentation and of interpretation. Such documents are best kept simple and are most appropriate for the full business case.

At the first level a simple spreadsheet is readily used to assist in calculations. At the next level, a pre-programmed spreadsheet will provide additional facilities. An example of this, used within IBM UK, is FINPAK, which handles multi-projects for multi-periods analysing the effects of major acquisition alternatives. It calculates values for NPV, IRR, payback period, discounted payback period, net annual benefits and average return on average investment and provides sensitivity analysis by applying different cash flows or different discount factors.

With some advanced evaluation models (such as IBM IS/IS, Chapter 9) the costs and benefits for each project can be loaded on to a base model containing the profit and loss and balance sheet projections for five to ten years ahead. Standard financial evaluations of the projects are then made by the model, as well as an assessment of the effects of the project on key performance measures such as the price/earnings ratio.

Many individuals across the organization are likely to contribute to the business case. This means that business cases, including spreadsheets, need to be communicated to others as they are developed. The ability to do this electronically is becoming at least as important, if not more so, as the ability to prepare the business case on a standalone system, however sophisticated that may be.

Finally, on a cautionary note, whatever IT support is used, the quality of the financial case will depend far more on the credibility of the basic data and estimates than on the processing and presentation subsequently applied to them. It is important to avoid being seduced by the technology. For project managers, effort spent in refining and validating the base data will be well spent. Once these data are sound then it will be to their advantage to have access to an appropriate financial modelling tool and guidance in its use.

11.3.6 Comparison of IT investment with other capital investments

The question is often asked, 'Are IT investments different from other capital investments?' Hochstrasser and Griffiths, in surveying 'value for money' obtained from IT, found that 68% of their respondents treated IT expenditures as normal capital investment, needing to show a definite return.[2] Conversely, 32% did not

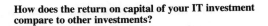

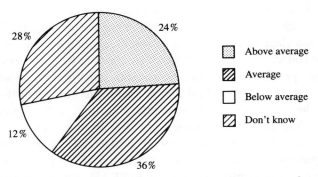

Figure 11.5.   Comparison of IT investment to other investments.[2]

require IT to show a specific return. The diversity of opinion relating to the ROC from IT compared with other investments is illustrated in Fig. 11.5. This shows that 60% of the sample surveyed see the ROC from IT as equal to or better than other investments, 12% see IT as below average and 28% don't know. (The survey did not make clear how far these responses were supported by statistics, or to what extent they were based on the subjective views of the individuals questioned.)

In making comparisons we need to consider both the nature of an IT investment and its treatment in the enterprise's accounts. Investments often have a stronger association with one specific activity. Primary activities are those concerned with the direct conversion of resources, such as raw materials, into the final product and its delivery to the customer. Secondary activities are those concerned with the support of primary activities, and include purchasing and marketing. Tertiary activities support the primary and secondary activities and include human resources and financial and facilities management. These make up the infrastructure of the enterprise. In general, it is easier to quantify the benefits from investments which aim to improve the primary activities than from investments in secondary and tertiary activities. Thus it can be expected that the benefits of an investment in production capacity for a manufacturing company or in transaction processing for a service company will be easier to quantify than an investment made to improve internal communications or to improve management information, although these cases will still be based on assumptions regarding sales volumes, product mixes, money values and allocation of cost overheads. The business case made by a retailer for an investment to build a new shop is different in nature from the business case made by a holding company to build a new head office. To which of these should we compare an IT investment? The answer given almost certainly depends on the nature of the IT investment itself.

Furthermore, investment appraisal methods are often related to the type of

Table 11.8 Appraisal techniques for different investment types

Projects by type of investment	Some appraisal techniques
Buildings	Discounted ROI (NPV) > five years
Equipment, for example computers	Non-discounted payback < five years
Plant – manufacturing	Payback: product life/volumes
Non-project-related expense	Profit and loss effect

investment involved. Some investments are concerned with capital assets and some are concerned with expense. Capital assets are depreciated over a period of years. Many projects involve both capital and expense items and IT is no exception. Which outgoings are allocated to capital and to expense is a matter of both national and in-house accounting standards and practice. Typically, for IT, equipment is capitalized and in-house systems development is expensed. Purchased software is often treated as an expense. Projects, IT or not, with a high capital component are more likely to be required to show a financial return, such as a break-even period. The different mix between capital and expense can be largely removed by considering project cash flows, as discussed earlier in this chapter. Variations regarding the mix of capital and expense in different types of investment, can lead to invalid comparisons of returns on those investments.

Some examples of how different types of investment might be treated so that financially acceptable projects can be selected from within each type are given in Table 11.8. Within IT investments, Weill and Olson have suggested that strategic investments be measured against revenue growth rate, investment in information infrastructure be measured against return on assets and transaction system investments be measured against change in labour and product costs.[3]

11.4   The evaluation of intangibles

11.4.1 The principles of evaluation

By definition, the intangible benefit is one which cannot be confidently quantified or directly and solely related to the implementation of an IT application. It does not give an absolute measure of the impact of the change brought about by the new investment. Tangible benefits are those that can be measured, often financially.

Intangible benefits are statements of what will be relatively better. Therefore their evaluation needs to be made in relative terms. Similar intangible benefits can be compared across projects. Within a project, different benefit types can be compared with each other.

In Chapter 10 we quoted Sharp, who wrote, '. . . experienced management judgement is an excellent, practical substitute for exact option analysis . . .'. He continued, '. . . and that managerial judgement must be embedded in a formal decision-making process'. This is what we have used for the last decade in the

Table 11.9   Examples of criteria for evaluating benefits

Positive impacts	Negative impacts
1 Revenue – sales	10 Equipment costs
2 Income – interest	11 Network needs
3 Direct costs – people	12 IT development cost
4 Direct costs – materials	13 Users involved
5 Direct costs – space	14 Level of technology
6 Indirect costs	15 Dependencies
7 Management control	
8 Customer service	
9 Employee morale	

evaluation of intangible benefits within application planning studies. It is just how many enterprises actually do it.

Moreover, the use of management judgement is neither peculiar to IT projects, nor to intangible benefits. It is also used for estimating and forecasting the size of tangible benefits, which are then expressed in measurable terms.

Management judgement means that managers – that is, accountable, well-informed and experienced managers – have to be involved. It needs managers who will be responsible for using the systems and who understand what the systems will do for them. Who makes the judgement is as important as how they make it.

A financial evaluation quantifies benefits numerically, and ultimately in units of money, and they become tangible benefits. The evaluation of intangibles can be similar, notional values being assigned to them. The intangibles are 'weighted' or 'scored'; it is the assignment of the weighting which needs the judgement. The values are not absolute, but they can be compared with similarly derived values. The weightings do not provide a basis of more universal comparison, as do financial values, and generally they are not used as a basis of measurement. However, they can be used as relative measures of value, and thus lead to statements of priority and ranking.

An example will illustrate the evaluation of intangibles. It is drawn from our own practical experience of building business cases. In Chapter 9 we discussed the use of an impact matrix in a benefits assessment workshop to evaluate both tangible and intangible benefits, within and across five application projects. The workshop participants will typically be a multi-disciplinary group given this special responsibility or an IT steering group. To be fully effective the method needs to be consistently used, and initially a skilled facilitator will help to ensure that the process achieves a solid consensus.

The criteria against which each project is assessed in the impact matrix need further inspection (Table 11.9). It can be seen that:

1   Criteria 1 to 6 are all potentially tangible benefits.
2   Criteria 7 to 9 are likely to be intangible benefits.

Table 11.10 The impact matrix with weighted criteria. See Table 11.9 for positive (1–9) and negative (10–15) impacts

IT application	Positive impacts									Negative impacts					
	1	2	3	4	5	6	7	8	9	10	11	12	13	14	15
	Sample weightings on a scale of 1 to 5														
	4	2	5	5	5	3	2	2	4	3	4	5	2	5	2
A	3	—	2	2	1	—	1	3	3	2	2	3	2	2	1
B	—	2	1	—	—	—	3	1	1	1	—	2	1	1	1
C	—	—	3	1	3	1	3	—	2	2	1	3	3	1	3
D	1	1	1	—	—	1	2	1	—	2	1	3	2	1	2
E	3	1	3	2	2	2	3	3	1	3	2	2	2	2	3

Impact rating: High = 3
               Medium = 2
               Low = 1

3   Criteria 10 to 12 are items of cost.
4   Criteria 13 to 15 indicate levels of risk.

In the cells of the matrix (Fig. 9.2), the weighting of benefits has been made on a four-point scale; high, medium and low and zero impact. Sometimes, a six-point scale can be handled; a ten point scale is generally too fine a cut. In some situations it is possible go further and relate the scale to approximate ranges of tangible benefit (or cost), for example, high = over £100 000, medium = £50 000–£100 000 and low = under £50 000. For small projects the ranges would be substantially lower.

Further refinements can be made to the evaluation as follows:

1   As a high/medium/low rating is given for each application against each benefit, reasons for the rating can be noted. Elements of quantifiable saving can be identified in this way.
2   The evaluation has only covered the relative potential of the benefits. Their achievability can also be rated. This is often conveniently mapped into the same cell by dividing each cell with a diagonal. Thus the top left rating will be a measure of the benefit, while the bottom right rating will be its achievability. In a similar way, costs can be given a certainty rating.
3   Each criterion can be given a numeric weighting as well, for example on a scale of 1 to 5, to provide a measure of importance given to the criterion.

    In this case the high/medium/low weightings in the matrix cells are best converted to numbers also. The weighting in each cell is then multiplied by the weighting assigned to the criterion and the results entered into a new matrix. To complete the analysis the results in each cell can be summed to give the total for positive and negative impacts respectively, for each project. This is illustrated in Table 11.10.

In the last step, however, management judgement has been replaced by an apparently statistical result. The question is whether a ranking of projects deduced from these statistics alone is really credible, and it is important for the group to discuss this. In our experience it is often best to use management judgement to make the final ranking rather than switch to statistics. It is the discussion and the analytical process which is of prime importance, not the arithmetic.

The process provides a statement, with reasons, of the relative importance of potential IT investments, but it has two limitations.

Firstly, in considering the evaluation of a *single* project, it does not provide a clear-cut answer as to whether it is worth approving; it only provides a profile of unquantified benefits, costs and risks. Secondly, as the matrix does not provide a quantified statement of benefits and costs these need to be identified in addition to the matrix-based analysis.

In the next section other sets of criteria will be discussed, which can also be used to evaluate intangible benefits and other project characteristics. Risk assessment is covered at the end of this chapter and we shall consider further the ranking and classification of projects in Chapter 12.

11.4.2 *Further criteria and methods for the evaluation of intangibles*

We now discuss six specific approaches to evaluating the intangible benefit components of a project. The methods have strong similarities: each asks the question, 'What is the impact of this project?' The first two methods consider the project as a whole. The second two methods analyse the project against types of intangible benefits. The last two methods include other criteria in the evaluation, as did the impact matrix example above.

Project classification

A single criterion can be applied to a project – it can be classified by its type according to a predetermined set of types, for example, mandatory, necessary or desirable. This imputes value to the whole project and is often used as a means of ranking projects. Classification by type is used for priority setting across projects, rather than providing an assessment of their standalone value.

Business processes

IT applications are developed to support business processes. Therefore assessing the impact of an application on a set of business processes will give a measure of its value. Identifying how it affects each process will help to identify specific, and even tangible, benefits. Processes may be weighted and key business processes will be given the higher weighting.

Discrete intangible items

In section 10.2.4 we described 17 intangible benefits, against which any application project might be given a numerical evaluation. They were:

- Improved planning and forecasting.
- Improved levels of management control.
- The time value of information.
- Improved quality of decisions.
- Organizational excellence and flexibilty.
- Customer service.
- Enterprise image.
- Better market development and market share.
- Employee morale.
- Product development.
- Manufacturing/processing responsiveness.
- Support for business policies and strategies.
- Fit with technical policies and architectures.
- Availability of future options.
- Legal and government.
- Security.
- Relative loss of position – what if we don't invest?

Benefits groups

Benefits in the above list were placed in five groups, namely management and organization, external, internal, strategic and high downside risk. Each group can be used as a criterion against which to measure the impact of an investment.

Another set of groups has been described by Willcocks and Lester. In their survey, they report on the criteria actually used by organizations for project evaluation.[4]

Overall the most popular combinations are: Cost Benefit, Competitive Advantage and Service to the Public (14%); Cost Benefit, Competitive Advantage and Service to the Public and Quality of Product (12%); Cost Benefit, Competitive Advantage and Service to the Public, Quality of Product and Job Enhancement (10%).

Only 16% of the organizations use more than four criteria on which to base their evaluation. Only one of the organizations who felt 'very satisified' with the results actually uses more than four criteria. It is no surprise that the most popular of the combinations offered is also the simplest.

Compound criteria – Buss

A further example of evaluation is provided by Buss in 'How to rank computer projects'.[5] This combines both financial and intangible criteria and goes further to include technical and operational assessments. This approach is widely used to set priorities across projects, and the criteria employed are:

1 *Business*: to evaluate the project in terms of its fit with enterprise or business unit objectives.
2 *Financial*: to evaluate the project in terms of, for example, its payback or return on investment.
3 *Intangible*: to evaluate those benefits that are identified but not quantified.
4 *Technical/operational*: to evaluate its significance in technical terms.

The first three Buss criteria match the project against the needs of the business, financial hurdles and resource constraints. The fourth criterion recognizes that, for IT resources to be used effectively, there must be an appropriate mix of development projects. Account needs to be taken of the level and mix of available skills, technical strategies, IT infrastructure developments and operational capabilities. Additional considerations are the level of risk and the quality of sponsorship associated with individual projects.

Information economics

Information economics has been proposed and described, thoroughly and comprehensively, by Parker and Benson.[6] Information economics is a framework of concepts and tools.

At one level, information economics is a collection of computational tools for quantifying benefits and costs for IT projects. This is the traditional role of cost–benefit analysis (CBA). Information economics looks beyond CBA to deal with value based on business performance – to handle projects that have strategic impact on the company. Information economics also looks at the IT infrastructure – the supply side investment in the infrastructure. At a second level, information economics is a process of decision-making.

At the centre of the approach are four techniques for financial justification. All of these aim to identify and quantify the potential benefits of a project. The financial factor consists of the following:

1 Traditional cost–benefit analysis.
2 Value linking and acceleration; in which benefits are achieved by other

departments, and are achieved more quickly, than simply those benefits projected for the department in which the investment was primarily made.

3   Value restructuring; in which the effects of modifying an existing job function or department are analysed.

4   Innovation valuation; in which alternatives among new applications of IT are assessed.

Additionally, nine other factors are proposed to extend the analysis beyond the return on investment of the financial calculations. These factors relate to business performance and to business and technical risk. The ten criteria are, therefore, in two groups:

1   Business domain values and risks:

- Return on investment
- Strategic match
- Competitive advantage
- Management information support
- Competitive response
- Project or organizational risk

2   Technical domain values and risks:

- Strategic systems achitecture
- Definitional uncertainty
- Technical uncertainty
- Systems infrastructure risk

For a project, or for each project in a group, scores (or weights) are proposed against each criterion. The criteria are themselves weighted and the scores multiplied by the weights to provide an overall factor for each project and a ranking of the projects.

The similarities of this approach with our own, the impact matrix, will be noted. The method is attractive because Parker and Benson have been careful to define their criteria, and to define what is meant by each level of the scores and weights. These definitions are fundamental to a consistent and reproducible application of information economics, and they require a good level of understanding on the part of those applying them. The importance of corporate cultures and management involvement and consensus in this process is emphasized by Parker and Benson.

A clear account of the application of information economics in a UK government department has been given by Wiseman.[7]

The approaches of both Buss and of Parker and Benson are attractive. The former is simple and robust; the latter is exhaustive and well-documented. They both illustrate that a combination of techniques is almost always needed to assess rightly the true value of any IT project.

The search for the perfect investment appraisal method continues. It is not only technology which requires investment decisions. Shank and Govindarajan have reviewed four approaches to capital investment appraisal: one discards financial analysis; one uses a refined NPV model; one links technology decisions to strategic analysis; and one proposes an integrated 'strategic–financial' analysis framework.[8] The authors find all four approaches lacking. They propose a framework of strategic cost management with three components: value chain analysis, cost driver analysis and competitive advantage analysis. They illustrate the strategic cost management framework with an impressive analysis of a capital investment. However, their framework does not include risk analysis – a vital component of decision-making.

Evaluation methods tend to come and go with people and with time, possibly suggesting that current fashion can play a major part in method selection, but also recognizing the continuing search for practical and effective methods. Carlson and McNurlin, writing in 'Measuring the value of information systems',[9] note that most thoughtful ideas come from researchers and consultants rather than from user companies. This may be so, but thoughtful ideas are not always practicable ideas. Rigorous methods are not necessarily preferable to usable methods. The best can be the enemy of the good. Moreover, it must also be said that much of the literature is complicated and often beyond application other than by a few individuals.

Making business cases and decisions to invest are team activities, which demand understanding from a wide cross-section of (fairly) ordinary business managers. Nevertheless, while some methods may need understanding and experience for their effective application, it is no good user companies complaining about the difficulties of measuring or predicting the value of IT if no practicable management systems are introduced to do it. Within the methods that we have described lie the principles on which such management systems can be, and have been, formulated.

11.5   Project risk evaluation

Risk appraisal is as much a part of the business case as financial appraisal, although in the past it has been less frequently and rigorously performed. Once identified, risks, like costs and benefits, must be managed.

Risk analysis can be applied to project implementation or to operation of the resulting system. In the former case, the concern is with successful project completion and this is important to the business case. In the latter case, the concern is with the continued integrity and availability of the system and these are best handled in detail during system design.

In the discussion of intangible benefit evaluation above, the question of benefit achievability was introduced. To achieve benefits the project must be completed, and there are many reasons why a project might not be successful. A project might be successful in terms of the function it delivers and yet still not deliver the forecast benefits, for a variety of other reasons. Some of these might have been foreseen, and some will have been quite unpredictable. Consequently, the assessment needs to include the risk of not completing the project successfully and of not achieving the benefits; both will influence the decision to invest.

How can risks be evaluated and, of more importance, how can they be minimized?

Risk management needs to be seen as complete process. The process will move through the steps of defining objectives, identifying and assessing risks, quantifying risks, building and evaluating a risk management plan, approving the plan and implementing and monitoring risk management activities.

Risk management needs to involve the right people, particluarly in the initial assessment and planning steps. Typical participants will have skills in risk and quality assurance, project management, functional business management and in those specialist areas which require risk assessment.

Risk assessment requires a high degree of judgement, based on experience and perception, as does the evaluation of intangible benefits. Consequently, the methods of evaluation are similar; both are best conducted by an appropriate team and both need a set of criteria for the assessment. The criteria can be weighted and scores given to the assessment of the project against each criterion. Each identified risk area can be factored by 'size of risk' (threat) and 'chance of occurring' (vulnerability). Some risks will be tangible and have a calculable cost associated with them, for example risks due to tight deadlines, while others will be intangible, such as the risks arising from poor project sponsorship.

A suitable set of risk assessment criteria has been provided by information economics. These were listed above as:

- Project or organizational risk
- Strategic systems achitecture
- Definitional uncertainty
- Technical uncertainty
- Systems infrastructure risk

A fuller list of criteria or parameters for risk evaluation is given in Fig. 11.6, grouped into five main areas. The parameters can be used for single projects, or in a 'risk matrix analysis' for multiple projects.

In the example shown the assessment is a binary one. For each project, each parameter is assessed for more risk or less risk, as shown by a tick in the appropriate column. For a single project, or for each project in a portfolio, the initial analysis is completed by identifying the five most serious risks. For a portfolio of projects, the number of ticks in each column against each project is totalled and the totals used as a basis for assessing and ranking the projects in order of their level of risk.

Risk assessment can now move to a second stage, for the most serious risks.

Project title:	Less risk	More risk

Project size
   Cost
   Duration
   Size and number of teams
   Number of departments and people affected
   Project experience and leadership skills		

Project structure and procedure
   Number of phases and tasks
   Probability of change to requirements
   Project planning and control
   Design and productivity tools		

Application and technology complexity
   New application area
   Stability and definition of requirements
   New hardware or software
   Leading-edge design or technology
   Experience with data management
   Technical competencies
   Supplier competencies
   Fit with technical policies		

Operational impact
   Organizational change
   Operational feasibility
   Operational complexity
   Level of training and education
   Number of departments and people affected		

Commitment of management
   Correct sponsorship
   Level of benefits and business need
   Level of involvement of users
   IT knowledge of the business community
   Effectiveness of steering committee reviews		

Number of ticks		

Figure 11.6.   Criteria for risk assessment.

Each can be assessed for its impact on the project in terms of resource and cost overruns, in delays to the project schedule or in the loss of function or quality delivered.

At the third stage, financial estimates are made of the impact on benefits, should the risk materialize. The results of this may be expressed in a financial sensitivity analysis (Chapter 10). However, in making a financial analysis it is vital not to lose sight of risks which may not have been quantified.

Identifying the risks of not achieving the benefits of a project is the first step, and arguably the most significant, towards avoiding the risks. Then it is vital to propose sensible actions to minimize or avoid the most important risks and to assign responsibility for those actions to individual managers. This involves additional project costs and these must be built into the project cost assessment.

Controls	Project risks			System risks				
	Improper scope	Cost and time overruns	Project prioritization	Functionality/performance	Maintainability	Controllability	Technology	Implementation
Management participation	X	X	X	X				
User participation	X		X	X		X	X	X
Information systems organization participation				X	X	X	X	X
Systems development methodology		X		X		X		X
Project planning tools		X						
Management report procedures	X	X	X					
Quality assurance	X	X	X	X	X	X	X	X
Audit involvement	X			X		X	X	X
Systems development standards				X	X	X	X	X

Figure 11.7.   Risks and controls matrix.[10]

Other risk management approaches will shift the impact of risk elsewhere or at least share it with other stakeholders. And some risks might simply be accepted. Management techniques which may be used to minimize the risks have been described by Institute of Internal Auditors Research Foundation and related to typical project and system risks (see Fig. 11.7).[10]

Finally, existing IT policies should be reviewed to ensure that they take account of significant risks which might affect any IT project.

11.6   Finalizing the business case

The second stage of proposing and authorizing the project will be completed as the staff work of evaluating the business case is finalized.

The content of the business case will vary from project to project and according to the stage of the project. The business case is likely to be embedded in a project proposal and in-house standards generally exist for the contents of this. For some projects and stages it may be appropriate to use a pro-forma (an example was shown in Fig. 10.6 to illustrate the contents and format). When used as a summary of the fuller project proposal, the pro-forma helps to achieve completeness and to aid comparisons across projects. There may be separate pro-formas for the initial proposal, for the full business case, and for approval of expenditure against agreed budgets. Whatever the form of the documentation, the finance function should be closely involved at an early stage to assist in structuring the proposal and to ensure that all the essential information is included and consistently formatted.

An oral 'presentation' is often more effective than formal documentation in communicating the essential contents of a project proposal, although it is no substitute for the permanent record of a document. Whatever communication medium is used, its 'packaging' must take account of the enterprise's culture.

Having concluded the staff work, gained the approval of all functions and finalized the business case, the project proposal is ready to be submitted to the next stage of decision-making for its authorization. This is the subject of the next chapter.

References

1 G. Roland Kaye, The role of management accountants in information strategy, *J. Information Technol.*, **3**(4), December 1988, pp. 251–264.
2 Beat Hochstrasser and Catherine Griffiths, *Regaining Control of IT Investments*, Kobler Unit, Imperial College, London, 1990.
3 P. Weill and M. Olson, Managing investment in information technology: Mini case examples and implications, *MIS Quarterly*, **13**(1), March 1989.
4 Leslie Willcocks and Stephanie Lester, Information systems investments: evaluation at the feasibility stage of projects, *Technovation*, **II**(5) (1991), 283–302.
5 Martin D. J. Buss, How to rank computer projects, *Harvard Business Review*, January–February 1983.
6 Marilyn M. Parker and Robert J. Benson with H. Edward Trainor, *Information Economics*, Prentice-Hall, Englewood Cliffs, NJ, 1988.
7 Devra Wiseman, Information economics: a practical approach to valuing information systems, *J. Information Technol.*, **7**(3), September 1992, pp. 169–176.
8 John K. Shank and Vijay Govindarajan, Strategic cost analysis of technological investments, *Sloan Management Review*, Fall 1992.
9 Walter M. Carlson and Barbara C. McNurlin, Measuring the value of information systems, *I/S Analyzer Special Report*, United Communications Group, 1989.
10 *Systems Audibility and Control (SAC)*, Research Report, Institute of Internal Auditors Research Foundation, 1991.

12
Stage 3: make the decision

12.1 Key factors in making decisions

We start by recalling some basic aspects of practical decision-making. To make sound decisions, good information is needed; but having good information does not guarantee a sound decision. Decisions are rarely made on the basis of having all the necessary information; the information that is available may be based on a number of assumptions and on forecasts of varying inaccuracy. The criteria against which the decision will be made must be understood. A good decision can be made that meets all the criteria at decision time, but the resulting project may not be well managed, the assumptions may prove to be invalid, or external events may frustrate it, resulting in only partial success.

Major decisions are rarely made by one person at one point in time, although some individuals will play a major role in shaping the decision. Decisions emerge after they have been understood by, and consensus gained from, all involved. Decisions are made in part on the absolute value of the proposed action but also on the merit of the action relative to alternatives. Decision-making is a blend of rational thinking and intuition working within the framework of an organization's culture and politics.

With such a background to the decision-making process there is not likely to be a well-defined process that will 'guarantee success'. This chapter discusses four topics that are vital to an understanding of good decision-making. These are the questions that must be asked of the proposed course of action (section 12.2), who makes the decision (section 12.3), the processes that can be used to establish priorities (section 12.4), and the nature of the framework within which investment project decisions will be made (section 12.5).

CASE STUDY

We return to Al Luchini, supermarket Store Manager in the case study we have followed in Chapters 10 and 11.

Al could make investment decisions, agreed by his accountant, of up to $15 000, without prior Executive approval. The $150 000 investment in a store refit needed Executive Board sign-off and to obtain this Al submitted a five-page investment proposal. Had he used one of the investment classifications described later in this chapter, he would have described it as a necessary business development. A $45 000 investment for computer systems was all part of the refit – it was totally consistent with business objectives and a significant 'agent of change' for the store. In a small business the cultural implications of change may be easier to contain – but Al did not anticipate that two of his check-out staff would leave with concerns over the new technology.

12.2   Key questions and criteria for a successful business case

There are seven key questions to be asked of a project and seven criteria that the project business case must meet. The questions aim to evaluate the content of the business case as well as its merit. The questions and criteria are important and can be applied however the business case is presented, whether it is written or oral, to a predefined format or in a less structured document. They search the aims, attitudes and abilities of those proposing the change.

12.2.1 Relevance to business objectives

Question: Why is this investment in IT being proposed? What is its relevance to the business objectives? What will be the result if it is not accepted?

Criterion: The proposal contributes to the enterprise's objectives and is consistent with business strategies, particularly with regard to customers, products and competition.

Many of the intangible benefits of a project will satisfy this criterion. To establish the true benefit of a project it may be necessary to assemble financial and statistical information about the enterprise, its industry sector and the markets within which it will be operating. Both current status and trend information may be needed. How competitors use or are planning to use technology may be a significant consideration and it is particularly relevant to identify the current competitive strategy of the enterprise itself. The investment climate both within and outside the enterprise will influence the decision.

Above all, the acceptability of the proposal depends on how it affects business strategies and plans. What are they? How important is the proposal to their achievement? Will it affect product development or manufacturing costs or is it customer- or supplier-orientated?

12.2.2 *Implications clearly understood*

Question: How well do key individuals understand the full extent of changes that are being proposed? Are they committed to making the changes?

Criterion: The proposal and the implied changes are visible to and understood by executive and middle managers.

Some of the most imaginative and competitively effective uses of technology have been the 'brainchildren' of a chief executive. All the real success stories have been heavily supported by the Chief Executive Officer. One of the key requirements for good decisions and implementations is the participation of appropriate executive and middle managers in the planning process and in the overall formulation of the systems solution. It is even better where there is previous experience to draw on of similar projects or of well conceived pilot projects.

The essence of meeting this criterion is to have a shared vision, beyond just the systems implications, of what is wanted, and to have a commitment to achieving it. It demands a clear understanding of what the change means, in the most tangible terms and beyond those groups of people directly affected. Both the opportunity that is there to be taken and the downside risk of what is proposed need to be appreciated.

12.2.3 *Requirements defined: solution available*

Question: Have the requirements been specified by the users in sufficient detail? What is the technical feasibility of the solution? How well will it meet the requirements?

Criterion: The requirements are defined in sufficient detail by the users and a feasible solution is available.

The foundation stone of any business case is the documented statement of business requirements provided by the users. This is a more rigorous statement of the required change than that needed to meet the second criterion. The managers whose business units will use the systems are the owners of the requirements. Often they will lack the time and possibly the skills to think through their current requirements, let alone to think creatively about the future. Many of the requirements will be jointly owned and will need a structured, team-based approach to achieve the most stable definition of them.

The requirements may well be influenced by the selected systems solution, and this calls for an iterative process for requirements definition. In any case, there will be trade-offs between what is required and the feasibility and cost of providing it. Often there will be options, the selection of which may appear to depend on technical considerations, but which involve assumptions affecting the business. In particular, the solution will need to fit with technical strategies that have been adopted to achieve technical efficiency and effectiveness. The solution will be described in terms of outline systems designs, software packages, networks, machines and equipment.

Finally, although imagination has its place, the proposed solution needs to be grounded in the reality of what is technically proven, or, where there are uncertainties, these need to be understood by the sponsor and users. Any lack of confidence by systems providers in their ability to deliver a solution will, and should, stop in their tracks any decision-makers who are considering the proposal.

12.2.4 People resources available

Question: What people resources will be required to implement it and are they available within the proposed time-scale? What tasks need to be performed?

Criterion: The estimated amount and type of resource needed to implement is available and the project time-scale is realistic.

To meet this criterion the business case needs to contain answers to the 'who' and 'how' of implementation. It will contain the tasks making up the project implementation plan. It will contain estimates of the amount and types of development resources on a period by period basis required to complete the tasks. The resources of those directly involved in the implementation, both users and IT, will necessarily be included; the resources of support groups (for example, training and contractor personnel) must be identified and be available to the project when needed. Assumptions about resource estimates need to be documented.

12.2.5 Return on investment

Question: What return can be expected on the investment and when? Can it be afforded within the planned time-scale?

Criterion: Estimated costs and benefits are within acceptable financial boundaries.

The potential return on investment will be deduced from estimates of the real costs and the tangible benefits, and of their phasing relative to each other. The costs and benefits (or their profit or loss component) will need to be collected and aggregated by type for the periods in which they will occur (for example, monthly, quarterly or yearly), and as far as possible for each project or sub-project. Thus the cash flows, or the profit effects where capital costs are spread over several years, will be derived for each project.

Provision should be made for inflation or falling costs. Net cash flows will be calculated and, after discounting (where this technique is to be used), they will be analysed to establish paybacks from break-even points and rates of return on investment. To take account of some of the uncertainties, sensitivity analysis techniques may be used.

The financial evaluation of the project should be accompanied by a benefits delivery plan, agreed and signed by the relevant budget managers. This plan might be in terms of improvements to either budget items or to key performance indicators.

12.2.6 Achievable and operable

Questions: How achievable is it? Is it operationally feasible? What is the impact if it is partially successful? What should be done to help ensure success?

Criterion: It has been assessed in terms of project size and complexity, for the technology to be used and for the experience of all those involved. Its mode of operation is understood.

This analyses constraints which may be imposed on the project and to assess the major areas of risk, firstly for its implementation and then for its operation. The main considerations are:

- The project and sub-project size, time-scale and the numbers of people involved.
- The experience of the technical team gained from a project needing similar skills.
- The reliance placed on new hardware, software and methodologies.
- The continuing availability of the appropriate skills and resources.
- The degree and the rate of change for technical people and users.
- The dependence on other business and technical decisions.
- The level of commitment to the project that will be maintained by the executive and user managers.

12.2.7 Synergy or contention

Question: Are we too stretched in other areas to take on this project?

Criterion: It fits well with other planned activities, and complements them rather than complicates them.

This criterion checks for projects or management programmes that are associated with, supportive of, or depend on the proposed project. The project objectives need to find synergy with other projects and programmes. For example, to achieve savings by making productivity improvements from an investment in IT requires an overall productivity strategy.

Some projects will need a policy framework within which to be effective. In making worthwhile productivity savings, progressive personnel policies will be needed if the project is not to run into industrial relations problems.

There has to be no significant contention for resources with other apparently disconnected projects. For example, a project requiring procedural changes implies further training for users. If other non-IT projects are also placing a heavy load on training resources, then both projects may be in jeopardy. Any major project will place a heavier workload on management. However well the project is financially justified, its business case may need to recognize other contenders for management attention.

CASE STUDY

We return to the project proposal used as an illustration at the end of Chapter 1. Based on the information given in the case study and the above criteria, we put questions which might have helped Dr Frank to improve the presentation of his proposal.

Relevance to business objectives: The reservoir visualization application was directly relevant to the oil company's main objective – the successful recovery of oil. Was this connection clear and the consequent priority of the proposal established?

Implications clearly understood: The geophysicist understood its potential impact. He returned from the trade show with a vision. Did it need to be demonstrated to a wider community?

Requirements defined – solution available: At this stage even Dr Frank was uncertain about the solution. Did the full $30 000 have to be spent to answer this, or would a prototype help to resolve its applicability? What was the case for reviewing the workstation type, or the policy?

Resources available: The vendor would provide the main resource. Were other resources needed too?

Return on investment: The proposal was for a 'proof of concept', with no expected return in the short term. With which other types of project did this really compete? What was the IT budget for R&D type projects?

Achievable and operable: Risks were recognized; for one, its conversion for his use might hit snags. Could actions have been taken to manage that risk?

Synergy or contention: The timing of the request had more to do with the date of the trade show than the preparedness of the decision-makers to consider it! When could their interest have been focused on the benefit of the proposal?

Our key questions and criteria for a business case are applicable to all types of investment project, for both large and small business units.

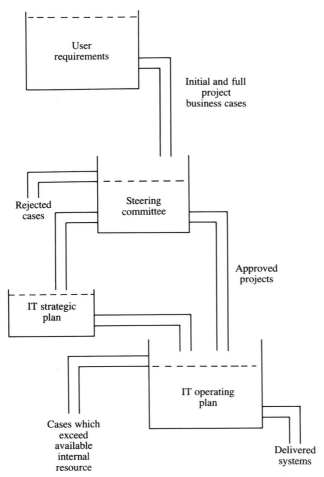

Figure 12.1. Process for project and business case approval. (*Source*: IBM UK ISL.)

12.3 Making the decision

12.3.1 Decision options and types

The decision to be made is whether to accept or reject a proposed IT investment project and/or to set it in order of priority among other proposed projects. Resources are likely to be already stretched this year and there will be contention for development resources for next year.

For a new proposal there will be several possible decisions, based on the business case presented for it, the timing of it and the relative priority this establishes. These are illustrated in Figure 12.1.

1   Based on the initial proposal, a steering committee may approve its develop-
    ment with resources allocated in the current strategic (two-year) plan. In this
    case, preparation of the full business case will be requested with a view to full
    implementation in 12 months' time.
2   Based on the submission of a proposal with a full business case, the project
    may be approved for inclusion in the IT development budget covered by the
    next 12 months' operating plan.
3   The project may be rejected.
4   Finally, if the necessary provision has not been made for a project in the
    current plan and it cannot be accommodated within the sponsor's annual
    budget for IT, or within any other budget for that year, then this project would
    be relegated to a later year.

Overlaying this process are two further considerations that will need to be
managed. First, project proposals tend not to be presented to the steering
committee in line with the business planning cycle. They arrive throughout the
year. Second, the committee's time is likely to be taken up with resolving issues on
projects already committed. The decision processes discussed in section 12.4 will
help to address these issues, but before that we consider who is involved in
decision-making.

12.3.2 *Participants in setting priorities*

For any enterprise, decisions are made within the context of its own organizational framework. Where in the organization the decision is made depends on the
size and nature of the decision. Decision-making is a political activity; it can never
be totally rationalized or set in procedures. A project sponsor always needs to
understand who has to be persuaded, and on what basis the project is likely to be
approved.

In many enterprises it may seem that priorities for IT investment projects are set
by 'the person who shouts loudest', and there is something to be said for this
approach, particularly if the person is the chief executive. This shows that
someone has a strong commitment to the successful implementation of the
project. Taken together, the chief executive's feeling for what is right and the
enthusiast's commitment to deliver results need only to have added to them the
specialist's appreciation of what is feasible to have a very workable priority setting
process.

Priorities almost certainly need to be agreed by a group of people, rather than
by an individual. The task may well be delegated from the Executive Board to
the Chief Information Officer. Such delegation may not be wrong, but it is not
normally the most effective. The theme is developed in 'How executives can shape
their company's information systems',[1] which describes the use of a task force to

help set priorities. The need for multiple views of priorities is supported by Hochstrasser and Griffiths,[2] who describe some of the issues this way:

> If senior managers with little knowledge of IT take charge of IT, the resulting systems tend to be expensive, patchy and only used to a fraction of their full potential. Incompatibility problems between different in-house installations often arise and the same data has to be input repeatedly for different functions, leading to duplication and error. Eventually, further technology has to be brought in, in the attempt to correct original mistakes.
>
> If IT managers with little knowledge of business goals are left in charge of IT, the emphasis in planning IT projects tends to be placed on the technological aspects of IT, such as the accuracy and speed of output rather than the appropriateness of the business functions supported.

Sometimes, where there is a particularly clear policy to integrate IT with the business, setting IT investment priorities may be delegated to a financial or business planner, within agreed procedures and criteria. This arrangement claims an advantage in that IT priorities are proposed by an objective and consistent professional, for ratification by an executive committee, after the necessary investigations and staff work have been completed. It will need a means by which recommended priorities can be challenged and by which issues can be escalated for resolution at an appropriate level of management.

Where appraisal of IT investment involves highly specialized knowledge, as for example in scientific or engineering computing, then investment reviews may involve peer specialist professionals.

In most instances, final decisions on priorities (at least for major projects) are rightly the responsiblity of an IT steering committee, which consists of senior representatives from the business functions committing to deliver the benefits, of the CIO committing to deliver the systems and of planning functions committing to take account of both in the strategic or operating plan.

Any of these arrangements can apply to both strategic and operational priority setting, but are more likely to apply to the latter. The CIO will assume more responsibility for proposing the strategic resourcing levels of IT and for the priorities of investments in IT facilities and infrastructure. For smaller projects (for example, minicomputers and PCs), where the IT expenditure is within agreed budgets and conforms with technical strategies, the priority might well be set by the departmental head of the function concerned.

Whoever has the task of setting priorities for IT developments, the priorities need to be aligned with business plans and goals. This requires a well-defined relationship between the procedures and the people responsible for business plans and for IT priorities. The quality of business cases will be improved if the criteria for their acceptance and prioritization are understood and applied.

The next section looks at the creative and analytical procedures that can be used for setting priorities. These processes can be used to help in setting priorities both for the strategic and for the operational business plan, but the creative processes are more applicable to the strategic time frame and to the overall allocation of resources to IT.

12.4   Decision processes

The decision to invest will be a 'go' or a 'no-go' decision, project by project, and then a decision as to which to do first. The evaluation of an individual project was discussed in Chapter 11.

This section focuses on the priorities of projects, on identifying which are the more important to the enterprise. It is vital that a decision is based not only on what is proposed, but also on what should be proposed. Therefore, the methods used need to be both creative and analytical. The tools are those of classification and ranking. Classification of projects tends to be more relevant in the creative process and ranking more relevant in the analytical process, and our discussion will reflect this.

12.4.1 Creative processes for setting priorities

The creative processes are those that facilitate the search for new applications of IT to support the strategic direction of the business. They start by asking, 'If this is the business plan, then how might IT be developed to support it?' But they go further and ask, 'What opportunities does the use of IT present? How can we exploit them?' The processes help to identify potential new application areas based on business needs, on industry trends and on technological developments. They generate ideas and visions for the use of IT. They will suggest the criteria by which IT investments should be judged.

The creative decision process is more relevant to early project selection, rather than later project approval, but we include it here, in Stage 3 of our decision-making process, because it is one aspect of making decisions.

These creative processes have been called 'inside-out' planning (as compared with top–down, analytical or bottom–up evaluation) by Earl and others.[3] These processes consider the project as a whole, rather than its internal components and position the project relative to other projects. By comparison, the analytical processes start by taking project proposals from business managers and from IT managers and then evaluating the proposals against a set of criteria, based on business plans.

The creative processes are typically offered by consultants who bring skills and perceptions which may not be readily 'home-grown'. Such consultants will work with a group of executives in a creative, but structured, planning activity. They will often prompt the question, 'What sort of company are we, and in what industry?', and endeavour to position the enterprise relative to its competitors. The process is illustrated in Fig. 12.2.

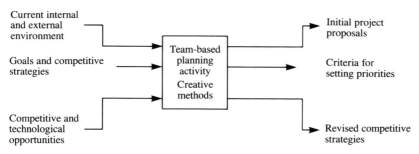

Figure 12.2.   Creative priority setting processes.

There are many established methods. Several have been pioneered by IBM UK and these have now been subsumed into the IBM Consulting Group practice for IT Strategy and Planning and for Business Transformation. Creative, inside-out planning is provided by the early modules of these methodologies (Fig. 4.6). Other frameworks are used to stimulate a creative approach to establishing IT priorities. Some typical examples are as follows.

1   *The value chain and competitive forces*
    Porter and Millar[4] describe the use of the value chain for analysing the strategic significance of IT.

    This concept divides a company's activities into the technologically and economically distinct activities it performs to do business. We call these 'value activities' . . . . To gain competitive advantage over its rivals, a company must either perform these activities at a lower cost or perform them in a way that leads to differentiation and a premium price (more value).

    The value chain helps to identify those line activities in which there is an opportunity for the application of IT.
    Porter and Millar also describe the structure of an industry by reference to the five competitive forces – the power of the buyers, the power of the suppliers, the threat of new entrants, the threat of substitute products and rivalry among existing competitors. Understanding these forces can help to determine competitive strategies and to identify IT applications to support them.

2   *Process and critical success factor analyses*
    A business process framework may be used as an alternative to the value chain. The key processes are identified using enterprise CSFs as evaluation criteria. Investigations then focus on how IT can be used to support and to transform the key processes. This approach has been described by Ward and Hardaker.[5]

3   *Matrices and four-square grids*
    Further creative approaches to identifying IT opportunities use portfolio analysis. In this, existing IT applications are positioned on a matrix.

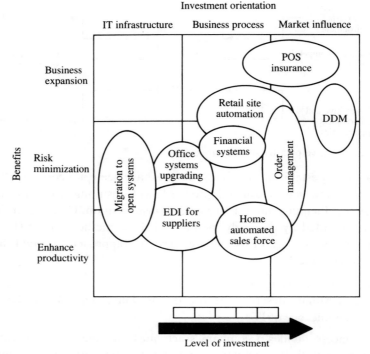

Figure 12.3. An example of an application map to evaluate IT investments. (*Source*: Glen Peters, Beyond strategy – benefits identification and management of specific IT investments, *J. Information Technol.* (1990), **5**(4), pp. 205–214.)

MacFarlan, McKenny and Pyburn have described four segments of a matrix, namely strategic, turnaround, factory and support.[6] The distribution of applications across the segments clarifies weak areas in the portfolio and suggests potential development needs.

The Boston Consultancy Group have used more imaginative names for the segments: cash cow, dog, star and ?, but their purpose is the same: to help identify gaps in IT support.

Writing in the *Journal of Information Technology*, in separate papers, Silk and Ward have developed the use of these matrices in portfolio evaluation. Silk proposed a practical benefit-level matrix of nine cells to distinguish between the investment types of strategic, tactical and operational on one axis, and investment consequences of efficiency, effectiveness and competitive edge on the other. Ward has usefully related the Macfarlane segments to the concepts and terminology of information economics.

There are other matrices. Price Waterhouse use the categories for rows and columns as shown in Fig. 12.3. The applications rarely fit within one cell and normally span two or more. Such a matrix would be constructed by a management group in a planning workshop.

A planning workshop is generally used with any of the above methods, and a typical example, the Strategic Information Systems (SIS) Study, has been described by Rackoff, Wiseman and Ullrich.[8] This provides a methodology by which to make a systematic search for the best way to use IT to gain competitive advantage. The study uses executive workshops to analyse the market in which the company operates, to review the company's competitive strategy and to identify specific IT opportunities to support the competitive strategy. The output is an outline plan for the implementation of one or more strategic applications together with an ITD support programme.

The purpose of the creative priority setting processes and the techniques they invoke is the same: to ensure that new investments in IT (and the existing portfolio) support the key competitive strategies of the business. They generate specific ideas for the application of technology and establish criteria against which projects can be prioritized. However, many of the ideas have then to be converted into viable projects and re-evaluated as they are first incorporated into business plans and then implemented.

This brings us to the analytical processes for setting priorities, which are essential to Stage 3 of the decision-making process.

12.4.2 *Analytical processes for setting priorities*

'Analytical' is used here to signify that priorities are set against a previously agreed business plan and criteria.

It is important that IT applications proposed for development, or under development, are visible and published in a prioritized, up-to-date and time-related list. This is generally referred to as the application backlog or development portfolio.

There are two stages to the analytical process of prioritizing applications, categorizing and ranking.

Categorizing applications helps to clarify how each may support the business and to establish a balanced development portfolio. Such a portfolio will contribute to major new competitive strategies and also provide the necessary enhancements to existing systems. It will include potentially risky research projects based on leading-edge technology as well as investments in the IT infrastructure. It is similar to the 'creative' processes described above. Figure 12.4 shows a simple and powerful way of categorizing applications on a matrix which sets applications 'necessary to the business' against those 'adding value to the business'. Other categories typical of those used by many enterprises and similar to those employed by IBM UK, are:

1 *Mandatory*: to meet legal, safety or security requirements.
2 *Essential investment*: vital support for a business initiative.
3 *Necessary for the business*: income- or profit-related.

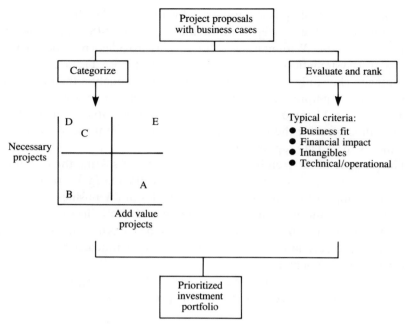

Figure 12.4.   Analytical processes for setting priorities.

4   *Desirable payback* projects with an attainable financial return.
5   Other investments with less clear business cases, which will *contend for any remaining IT resource*.

This list of investment types has been reinterpreted and expanded by many others. Five main types are described in more detail in *Getting value from information technology* (Butler Cox Research Foundation).[9] Their investment types are: mandatory, performance improvement, competitive advantage, infrastructure and research. Their analysis of some of the characteristics of these investments is reproduced in Table 12.1. This table also suggests which technique it is appropriate to use in evaluating different types of investment and indicates the likely importance of management judgement in each case. Management judgement is crucial for strategic investments, but of more limited applicability for mandatory investments, in which affordability and timing are likely to be key considerations.

Ranking applications is facilitated by evaluating each project against a set of criteria. Ranking projects solely by 'return on investment' is not likely to be satisfactory, even if that measure were to be available for all projects.

The evaluation criteria proposed by Buss were described in Chapter 11. Here, projects are scored on their financial benefits, intangible benefits, technical importance and business fit. Buss also describes eight steps by which priorities can

Table 12.1 Classification of IT projects[9]

Type of investment	Business benefit	Main formal aids to investment evaluation	Importance of management judgement	Main aspects of management judgement
Mandatory investments as a result of:				
Regulatory requirements.	Satisfy minimum legal requirement.	Analysis of cost.	Low	Fitness of the system for the purpose.
Organizational requirements.	Facilitate business operations.	Analysis of costs.	Low	Fitness of the system for the purpose. Best option for variable organizational requirements.
Competitive pressure.	Keep up with the competition.	Analysis of costs to achieve parity with the competition. Marginal cost to differentiate from the competition, providing the opportunity for competitive advantage.	Crucial	Competitive need to introduce the system at all. Effect of introducing the system into the marketplace. Commercial risk. Ability to sustain competitive advantage.
Investments to improve performance.	Reduce costs.	Cost–benefit analyses.	Medium	Validity of the assumptions behind the case.
	Increase revenues.	Cost–benefit analyses. Assessment of hard-to-quantify benefits. Pilots for high-risk investment.	High	Validity of the assumptions behind the case. Real value of hard-to-quantify benefits. Risk involved.
Investments to achieve competitive advantage.	Achieve a competitive leap.	Analysis of costs and risks.	Crucial	Competitive aim of the system. Impact on the market and the organization. Risk involved.
Infrastructure investment.	Enable the benefits of other applications to be realized.	Setting of performance standards. Analysis of costs.	Crucial	Corporate need and benefit, both short- and long-term.
Investment in research.	Be prepared for the future.	Setting objectives within cost limits.	High	Long-term corporate benefit. Amount of money to be allocated.

Table 12.2 Summary of eight steps for prioritizing IT projects
(*Source*: Martin D. J. Buss, 'How to rank computer projects',
Harvard Business Review, January–February 1983)

Step 1	Get control of data processing.
Step 2	Document systematically.
Step 3	Clarify business objectives.
Step 4	Rank against financial costs and benefits.
Step 5	Rank intangible benefits.
Step 6	Rank according to technical importance.
Step 7	Assess fit with objectives.
Step 8	Summarize priorities.

be established (Table 12.2). These steps could be used by a steering committee wishing to prioritize applications.

Critical success factors (CSFs) can also be used as criteria, and IBM UK compares application proposals with its CSFs. The impact of each application on the CSFs is given a high, medium or low rating. This, together with other considerations, provides a basis for agreeing the priority of proposed applications.

Clearly, it may not be feasible to consider the priority of each new project proposal regardless of its timing relative to business planning and IT priority-setting deadlines. A policy will be needed for handling potentially high-benefit projects that emerge between planning deadlines. The best approach can be to make such a project inadmissible other than in exceptional circumstances, and this principle will need support at the highest level. The output of the ranking process will be a list of agreed IT investment priorities.

12.5 Decision constraints

12.5.1 Investment culture

The investment culture of an enterprise is largely described by the answer to the question, 'How is the business case to be prepared and what are the key ingredients that may influence the investment decisions?' This was the last of thirteen questions indicating the information required for capital investment appraisal (Table 11.7). If a financial case is not expected or wanted, then there may be little value in preparing one. If the first question to be asked is about the project's financial performance, then a financial case, in one form or another, is vital. Taken together, the answers to the questions largely describe the investment culture of an organization.

12.5.2 Enterprise culture

Decisions generally mature, rather than happen precipitously. Decision-making – how it is performed, rather than its correctness – reflects the culture of the organization in a way that few other activities do. Culture affects the nature of the decision, because decisions to invest are about decisions to change, and change can affect the culture. For example, a decision can be creative or cautious, strategic or tactical; it can involve ethical considerations or not.

Culture has been defined as, 'the way we get things done around here'. Culture emanates from the values of the organization's leaders; it manifests itself in the attitude and behaviour of its people, and chiefly those of its managers.

The basic 'beliefs' of IBM, established by its founder, Thomas J. Watson Sr, are service to the customer, respect for the individual and the pursuit of excellence. At the other end of the scale, where these values are interpreted into actions, IBM has maintained a recognizable corporate style, for example in office accommodation and procedures, in guidelines for business entertainment and hospitality and in its role in the community. Some aspects of IBM culture are changing rapidly, for example, in its decentralized decision-making, as it seeks to achieve a fundamental redefinition of its business.

The parameters by which to describe culture are potentially many. We identify 10 that can affect investment decision-making. They are presented in no order of priority.

1   *Peoples' compensation*
    Payment by results focuses the minds of those who make decisions, both on their own objectives and on the cooperation that they can expect from others with different objectives. To work properly, payment by results needs a carefully balanced interdependence of groups with different missions. The basis of compensation is one element which sets the tone of an organization; in the 1990s, IBM extended its measures of performance to include quantified customer satisfaction. Managers are more likely to give special attention to achieving objectives that are financially rewarded.

2   *Centrally directed versus autonomous units*
    The forces of centralization and decentralization have always operated. Today they are called harmonization and empowerment. The balance of corporate power and specific need will affect decisions. For example, with a centrally focused corporate culture, the need for corporate IT infrastructure investments will be better understood.

3   *Cross-functional project teams*
    Hierarchy is necessary for command and control; specialization is fundamental to excellence. Most activities are conducted in accordance with repeatable processes. However, the task force working in project mode is a sure way of solving a one-off tough problem in a short time-scale. The task force pulls together a multi-disciplinary team, working as peers in project mode, to do a job or to produce practical recommendations. Some organizations never use them; others are never without them.

4   *Trade union versus non-trade union*
    Decisions are measurably affected by the additional interest of a union of employees that is external to the enterprise. The direct relationship between

people who have the role of manager and those who have the role of employee is no longer as simple. Additional considerations are likely to be introduced by trade union representatives; the human factors of change generally receive greater emphasis.

5   *Amount of planning and planning horizons*
Planning can be bureaucratic, but it ensures consistency of direction and optimizes the use of resources. Fashion-driven retail companies plan over shorter time-scales. Of recent years, the trend to 'just-in-time' techniques has moved planning boundaries back into suppliers' operations. These affect the criteria against which IT investments have been selected.

6   *Methods of communication*
Accountability and auditability are fundamental to government and public service. Written communication is part of the culture. The details of agreements struck by a handshake in a face-to-face meeting are generally confirmed in writing. The spoken word is needed to generate a vision and commitment, but wise project managers know the value of clear understandings – 'what isn't written down, isn't said'. How people communicate is vital to the dynamics of decision-making.

7   *Organizational stability*
Organizational change is, of all types of change, largely under management control. It is vital to change to ensure that the organization is responsive and competitive. Whether an enterprise is skilled in managing organizational change will affect its ability to make investment decisions which involve change.

8   *Consensus versus directive decision-making*
The Japanese are reputed to take time and trouble to reach consensus decisions in their corporations, but military operations are directed from a small core of senior officers, with one overall commander. These management styles affect decisions, and either can be effective. It is how the styles are blended that makes for good decisions and successful implementations.

9   *Product versus customer orientation*
Enterprise strategies can be based on a product or customer emphasis. Pharmaceutical companies need to be concerned with the quality and reliability of their product. The staff of financial services suppliers have direct contact with customers, and often the product is quite simply the service that they are perceived to provide. The attitudes and culture of these enterprises tend to be product- or customer-orientated.

10 *People-orientated personnel policies*
Sometimes personnel policies are determined by what is affordable, but more often they are a direct expression of the culture, by design or by default. In IBM, as well as policies which determine the environment of employment,

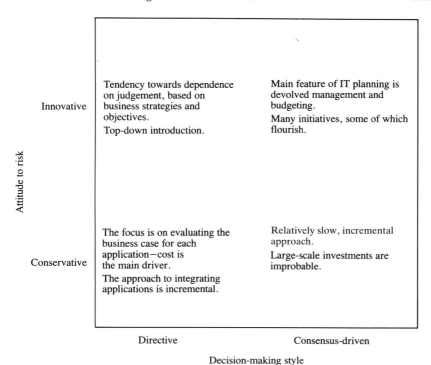

Figure 12.5.   Management style has a marked influence on attitudes to IT investment.[9]

there are those that actively declare 'respect for the individual'. Whatever the personnel policies, they will be the backdrop against which investment decisions are being made.

These ten parameters of an enterprise's culture provide a checklist of factors that may have a bearing on the timing, and possibly on the nature, of the decision. Butler Cox have also considered the effect of management style on investment appraisal, and a summary their analysis is reproduced in Fig. 12.5.[9]

An example, taken from our own observations, is shown in Table 12.3, which provides a tangible illustration of the effect of culture, simply in the area of presenting IT project proposals. In summary, large, structured bureaucratic organizations may be prepared to invest considerable resources in reports, business cases and presentations. In contrast, smaller, less structured organizations may be satisfied with less formal presentations, although often expecting more detailed reports and business cases. Consideration of the company culture can mean the difference between success and failure in the acceptance of an otherwise 'technically correct' project proposal.

Table 12.3   Observations in two different cultures of attitudes towards business case documents

Major clearing banks	Manufacturing and distribution
Considerable importance is attached to reports or business cases so that virtually every word is scrutinized.	Organizations tend to be less hierarchical and more personal relationships are formed.
Reports are invariably precise and economical.	Reports are often voluminous and less attention paid to detailed wording.
Presentations are regarded as a major activity. High standard deliverables, rehearsed and criticized beforehand are normal. A single person would manage the presentation.	Presentations are considered as important and are rehearsed. Generally, all team members would be involved in and contribute to the presentation.
Report distributed before the presentation.	Report delivered at the end of the presentation.
Organizational structures are elongated and hierarchical. Interpersonal and business relationships are often formal and at 'arm's length'.	With normally more daily contact between team members and other senior managers and directors, presentations are less awesome events.
Benefit quantification is always required.	Business cases need to be well researched and to satisfy detailed procedural requirements and financial criteria.
IT justification easier, probably because of fewer other competing demands on the capital budget.	IT justification often difficult when competing with other capital projects, which are seen from within as easier to justify.
Team includes a financial person, familiar with capital budgeting and evaluation process.	Team includes a financial person, familiar with the capital budgeting and evaluation process.

12.5.3 The culture gap

In Chapter 6 we noted a gap between the ITD and other business functions that needed to be bridged, and identified some reasons for its existence and suggested some ways of bridging it. This gap is often referred to as a communications or culture gap. It impedes decision-making.

Two clear indicators of the gap are to be found in 'priorities' and in 'jargon'. Priorities are a statement of what is important; jargon is the everyday language used to talk about a subject. Priorities and jargon must be commonly owned by the ITD and business functions for good decisions to be made and to be implemented effectively.

The existence of the culture gap and its effects have been the subject of comment in the Price Waterhouse *Information Technology Review 1991/92*.[10] Based on the 1990 Price Waterhouse/Financial Times IT Directors Survey, the culture gap was the highest rated in a set of problem areas. The problems and their ranking are reproduced in Fig. 12.6 and the recorded effects of the culture gap in Fig. 12.7. The authors of the review summarized the impact of the culture gap on decision-making:

Losing opportunities to exploit IT for business advantage is held by most IT directors to be the worst result of the culture gap. [Figure 12.7] shows three

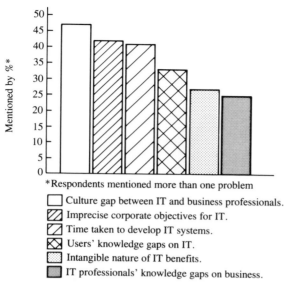

*Respondents mentioned more than one problem

☐ Culture gap between IT and business professionals.
▨ Imprecise corporate objectives for IT.
▧ Time taken to develop IT systems.
⧆ Users' knowledge gaps on IT.
▩ Intangible nature of IT benefits.
▪ IT professionals' knowledge gaps on business.

Figure 12.6. IT directors' problems.[9]

related problems: artificial justification methods, putting in the wrong systems, and over concentration on cost-cutting applications.

Together they amount to a more serious consequence, however. They reflect a three stage syndrome:

1 Accused of providing insufficient return on investment, the IT director, aware that computer systems on their own cannot advance the business, and that improved information on its own has no value, attempts to put values on the intangible benefits.

2 Disillusioned by these attempts, his board colleagues become cynical and demand 'bottom line'. The only bottom line benefits the computer can provide on its own are to reduce costs. By saving clerks; or, ironically, cutting its own budget.

3 These cost-saving applications are popular with the board. The IT director is thus reduced to preparing cost–benefit statements showing doubtful savings, and proposing non-strategic systems, meanwhile putting in the vital systems he believes will ensure the company's survival by means of a hidden agenda.

12.5.4 *Enterprise politics*

The final constraint on decision-making discussed here is that of politics. Politics is about people and power. Earlier we noted that people and information were inseparable; and information is an important basis of power. When information is linked to change, the *raison d'être* of the investment decision, then the significance of politics in decision-making should not be underestimated.

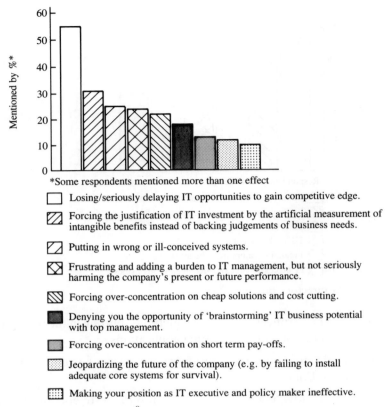

*Some respondents mentioned more than one effect

☐ Losing/seriously delaying IT opportunities to gain competitive edge.

▨ Forcing the justification of IT investment by the artificial measurement of intangible benefits instead of backing judgements of business needs.

▨ Putting in wrong or ill-conceived systems.

⧆ Frustrating and adding a burden to IT management, but not seriously harming the company's present or future performance.

▨ Forcing over-concentration on cheap solutions and cost cutting.

■ Denying you the opportunity of 'brainstorming' IT business potential with top management.

▨ Forcing over-concentration on short term pay-offs.

▨ Jeopardizing the future of the company (e.g. by failing to install adequate core systems for survival).

▨ Making your position as IT executive and policy maker ineffective.

Figure 12.7.   Culture gap effects.[9]

Telling phrases, used to criticize a person or a situation are 'vested interest', 'empire building' and 'personal power base'. However, within limits these are desirable characteristics. Ultimately, it is for the CEO to ensure that both purely personal motives and business objectives are held in the right balance through appropriate decision-making mechanisms, such as an IT steering committee.

Willcocks and Mark, writing about IT systems implementation, recount several examples from the public sector which illustrate that IT is as likely to reinforce political boundaries as it is to remove them.[11]

These examples demonstrate some of the IT implementation problems, many of which are, at root, political in nature, being experienced at regional, district and hospital levels within the NHS [National Health Service]. A major influence here is the limited power bases that the relatively new general managers have formed, and their over dependence on formal position (authority) even where those managers have been recruited from within the NHS. As a result they have rarely been able to act as a countervailing force against, and indeed most often have to work with, the grain of existing power structures whether these are of a central versus local power dimension, or consist of other powerful groupings and vested interests, in particular clinicians. The result is that whatever the policy is, in practice the needs and priorities of groups like clinicians, or of groups at regional level rather than district level, are the first to be embodied in what has actually been successfully implemented so far in the NHS.

Political considerations in decision-making are universal. Even technical decisions can reflect the personal preferences, ambitions and concerns of those involved. Within limits, this is not wrong, provided that the objectives, as much as the means, of the implementation are clearly defined and accepted by the implementors as their personal responsibility.

Good investment decisions can be put at risk because they are politically unacceptable. A good decision, like a harvest, is the result of multiple cross-fertilizations and a period of growth. Serious political contention is the canker which will ruin the crop.

References

1 Thomas H. Davenport, Michael Hammer and Tauno J. Metsisto, How executives can shape their company's information systems, *Harvard Business Review*, March–April 1989.
2 Beat Hochstrasser and Catherine Griffiths, *Regaining Control of IT Investments*, Kobler Unit, Imperial College, London, 1990.
3 M. J. Earl, *Management Strategies for Information Technology*, Prentice-Hall, Englewoods Cliffs, NJ, 1989.
4 Michael E. Porter and Victor E. Millar, How information gives you competitive advantage, *Harvard Business Review*, July–August 1985.
5 Bryan Ward and Maurice Hardaker, Getting things done, *Harvard Business Review*, November–December 1987.
6 F. Warren McFarlan, James L. McKenney and Philip Pyburn, The information archipelago – plotting a course, *Harvard Business Review*, January–February 1983.
7 David J. Silk, Managing IS benefits for the 1990s, *J. Information Technol.*, **5**(4), December 1990, pp. 185–193.
  John M. Ward, A portfolio approach to evaluating information systems investments and setting priorities, *J. Information Technol.*, **5**(4), December 1990, pp. 222–231.
8 Nick Rackoff, Charles Wiseman and Walter A. Ullrich, Information systems for competitive advantage: implementation of a planning process, *MIS Quarterly*, **9**(4), December 1985.
9 *Getting Value from Information Technology*, Research Report 75, Butler Cox Foundation, June 1990.
10 *Information Technology Review 1991/92*, Price Waterhouse, London, 1991.
11 Leslie P. Willcocks and Annabelle L. Mark, IT Systems Implementation: Research Findings from the Public Sector, *J. Information Technol.*, **4**(2), June 1989, pp. 92–103.

13
Stage 4: control the investment during implementation

It is one thing to make the right investment decision; it is something else to implement it successfully. The focus of this book is on making the decision to invest, and every decision will be affected by the past experience of the decision-maker – by the relative success of the previous investments. Implementing investment decisions and reviewing them post-implementation are, therefore, the subject matter of Stages 4 and 5 of the decision-making process, and they are covered in this and the next chapter, respectively. Moreover, here we are only concerned with *project* investment; managing and evaluating *non-project* investment in IT was the subject of Chapter 5.

This chapter is not intended to be a primer on project management. However, to realize value from an IT project, it must at least reach a successful conclusion. Therefore we review some of the reasons why a project might not be successful, and what can be done to make it successful, before briefly discussing the financial management of projects. Benefits management and realization is dealt with at the end of the chapter.

CASE STUDY

We continue with the example introduced in earlier chapters. Without Al Luchini's (the supermarket manager) commitment, the IT investment might never have been made and the staff could have been overcome by technical problems. Before the installation of the EPOS checkouts a stock audit was performed. In the event this had been done too early and had to be repeated at an additional cost of $3750. Few projects go without any hitch. Al felt he lacked proper advice on the timing of the audit from those who had done it before; his project plan did not show it to be time critical.

Al also realized that the total refit had been a big project. Next time he would take it in smaller and more discrete stages.

Once the new systems had bedded down the store soon began to feel the benefit. The checkouts proved easy to operate, enabling less-trained staff to use them. One person who had left returned. Invoices were easier to validate and to process. Queues were shorter. Stocks were better maintained. Al Luchini was soon able to exploit the sales information to improve store operations. And he recognized that achieving the full benefits of the investment was solely up to him.

In a period of continuing recession, through 1992, and with a squeeze on margins, the investment has enabled Al Luchini's supermarket to maintain its profitability and to improve its market position in 1993.

13.1 Managing successful projects

13.1.1 Project problems

For most of the 1980s, meeting project deadlines had been the number one problem on the minds of ITD managers. In 1988 it took second place to integrating IT with corporate plans. It held this position until 1991, when cost containment relegated project deadlines to third place.[1] The point is illustrated by a cartoon (Fig. 13.1), which originates from at least the 1960s (and most probably before 1960 BC – was everyone happy with the outcome of the pyramid

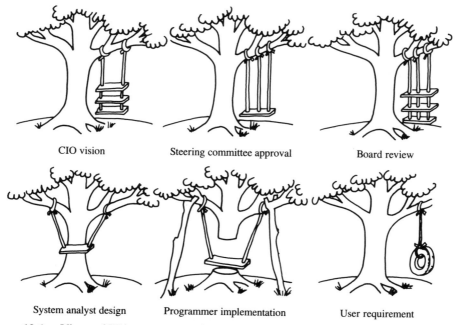

CIO vision   Steering committee approval   Board review

System analyst design   Programmer implementation   User requirement

Figure 13.1.   Views of IT investment projects.

projects?) It speaks for itself: success, like beauty, is largely in the eye of the beholder. A person's expectation for successful completion is dependent on their understanding of the scope of the project; on whether an IT project is a systems project or a business project.

Of course, the concern over not meeting project deadlines is still there. Success is rarely seen as 100% by all of those involved in IT projects. Several levels of success can be identified:

Success
- Product exceeds expectation, the customer is delighted.
- Product as defined, on schedule and within cost estimate.
- Unexpected results, but customer accepts product.
- Schedule missed and/or estimate exceeded but customer accepts product.
- Schedule or estimate missed and rework necessary.
- Customer dissatisfied and pays late (assuming a paying customer).
- Major functions missed and needed prior to implementation.
- Product developed does not do the job and major rework necessary.

Failure
- Product developed is totally unusable.

Many of these statements depend on the acceptability and usability of the project deliverables. This can depend on what the customer wants and expects as much as on the defined deliverables; even the 'top' level of success may fail to satisfy everyone.

The causes of project failure, partial or complete, can arise from within the project or they can be entirely external. Some of the internal reasons for failure are listed in Table 13.1, and these can lead to tangible and measurable losses against the project plan. The list is not exhaustive; note that it emphasizes the importance of pre-project planning activities. The internal reasons for project failure are largely about project management. The external reasons for failure arise from unanticipated change – often because the question, 'What might change during the life of the project?' was not asked of the right people. The procedures and skills needed for effective project management are understood, if

Table 13.1 Why projects fail

User requirements not properly defined.
Project does not have an owner, or user.
Project manager lacks status or skills.
Project objectives not defined or agreed.
High-risk project, but not recognized and planned for.
Changed requirements or priorities.
Estimates on fixed price and underestimated.
Poor selection of hardware or software.
Optimistic skill assumptions have been made.

not always applied; it is new technology and external change that often hurt. These will prevent projects from being completely successful.

13.1.2 *Project critical success factors*

If those are the problems, what can be done to promote project success?

The principles of good project management are well documented. Knight and Silk[2] provide a basic introduction and framework. Parker, writing in *Managing Information Systems for Profit*, describes many of the key techniques that he has employed in managing systems development within IBM UK.[3] Project experience outside IT has been collated in a series of booklets published by the Institute of Management.[4]

Our experience has been gained in IT application planning projects, and these have given us ample evidence of what is important to project success. These CSFs need to be seen within the wider context of:

- The CSFs of creating change (Chapter 9).
- The organizational obstacles and 'decision constraints' (Chapter 12).
- The project risks (Chapter 11).

The eight factors that need special attention to ensure effective implementation of the decision to invest are:

1   *Key roles in the project need to be filled by appropriate people*
    Three roles need to be recognized: the sponsor, the business owner and the project manager. The titles can vary; it is the role description which is important.

    The sponsor is often at an executive level. The initial idea may have originated with someone other than the sponsor, who is championing and driving the proposal. However, the sponsor accepts overall responsibility for the business case and for a successful implementation of the project. The sponsor's function, more than any other, needs the IT system or facilities.

    The sponsor has a particular role in protecting the investment of the project and to understand how benefits will be measured and verified. The sponsor will need to be informed, by means of project evaluation reviews, about changes to requirements, progress in developing systems function and the effectiveness of risk management. (This implies that the sponsor will have been assured that appropriate project procedures and standards are being followed. Project evaluation reviews for the sponsor must provide a broad view of the project, recalling why it was started, predicting how well it will achieve its aims and identifying issues that need to be resolved.)

    Of course, the sponsor does not directly manage the project. The sponsor will appoint the business owner to represent his or her interests and to manage business resources required in the project. For the business owner, sometimes called the project administrator, this may or may not need to be full-time. However, apportioning time for line and project management within one person's job is far from satisfactory, even if both project and line management skills are present.

The third key role is that of the experienced, full-time ITD project manager. The main activities of an IT project will be technical in nature and these will need to be understood by the project manager. The project manager, who may run several IT projects concurrently, depending on their size, will manage the project team, consisting of technical specialists and some functional specialists, committed to the project.

2 *The scope and potential impact of the project must be stated*
It sounds simple, but project objectives are not always well formulated and agreed. It is not unknown for the technical solution to be more visible, and its correct implementation to be of more concern, than the business problem it is solving. The objectives should at least make clear what business change is expected as a result of the investment; benefits can be set as targets.

3 *Project activities must be planned within an overall structure*
To monitor the progress of a project, its structure needs to be visible and appropriate. Where the elapsed time of an IT project is greater than 12 months the project should be staged or broken down into a series of smaller projects. This helps to convert uncertainty, which cannot easily be managed, to risk, which offers choices.[5] For a lengthy project, too much change can happen around it and the users get impatient.

4 *Expectations for the project deliverables must be primarily those of the client or system user*
This is an extension of stating objectives, but it recognizes that objectives and expectations may not remain in step, even if they start off together. The cartoon of Fig. 13.1 really says it all. The user is not singular, but many, and there are several stakeholders. Some change in expectations will be forced by other events; a process to appraise and to approve changes to requirements is vital. Manage change and many project uncertainties disappear.

5 *Ways of communicating about the project must be set up*
All sorts of communications are needed. They range from near-hype, in order to set the vision, to mundane progress reports; from briefings to feedback. There is a lot of fear about change, often based on misunderstandings or the fact that 'no one asked my views' – for communication is two-way. There needs to be a process for identifying and for dealing with problems and issues that, if not resolved, will seriously damage project completion. Apart from special issues, a framework of reviews needs to be established at regular intervals and at appropriate functional levels.

6 *Cost-effective procedures are needed for administration and control*
If the army marches on its stomach, then the army needs good catering logistics. A good administrative infrastructure, but not a bureaucratic one, is a

necessity for an effective project. This internal discipline helps to counteract organizational instability and the adverse effects on the project of people joining and leaving the team. Financial control will be part of this support, with its implied need for project records. The records will include documentation of project plans and deliverables and progress towards fulfilling the plans. Management systems and tools will be required to keep records; a central operations room, with up-to-date wall displays, visited regularly by senior managers, can maintain an awareness of project progress.

A project overrun of months generally takes place one day at a time. For this reason, at least the key projects in the development portfolio should be reviewed regularly by a group of senior managers.

7 *The planned amount and types of resource must be available*
There are many wise proverbs about projects. 'You can make a project manager promise, but you can't make him deliver' is one. If estimates are cut too fine, or if planned and requested resources are not available, the project time-scales are liable to extend or the function projected for delivery to be cut – despite any new promises that are forced out of the project manager. Likening a project to gestation, another proverb points out that 'Doubling the resource does not halve the time-scale'.

8 *Arrangements must be made for an effective handover of defect-free deliverables to the operational user*
This critical success factor implies adequate user testing of the system and thorough user training. These are both very different and important tasks, and it is hardly possible to do enough of either. Poor planning and execution of system testing and user training results in underperformance and a constant stream of cost-creating problems.

Following these critical success factors will provide a secure basis for a successful project implementation, and this is needed to achieve the project's financial targets. Some of the considerations of project financial management are discussed below.

13.1.3 Project financial management

The resources taken up by a project, measured by their monetary value, provide the costs; the outputs, or results, of the project generate the benefits; the risks give levels of uncertainty that the actual costs and benefits will be the same as the estimates made during planning.

The purpose of project financial management is to forecast, monitor and control the financial values of the inputs and outputs, so that the project can achieve the planned financial result. It is not management of the finances that produces the result, but rather management of the project; finances are a key indicator of implementation performance.

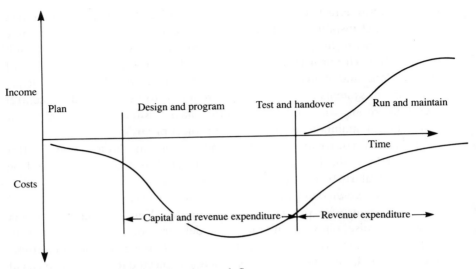

Figure 13.2. Typical profile of project cash flow.

Project cash flows normally follow a standard profile, which is shown in Fig. 13.2. Cash expenditure will be either capital or revenue. Capital expenditure will appear as a fixed asset in the enterprise balance sheet and revenue expenditure will be set against income in the profit and loss account.

The distinction between capital and revenue expenditure may be important to the project financial result in that:

1 Capital costs can be spread over a period of years, by means of an annual depreciation charge.
2 Excess capital or revenue expenditure can be 'hidden' by misallocation to the other category.

Thus the financial progress of the project is best reflected in cash terms. The rules used for allocation to capital and revenue need to be agreed at the planning stage. Typically, IT equipment and its accommodation will be capital; purchased software might also be capitalized, but is more often treated as revenue; system design, programming, purchasing, testing and handover are usually tracked in revenue items. Early project planning, research and development and post-project appraisal are rarely charged to the project; system operation and maintenance are not project costs.

It is by breaking down the total project into these activity and cost areas, and into sub-areas, and by assigning responsibilities for their completion, that financial control is achieved. However, for the sound prediction of financial progress, expenses data have to be recorded and allocated, and the proportion of work completed correctly estimated. Regular reporting of expenditures and commitments is essential for good control.

The 'test and handover' stage (Fig. 13.2), is a key part of any project and the resource required for it is easily underestimated. Moreover, there is likely to be a loss of efficiency in the early days of the system, while initial learning and familiarization takes place. Add to this the potential for a late inflow of tangible savings from the system and the scene is set for financial targets to be seriously missed. This is when many of the human and organizational costs will be incurred, and they are likely to be a significant proportion of total costs.

Identifying and monitoring the costs is an essential discipline; benefits should be treated likewise. Benefits can be expected to flow from the time the system is operational and will increase as more system function is made available to fully trained users. Indeed, systems improvements, aimed at improving benefits, for many projects should be driven by regular post-project appraisals. Quality is a journey, not a destination; so is benefits achievement.

The final cost area identified in Fig. 13.2 is that of system maintenance. No system will be maintenance-free, but the level of cost experienced in this area will depend on:

- How much rework may be necessary to meet the original specification.
- The attention paid to producing defect-free program code.
- Extensions now required to the function provided by the system.
- The level of flexibility designed into the system to accommodate new requirements.
- How much additional function it was planned to deliver in a second stage of the project to facilitate a quick delivery of the first stage.

In practice, a distinction will be made between correcting defects and major new extensions. However, both of these will be costs and will be a function of decisions and assumptions made, or not made, in the original project proposal. The running and maintenance costs of middle-aged systems (five to ten years old) will be substantial, and can be affected by the original level of investment.

For control purposes a graph of cumulative costs and benefits is most helpful (Fig. 13.3). It shows the payback period and the percentage return on investment over a given time period. The curves also show the ongoing costs and benefits. Many projects experience ongoing benefits improvement, especially where initial benefits management and subsequent auditing are performed in a determined effort to harvest further tangible savings.

For most enterprises the costs of small computers, such as PCs, are a significant concern. Their purchase price is generally capitalized, but their location and utilization may be hard to monitor. The costs of installing small computers is often not even recorded, and the value of their associated software is hidden in 'revenue' budgets. User training, or lack of it, is all too often an unrecognized expense of the small system. On the other hand, the user will have a clear, if subjective, view of the benefits provided by the investment.

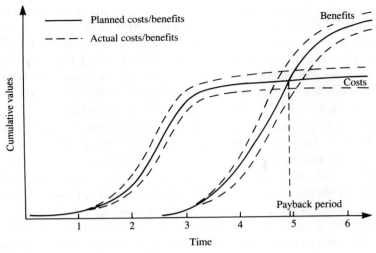

Figure 13.3. Cumulative costs and benefits.

Some of the issues discussed above are illustrated in the case study below.

CASE STUDY

In October 1991 the Channel Tunnel project was reported to be over-spending by twice the original estimates. Costs had risen from £3.7 billion to £8 billion. The reasons given for the overrun were:

- Loose contracts, containing rather general specifications of requirements, were awarded in order to get the project under way.
- Changes to requirements, which implied higher quality deliverables, were not properly costed.
- The project managers were concerned about the potential this could give for exploitation by their contractors.

Even after some one hundred years of planning the tunnel (although much of it not relevant to this issue), the need to 'get the show on the road' meant that the age-old cause of cost overrun, changed requirements, appears to have beset the project.

13.2   Benefits management

Benefits management is part of a wider issue, which is how to manage the successful implementation of large-scale change. How change is managed depends in part on how the project is viewed: whether it is a technical project to install a system, or a business project to adopt new methods and processes. The question of responsibility is put well by Angell and Straub, in their 'Manifesto for information systems',[1]

> The real task of IT management is to cope with the manifestations and consequences of technological change. . . . We must accept that we cannot shift responsibility for tangible consequences onto a technology that ultimately cannot be culpable.

This stresses the responsibilty of IT management, but Angell and Straub do not imply that it is theirs alone. They point out that we may be deluding ourselves if we imagine that we can be totally in control of the apparent consequences of applying technology.

However, overall responsibility for the investment that an enterprise makes in IT will rest with a corporate steering group, as for example the IT steering committee, or with the director responsible for IT. To discharge this responsibility and to ensure value for money, some management systems will be required. Throughout this book we have discussed aspects of managing the planning of IT, the IT department, the preparation of the business case, and the IT project. Although there is much less established practice for managing benefits, the IT steering committee has a particular responsibility to ensure that relevant procedures are established. The project sponsor must see that benefits are achieved in the project.

Often benefits management does not occur because:

- Thought and effort are required to determine the base position.
- Measurement procedures and disciplines are not established early in the project.
- The initial forecast and final assessment of tangible benefits involves an element of management judgement.
- When forecast benefits are not achieved, the result may be disguised or suppressed and there is little possibility of making good the loss. Why waste effort asking the question?

For whatever reason, not much attention has been paid to benefits management, so there is scope for doing better. Benefits management cannot be ignored if questions about the value of IT are to be answered. Effective benefits management turns on three key activities, and these are discussed below: setting performance criteria; measuring the change; and delivering the benefit.

13.2.1 Establishing the baseline and performance measures

Accepting the need for project objectives to be expressed in quantified terms and for these to reflect the business benefit that the project is expected to deliver, what measurement criteria should be chosen?

The criteria should reflect the changes expected in key variables or perform-ance indicators. For example, for finance, credit days or cash balances might be indicators; for stockholding, turnovers or stock-outs; for sales, order processing costs or sales volumes and values; for customer service, satisfaction levels and waiting times; and for manufacturing, capacity utilization or unit administration costs. These will be more directly affected by IT. At a higher level of measure-ment, any of the tangible benefits of cost reduction, cost avoidance or revenue increase (Chapter 10) may be used as measures of change, but the connection with IT may be less direct. Only for large IT investments and over a longer period of time will 'bottom line' and profit measures of the enterprise be impacted. The nature of the benefits will be a key factor in the type of benefit management programme established for that project.

The indicators and parameters need to be part of the project objectives, as it will be too late to apply them post-implementation.

13.2.2 Measuring the change

The method most generally used is that of the post-implementation review. This looks back at what has been achieved and may take corrective action to take benefits, where appropriate and possible. Typically, it is concerned with the function delivered and the project cost rather than focusing on benefits. It is most likely to be conducted by the IT department, although its results will be reviewed by users. For any given project it is reactive rather than proactive; it shuts the stable door, and possibly checks that other stable doors are not open. It is a step in the right direction towards effective benefits management, but it rarely does what is really required.

Indeed, the levels of each indicator chosen as a measure of system performance must be determined before system handover is commenced, tracked while system roll-out continues, and recorded again when the systems are fully operational. To help identify changes arising from external factors it might be necessary to establish a 'control' situation, in which no system changes are introduced and with which comparisons can be made.

Some techniques for measuring change are discussed in Chapter 14 in the context of post-project appraisal. These techniques can be used in conjunction with the management approaches discussed below.

13.2.3 Delivering the change

The four methods discussed below are complementary to each other; they may all need to be employed to ensure that the benefits of an IT investment are taken and used to improve the business. Their overall purpose is to ensure that forecast, tangible benefits result from the change of measurable parameters of the enter-prise. The first method is a precursor to, and an enabler for, the other three.

The benefits project

For a large project it might well be necessary to define a sub-project to manage the benefits. Such a project is likely to start before, and to end after, the main project; in importance it will not be subservient to the main project. Responsibility will be separately given to a sub-project manager. A small project team will establish measures, pre- and post-project implementation, against which the impact of the installed system can be assessed. The approach is more proactive than simply auditing. It implies gaining written agreement from line management to reduce budgets and accept responsibility for other change once the system is delivered and working. It implies feedback to an executive manager or committee for action throughout the main project, and particularly where the agreed steps have not been taken by line management to realize the benefits after implementation.

This approach has not been widely adopted so far; it can raise contentious issues between the sub-project manager and line managers. The use of a benefits sub-project team is described in Chapter 14 for the IBM UK National Office Support Services project, in which it was used for benefits management through business planning.

Line manager responsibility

Benefits management is best made a line management responsibility. However, without the discipline and verification of the benefits project, the assignment of responsibility may lack the teeth needed for its fulfilment.

Nevertheless, where the benefits are measurable then responsibility can be set for their realization once the system is performing to specification. For the responsibility to be meaningful the targets will need to be agreed before implementation, probably as part of the individual's business objectives, and their achievement will need to be audited. Responsibility for benefits achievement may be taken by the project sponsor, who may choose to delegate responsibility for benefit management to line managers and to use the normal management processes for setting and monitoring targets.

For benefits management by line management to be effective, benefits must be taken from projects and built into business-as-usual management systems. There are two interrelated approaches, through the financial planning processes and by charging out IT costs to users, discussed below.

Financial and business planning

Ultimately, the cost of IT has to be borne by the business. Profits will either be reduced, or else the costs will be absorbed by savings or increased income, consciously or unconsciously on the part of the enterprise. Cost recovery can be planned into budgets and kept visible as cross-charge items.

The argument here is that it is best to make provision for IT investment and benefits consciously, before the event, rather than try to do it historically. IT costs have to be planned into the business; benefits should be too.

The business plan is the product of many complex interactions – proposed management actions and forecast market conditions. The result of an IT investment project has similar complexity; the link between cause (investment) and effect (benefit) can be impossible to quantify with certainty. While strategic and intangible benefits are not the material for tight management controls, they are real and can be taken into account in the overall planning algorithm.

For this to be effective there must be a tradition of mid-term planning in the enterprise. The projected benefits, tangible and intangible, need to be visible to and understood by those providing the inputs to the business plan. This means that initial project proposals, with at least outline business cases, be available for most large IT investments six to twelve months before the start of the year in which the system is implemented. If the business case, signed off by the user sponsor, the ITD, finance and other affected functions, proposes an investment in IT to reduce headcount, material wastage, reduced space requirements or lower logistics costs, then these changes will be built into the budget to take effect in the appropriate period. If the business case predicts increased product sales, sharper pricing, more effective publicity or mailing, or an earlier product launch, the planners will more carefully assess the realism of the estimates and then, all other things being equal, expect higher sales targets to be set and to be achieved once the system has gone live. Even if quantified benefits cannot be predicted with certainty, they can still be reflected as business performance measures.

Of course, IT investment projects will not be the only factors affecting the business plan. In the committed plan, significant increases in material costs might mask the smaller advantage from an IT system. An expected downturn in business might make higher sales targets a pipedream, even if market share projections are better as a result of the IT investment. In addition, new product launches, legislation, alliances and manufacturing facilities, to name but a few, will all need to be taken into account in setting the expectations for future business results.

Naturally, performing to budget will be dependent on the timely delivery of the promised system – and on many other factors, apparently beyond the control of the budget manager. The ITD is responsible for timely delivery, which often depends on factors apparently beyond its control, like the availability of resources from the user community for requirements specification or for systems testing. The factors that contribute to project delays will need careful control and the sponsor's commitment to resolve key issues.

Building benefits into the business plan and into operational budgets puts responsibility for their achievement where it belongs, individually and corporately, and recognizes the complex interactions that take place internally and externally to move the business forward. As a by-product of this approach, minds are focused so that the business plan and its control become all the more real and necessary.

This approach has been used by IBM UK, and a case study describes its application in Chapter 14.

Finally, there is an element of benefits management that can be obtained through charge-out.

Charge-out procedures

The procedures and considerations relating to charge-out were introduced in Chapter 6, in the context of aligning IT with the business strategies. If it is effective in doing that, then it must also play a part in benefit management, and vice versa.

The principle of charge-out is simply stated. IT costs are allocated to operational budgets to reflect the use made of IT resources and facilities. The assumption then is that the budget holders will absorb the costs within their planned limits or will offset an increase in cost against savings and income from other areas. Above all, the users will be in the driving seat in deciding how to use IT to meet their objectives.

Butler Cox have referred to charge-out as 'Creating a commercial relationship between the systems department and business units'.[6] Taking this relationship to the extreme, the IT department becomes a subcontractor to the enterprise, and may then sell its services to other organizations as well. The practice of subcontracting, or outsourcing, has been widely applied by local government in recent years, and it can be expected to expand in all sectors.

We conclude this chapter with a case study of benefits management from the Trustee Savings Bank, as described by Des Glover, Director, Network Project Re-design.[7]

CASE STUDY

Introduction

From the mid 1980s onwards the financial services sector came under pressure, the like of which it had never experienced. The rate of change rocketed. At the same time earnings derived from interest rate margins, the major source of income, started to decline dramatically as new players came into the market and customers were no longer prepared to leave money in cheque accounts without interest. This led most financial organizations into dramatic reviews of their strategy particularly regarding the viability of their branch networks.

The TSB Banking Division is the retail banking arm of TSB Group Plc, a full financial services group. It has approaching 1600 branches spread throughout England, Wales, Scotland, Northern Ireland and the Channel Islands.

The strategy devised by TSB Banking Division was a mixture of organizational engineering and automation, each having a clear aim of bottom line benefits. It commenced with a decision in October 1987 and will be fully in place by 1993.

Automate administration

The initial move was to automate those processes in the branch which were not covered by our already sophisticated counter automation systems, that is, the branch administration and the sales support functions. These two distinctly different systems applications areas both needed access to the same customer and financial information held both locally and at the central host systems.

The equipment chosen for this task was the Unisys 'B' series equipment. Each branch was to be equipped with a branch controller, a B39 series device, on which all the local customer information would be held. This controller would serve all the existing front office terminals and autotellers within the branch plus the back office and sales support systems.

In order to receive an early payback and because it was a familiar area, the first two years of the project involved the installation of the systems in all branches with the initial phases of automation being that of administrative tasks. That established the base level of automation and replacement of paper records, the savings which paid for the equipment.

Provide the sales environment

The automation of the customer information along with the use of teller assist units, which are cash dispensing devices linked to the teller's terminal, has enabled the branches to be refurbished and to turn them into almost exclusively open plan areas.

The turn around in space allocation here has been most remarkable, 55% of the total branch space has been reallocated to the customer making their total share 80%. The opportunity has been taken to increase the number of interview areas. The only area which is now reserved for bank administration work is 20% and this is largely allocated to a secure area for handling high cash amounts.

The technology support for the sales and marketing function was provided using the same range of Unisys equipment. A set of applications was implemented which was specifically designed to support selling and marketing functions within the branch – Super Service.

Justification and control

The amount of funding required by the project needed full Board approval. To achieve this a fully comprehensive business case was prepared and a rigorous control mechanism set in place.

It was essential to be able to demonstrate clear benefits in line with spend and the emphasis was on what could be proven and measured rather than claim quality improvements which, while expected and important, were not reflected as a financial value.

Throughout implementation branch staff numbers were adjusted in line with the project plan, as systems were delivered to branches. Work measurement techniques were used to confirm that savings had been achieved. At one stage, benefits were not being achieved and the roll-out of systems to branches was halted and systems and plans were modified. Overall, some of the key quantified benefits were:

- some 20% increase in sales
- reduction of administrative costs by 50 to 60%
- floor space savings of £15 million

The project was about more than investing in IT, although that was a substantial part. It was a business project initiated to improve the competitive position of the Bank. The Trustee Savings Bank is not an isolated case in which benefits have been identified and reported from such a project. The Woolwich Building Society, in a similar project named 'Counter Attack', '. . . recorded a 10 to 60 per cent increase in business across its product range as a direct result of the project'.[8]

References

1 *Information Technology Review 1991/92*, Price Waterhouse, London, 1991.
2 A. V. Knight and D. J. Silk, *Managing Information: Information systems for today's general manager*, McGraw-Hill, Maidenhead, 1990.
3 Tim Lincoln (Ed.), *Managing Information Systems for Profit*, John Wiley & Sons, Chichester, 1990.
4 *Total Project Management*, The Asset Management Group of the Institute of Management, London, 1991.
5 Philip A. Roussel, Cutting the guesswork in R&D, *Harvard Business Review*, September–October 1983.
6 *Getting Value from Information Technology*, Research Report 75, Butler Cox Foundation, June 1990.
7 Des Glover, Cost Justifying very Large, Strategic IT Projects, *Managing IT Investment Conference Proceedings*, British Intelligence in association with *Computer Weekly*, May 1991.
8 Stephen Quigley, A British savings and loan profits by 'counter attacking' customers, *IBM Think Magazine*, No. 1, 1991.

14
Stage 5: review the decision – audit the investment

14.1 The purpose and scope of post-project appraisal

CASE STUDY

We conclude our supermarket story with this instalment.

Al Luchini did not conduct a post-project appraisal until we interviewed him. The five steps of our investment decision-making process sharpened his understanding of what he had done. It helped him to focus on the hard lessons to be learned at each stage. As he recounted the results of his investment, he recognized one benefit not originally foreseen. Simpler checkouts, requiring less keying skill, helped to achieve a balanced use of staff.

At peak times, all checkouts can be quickly opened and long queues avoided. In tough business conditions good stock availability of popular items and quick checkout service are fundamental to customer satisfaction and loyalty.

14.1.1 Why audit?

At first sight, the questions posed in our first chapter regarding the value for money obtained from IT may be best answered by looking at what IT investments actually achieve.

A headline in *Management Today* has proclaimed, 'Managers are being laid off in their thousands. Computers are the cause and recession the catalyst'.[1] This seems to indicate a clear result of using computers, but is it a benefit or a disaster? Is not the recession the cause and the computer the catalyst? Clearly, finding ultimate answers to the questions might not be straightforward.

Perhaps for this reason, the practice of post-project appraisal is not as widespread as it might be. In a survey in 1988 of the top 1000 companies, of the 385 respondents, 48% used post-project audits in some form,[2] and this applied to all kinds of projects, not only those concerned with the application of IT. The survey also showed that those who practice post-project appraisal speak well of it. They found that it enhanced initial project appraisal and decision-making and gave an improved ability to control and direct similar projects and to improve corporate performance. More recent surveys show similar results. However, it is not clear how far these surveys determined return on investment for the projects or, more simply, the level of their 'customer' satisfaction.

Crosby, the quality guru, has said that, 'What gets measured gets done'. The old adage of 'practice makes perfect' is at no time more true than in estimating, taking and auditing benefits, that is, in completing all five stages of the decision-making process and in providing feedback from experience into forecasting and into managing. The post-project audit is a vital ingredient, at least for some projects, if questions about the value of IT are to be answered. The relevant question about post-audits is 'How?' rather than 'Whether?'

Take office automation, for example. This has traditionally been a difficult IT application for which to justify an investment. In improving productivity it provides the potential for staff cost savings. The Institute of Administrative Management (IAM) and Touche Ross survey found that over 70% of potential users of office automation have not proceeded, on account of the high cost and unclear or intangible benefits.[3] However, their investigation also found that the most significant benefits had been experienced when office automation facilities had helped to integrate other applications, by providing a common interface. Moreover, job satisfaction improved and staff skills and work profiles changed. (Of course, not all changes will be beneficial and perceived to be so; these must also be recorded in a post-project audit.)

14.1.2 What is to be audited

Audits at the business unit level, that is for the enterprise and for the IT department, were discussed in Chapter 5. Our focus in this chapter is at the functional and individual level; we are considering the audit of an IT project.

A project audit records the status of a project and the progress made since the previous audit. If a 'base case' for the investment does not already exist, then an audit will need to construct one. An audit must not ignore the unexpected result, because most projects produce benefits that were not anticipated and which need to be understood by the decision-makers. The purpose of an audit is to determine the degree of success of a project.

Project success must be measured against the original objectives and in the same terms as those objectives. This is often where the trouble starts, because project objectives can be woolly, not expressed in quantifiable terms and not agreed by interested parties. Even where the objectives are precise and agreed, the effects of the project can be far-reaching and often unforeseen. Those benefiting from the project may not have a single and simple view of the value of the project.

For example, an office automation project might simply be seen as facilities to *automate* what is already done, and this generally results in measurable efficiency improvements. Office automation can go well beyond this and '*informate*', in providing an enhanced level of information relevant to the work performed. This improves effectiveness, which is more difficult to measure. Even this level may not reflect what has really happened or what can happen with clear management direction over a longer period. Office automation can '*transformate*' the whole organization of work by enabling the business processes to be restructured and redefined. It provides an opportunity for innovation. (The words 'automate', 'informate' and 'transformate' have been used by Zuboff.[4])

Many office automation implementations have missed their full potential. IAM and Touche Ross concluded that 'Most Office Automation systems have been used to improve the productivity of individuals performing routine tasks, although greater gains are made when systems support key business functions at a higher level'.[3] Office automation in many situations only scratches the surface. Redesigning business processes, and using IT to perform them, has given productivity improvements of 60% and 75% at Mutual Benefit Life and Ford Motor Company, respectively.[5] Another example of knowing what to audit is provided by Gulliver.[6] He describes the construction of gasoline production plants in Australia and in Rotterdam and the subsequent post-project audits.

> Although the Rotterdam project had obvious problems, the market for the product remained strong in Europe. Thus that project's return on investment was in line with predictions, while that of its Australian counterpart was much lower. The Rotterdam project's success taught top managers at BP a valuable lesson: the planners needed to improve their market forecasting techniques.

Project outcomes can be affected by uncontrollable variables, and it may be hard to draw firm conclusions about project success, and it may even change the criteria by which success is to be judged. Disentangling the result of the project from its environment can be difficult. The post-project appraisal may have to understand the corporate thinking of the enterprise of three or four years ago to assess project results rightly.

Finding absolute measures for the value of information is difficult – even impossible. It is often possible to identify operational parameters, such as service levels and utilizations, that can be measured and which change through use of IT; and operational parameters can be related to financial parameters.

14.1.3 Audit timings

A project audit may be performed before the project starts, as soon as the decision has been made, during the project, after its completion and at regular intervals thereafter. A post-project appraisal will make useful recommendations for future projects, but the reviewed project will not significantly benefit. In the case of a 'strategic' project it is not likely that conclusions regarding the benefits delivered will be available in the short term, by which time many parameters will have changed, potentially invalidating attempts to quantify returns on the investment. Consequently, there is advantage in considering appraisals at times other than post-project, that is at some point before full project success can be measured.

1   *Pilot projects as pre-implementation audits*
    Some of the risks and unknowns that surround a project can be resolved by a pilot, or small-scale, implementation. Typically, questions of technical design and performance can be evaluated in a pilot; the skills and experience needed for a full-scale implementation can be built up.

    Measuring the impact of the pilot and its ability to provide benefit is often a secondary or poorly stated objective. For this reason, pilot projects are often less than effective in demonstrating the potential value of an investment. Moreover, even with a carefully constructed pilot, it is not always possible to deduce the real effect of a large-scale implementation or the possible return from a larger investment in IT. Many of the risks and uncertainties of the full project will relate to the extent of organizational changes it brings about and to the competitive environment in which the enterprise operates.

2   *Audits throughout implementation*
    Often project benefits are better monitored and audited within an initial, small-scale, but real implementation. Where working practices and business processes are changed, it is highly desirable to have an early review, and to continue the implementation with further iterations of review and development. A project audit should seek to do more than record the past. It must also search out what more can be done to improve what has been achieved; success so far might only be mediocrity. In many instances, measurement will be required before the project commences, during the project implementation and after project completion to determine the changes that have occurred as a direct result of the project and those that have occurred around the project.

3   *Audits in a 'controlled' environment*
    As an important variation on the pilot project, IBM has developed a Systems Usability Laboratory. This enables the interaction between a user and the system to be investigated objectively by designers, implementors and trainers and leads to improved human factors features.

    The facility consists of a studio equipped with the appropriate IT devices, typically computer terminals or personal computers. It is furnished to simulate the working environment of the system user and is divided off from an observation room by a large one-way window. The observation room accommodates the observation team and contains controls for video and audio recording equipment and has voice links with the user in the studio. The user in the studio enacts various operational scenarios, often following written instructions. Each member of the observation team has a task, some of which may include interaction with the user in the studio, to simulate normal business communications.

Full de-briefing is carried out at the end of the session. This often leads to dramatic improvements being made to the systems under test, frequently in unexpected areas.

The technique has special relevance in helping to predict and to achieve system benefits, which, in many cases, depend on the usability of the system and its interface with the user. As demands for 'getting it right first time' and for user-friendly systems increase, this novel approach is likely to be a key contribution to managing major change.

14.1.4 Project audit levels

In answer to the question, 'What should be audited?', there are several levels at which a project can be appraised both for the initial evaluation and after implementation. They are:

1   *Systems installation*
    At the base level, the direct results of installing the systems can be recorded: the function delivered, the system costs and the immediate benefits.
2   *Individual benefits*
    At the second level there will be improvements for the individual, typically associated with training, job improvement and personal development. These may not have happened without the stimulus of the new system, and are likely to be considered as part of the investment project.
3   *Departmental management initiatives*
    Thirdly, within the period of implementation and within the departments affected, other changes to resources and procedures may have been initiated, of which only some will have been inspired by the new systems. Their interactions can be hard to disentangle.
4   *Interactions with other systems*
    The system itself will interface with and use other systems and share computing facilities with them. These may well have been ignored during the original appraisal, possibly because the linkages were not then clear, and were certainly not quantified. Now that these costs, and benefits, can be more easily seen, there may be less justification for assessing project costs on a marginal basis, by not taking account of shared facilities. However, comparisons between pre-project and post-project costings will lose validity if the basis of the financial evaluation is changed.
5   *Enterprise level changes and programmes*
    At the fifth level, the enterprise might be looking for the effects of the system on profitability. If the investment project was large enough to do this it will have taken time to implement and other changes are bound to have occurred:

price changes, new products, a reorganization, a new chief executive – the possibilities are endless. Any one of these could have affected the bottom line as well.

6   *External environmental factors*
    The final level is the most difficult to forecast and control: it is that of the external environment; the effect of competitors, of government, of consumers and of trade unions.

Any post-project appraisal will need to be clear about which levels are to be included. Moreover, not all projects should be the subject of a post-project appraisal. Some will never be repeated; others, or projects much like them, have been repeatedly done before; others will be too small. (Individual 'smallness' may be relevant, but the aggregate of small investments made outside the IT department is often a significant proportion of the total investment in IT. This almost certainly warrants a more formal appraisal than it currently receives.)

Post-project appraisal is likely to be used for projects of significance, which imply high levels of change for the business or the use of new technology. For this reason, several conditions must be met for successful appraisal. Firstly, it must have the backing and attention of senior, if not top, management. Secondly, the appraisal must not become a witch hunt; successful projects must be appraised as much as the less successful. Thirdly, arrangements to audit, and to do so repeatedly at regular intervals, need to be made when the project is in the early planning stage.

14.1.5 *Who conducts the audit?*

In Chapter 4, reference was made to phase 5 of the project life cycle, the final project phase for review and audit. Many organizations will recognize phase 5, but not so many do it regularly – even for large projects. More often than not, ITD audit groups monitor project progress and the application of standards during implementation, rather than focusing on measures of the business value to be delivered by the project.

From within the ITD an audit group, or a quality assurance group, can be used to post-appraise projects. So too can IT requirements planners and analysts, who may also be called upon to assist in the preparation of the original business case and its appraisal. These professionals are likely to be well informed about the projects, about techniques used in post-appraisal, and to be well positioned to provide constructive feedback to project owners and managers. However, there will be concerns that they lack objectivity, unless they are part of a non-ITD function. Such an independent audit group is often situated in the finance function, although post-project appraisal skills are by no means the same as those needed to audit the processes of finance.

Where project appraisal is taken seriously, the best solution, as always, is to have a committed resource and clear responsibility for its performance. This post-project appraisal resource might be one person, full- or part-time, or a small group of people, building up the necessary experience over a period of time. Appropriate seniority and breadth of experience is vital, particularly for the manager, as sensitive political issues will inevitably arise. The manager will need credibility and clout. For any appraisal it may well be necessary to involve other functional specialists and representatives, to supplement the small core post-appraisal team. Using a specialist audit group, rather than an ITD group, has the advantage that non-IT projects will also be included in its work. Many companies are consciously using project-based initiatives to implement change, and most IT projects are better regarded as business projects that require the use of IT resources.

One example of a dedicated audit group is that of the UK National Audit Office, which has a wide-ranging remit covering government processes and projects in all central and local departments.

14.1.6 Problems with post-project appraisal

As with the initial investment appraisal, many reasons are given, explicit and implied, for not conducting post-project appraisal. These are summarized in Table 14.1.

The cost of appraisal is one further reason given for not doing post-project appraisal. There is considerable scope in post-project appraisal, as there is with initial planning procedures, for the growth of a bureaucratic empire. The right balance between effectiveness and cost is likely to be found, as usual, by setting clear objectives for the right person and ensuring that projects are selected for appraisal at an appropriately high level.

In spite of the problems, post-project appraisal is a vital technique for establishing and improving the value of information technology. It completes the process of making and implementing decisions to invest in technology by providing invaluable feedback to the planning and evaluation stage of future projects. Without some post-project appraisal, investment appraisal is not complete and the value of IT cannot be rightly assessed.

Table 14.1   Summary of reasons sometimes given for not conducting post-project appraisal

- It is a non-productive use of resource, because what has, or has not, been achieved is history and cannot be substantially changed.
- It does not always reveal the true result of a project, unpalatable truth being suppressed through vested interests.
- It cannot measure the financial results of a project or relate directly the cause and effect of intangible benefits.
- It generally has to be conducted when the baseline and environment of the project implementation have changed.

14.2   Post-project appraisal methods

14.2.1 Critical success factors and key questions

For effective post-project appraisal, appropriate sponsorship and choice of methodology are important. As for the initial estimation of benefits (Chapter 10), there are four key principles for post-project appraisal, namely:

1   The cornerstone of auditing the value of a project is in describing the change that has resulted from implementing the project. It might be a subjective description or a quantified description, but it must be a *visible* and an *agreed* description.
2   The effect of the change, the result of the project, must be accepted and owned by the person who was accountable for it – a technician's view of the value of the project will not suffice.
3   There are bound to be some 'reservations' about the project and what it achieved – cause and effect are not always easy to establish. Several factors and interacting causes external to the project might have been responsible for some results.
4   Finally, there might be no one individual who is in a position to perceive the more far-reaching results of the project, and it may need the synergy of a group to evaluate it and to affirm it.

In addition to these CSFs, there are four basic questions. These at least must be asked to determine the value of an IT project:

- How well has this project supported strategic elements of the business plan?
- What has been the effect on budgets, which would not have otherwise occurred?
- Has the specified function been delivered, and on time?
- Are the project costs as budgeted?

Those putting questions will need to understand the terms in which they will be answered. The project results may not have been amenable to direct measurement or the basis of measurement may not have been agreed. The project results might be measurable, but only by spending considerable time and effort in that measurement. In this case, more subjective views of project benefits might be obtained through interviews with key users. Management judgement can just as easily be invoked for post-appraisal, as for pre-appraisal. Just because project benefits cannot be conclusively measured, there is no more reason for not conducting a post-project appraisal than not to prepare a project business case.

14.2.2 Tools and techniques

Direct communication

Before coming to more formal methods of appraisal, the simple method of people talking to people needs to be considered.

At the top level the CIO should anyway, quite apart from any other audit activities, talk regularly to other heads of functions about their view of IT and about specific projects. This audit of value and service is arguably at least as relevant, if not more so, as any formal review.

An understanding of the 'customer's' perception of satisfaction is vital to the IT department. Business analysts and project managers and those in user support functions have many contacts with users and plenty of opportunity to invite and to listen to their views on the service that they provide. However, informal contact may not resolve real problems or correct wrong perceptions unless key issues can be identified and recommendations made to the appropriate management level for action.

To facilitate this process, questionnaires and interviews can be used to provide a more systematic collection of data about specific services or projects. This immediately incurs an overhead in the management and conduct of the survey process. Per respondent, questionnaires use less resource than interviews, but unambiguous questions, which collect data in a form suitable for later analysis, can be difficult to design. An experienced interviewer can explore issues in much more depth and can arrive at a more balanced view of the real success, or failure, of a project.

Useful guidelines for survey data collection are given in *A Guide to Measuring and Managing IT Benefits*.[7] The user satisfaction survey is an important audit technique and Fig. 14.1 shows a typical questionnaire that can be used to facilitate this communication process.[8]

Business as usual

In all cases, project benefits, such as reduction in expense budgets, are more secure when the project benefits are consciously built into the business-as-usual management systems for period-by-period control, as described in Chapter 13. Then the management systems that exist for monitoring and control of annual budgets are also those that 'audit' the financial and tangible results of a project. When operating budgets include the projected benefits of IT projects to be completed in that budget period, without waiting to see how well the system works, then the savings are, to that extent, self-auditing.

Project Phase 5 review

This activity is performed by the project team and identifies lessons to be learned from the project implementation. The review is likely to focus on the three parameters that a project manager has to balance: the quality of what is delivered, the time-scale within which it is delivered and the cost. However, it does not always amount to a full validation of the results of the project by the project beneficiaries and others, and this is essential for a full project audit.

Project name: _____

Release No: _____ First production run date: _____

Please rate IS performance in this project against the following criteria. (A guide to the criteria may be attached.) How satisfied are you with the IS performance in the following areas? Score →	Very good 5	Good 4	Fair 3	Poor 2	Very poor 1
1 Gathering and agreeing requirements					
2 Estimating and scheduling of project					
3 Applying appropriate level of control					
4 Communication of design of solution					
5 Allowing user to contribute to development					
6 Assessing and managing change controls					
7 Responsiveness to user queries/concerns					
8 Addressing audit/security aspects					
9 Quality of solution/function provided					
10 Ease of use of solution/ function/provided					
11 User documentation/ education provided					
12 IS/user relations during the project					
Totals					

User satisfaction index (please calculate to two decimal places $= \dfrac{\text{Sum of totals}}{\text{No. of questions answered}} = \underline{\quad} =$

Which one of the above areas do you feel IS should most concentrate upon to improve the overall service they provide? _____

Completed by: _____ Title: _____

Function (e.g. Admin., Personnel, Finance, etc.): _____

Signed: _____ Date: _____

Figure 14.1. User satisfaction index questionnaire.[8]

Table 14.2   Summary of results of SESAME investigations[10]

Break-even point (after system installation)	Mean benefit–cost ratio
• Median five months	• Median 2.4
• 50% between 1 and 21 months	• 50% between 1.7 and 1.8
• 77% less than two years	• 88% greater than 1.0

Many projects have post-implementation reviews, but these may not amount to a full post-implementation appraisal, which determines whether the original business case for the project has been realized. A typical situation has been reported by the National Audit Office in March 1991.[9] Prior to office automation in four government departments, thorough investment appraisals had been made. However, subsequent post-implementation reviews did not collect enough data to prove systematically that improved efficiency had been achieved.

Nevertheless, the Phase 5 post-implementation review is a valid audit technique, within its intended scope. Most organizations have some procedural guidelines for post-implementation reviews. Parker provides a useful pro forma in *Managing Information Systems for Profit*.[8]

IBM post-project appraisal methods: SESAME and the Four Layer Evaluation Method

The Systems Effectiveness Study and Management Endorsement (SESAME) has been used since the early 1970s by IBM UK consultants working with client organizations in post-project appraisal. These studies have demonstrated that, in most cases, substantial and tangible benefits have resulted from implementing IT projects. The results of sixteen of the investigations, covering 166 applications, have been reported by Lincoln.[10] Some of the results are summarized in Table 14.2.

In the 1980s SESAME was applied within IBM UK to audit the National Office Support Services (NOSS) project. (This project was based on the use of IBM Professional Office Service (PROFS).) For this the SESAME techniques were extended and the new process was called (by its main protagonist, Laking), the 'Four Layer Measurement Methodology'. Being more detailed than SESAME, the Four Layer Measurement Methodology requires more resource for its execution.

SESAME

The main features and steps of SESAME are summarized in Fig. 14.2. The success of SESAME depends on the use of a multi-disciplinary team, in-

A SESAME study focuses on systems that have been implemented for at least 12 months and identifies in considerable detail, by means of extensive user interviews, the full costs and benefits experienced to date. The SESAME approach identifies benefits by asking users to consider how they would meet their current objectives without the help of the system under review. Once these are established, projections will be made over the expected system life to a maximum of five years and the results presented to achieve management approval.

Main activities

- Set up meeting with the sponsor.
- Team briefing and planning.
- Overview of the systems installed; identify expected benefit areas.
- Identify organizational changes since planning the system.
- Agree a comparator and time-scale against which to measure the system.
- Collect data on the effect of introducing the system.
- Analyse the data and draw conclusions.
- Prepare report and presentation for the sponsor.

Figure 14.2.   Summary of features and activities of a Systems Effectiveness Study and Management Evaluation (SESAME).

cluding users, which reports to an executive sponsor. The approach seeks to recognize that, in most cases, there will not be a cut and dried answer to, 'Has the investment been worthwhile?' The answer will depend on what costs and benefits have been included, over what time frame, and what methods and criteria have been applied. Comparisons are needed of these with the original appraisal parameters. The approach also seeks to understand the 'political' and other forces at work throughout any implementation.

Experience has shown that no single financial measure adequately describes the full financial performance of a computer application. SESAME studies generally quote the break-even point, the mean benefit–cost ratio over the system life and an internal rate of return for all the applications reviewed. The vast majority of studies have demonstrated positive and acceptable financial post-audit evaluations.

SESAMEs have been conducted for both small and for large projects. However, we shall now describe how a stretched version of SESAME was applied to measure the results of implementing the IBM UK investment in PROFS.

Four Layer Measurement Method
Audits were conducted before the start-up of PROFS in 1983, and every two years thereafter. The regularity of PROFS audits has been fundamental to an appreciation of the benefits gained and to gaining more benefits.

The PROFS audit methods were based on four measurement approaches, which, taken together and over several successive audits, provided consistent views of the productivity gains. For an all-pervasive system like PROFS, which is not dedicated to processing transactions, different approaches need to be used to

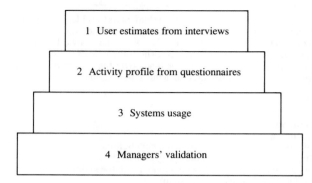

Figure 14.3. The IBM Four Layer Measurement Method.

build the whole picture. The audits had not only to record achievements in financial terms, but also what had not been achieved, in terms of perceived problems, and what users still required to be achieved, in terms of potential benefits.

The four strands of the Four Layer Measurement Method, Fig. 14.3, provided comparative views and measures – checks and balances for each other. Information was collected by means of questionnaires, by time logs, by interviews and from system statistics on:

1 Assessment of productivity gains by individual professionals and managers. These were determined by questionnaires.
2 Comparison of work profiles (that is, types of office activity), before and after installation of the system function. The work profiles were recorded by the individuals performing the work.
3 Analysis of the system usage by function by, for example, document production or diary usage.
4 Assessment by managers of the effective application of productivity gains, within work groups, sometimes with a recorded change in the headcount of the group. These assessments were made during interviews.

Many techniques were used within the four main methods. The time and effort spent in designing and developing the survey questionnaires, in interviewing and in information analysis, was considerable. The work was performed by the Systems Measurement Group in the IBM UKIIS (United Kingdom International Information Systems) department. Although the group might have been seen as an interested party, it reflected the company's emphasis on improvement through audit rather than just historical investigation. Moreover, the group acted as the market research ear of a user-orientated IS department. The small core team had a background in, and management experience of, work study, office services and

IT systems. Their competence was built over the years; it was their skill and dedication which produced the results, as much as the methodology.

14.3 Case study: audits of IBM UK National Office Support Service (NOSS)

CASE STUDY

Early in the 1980s the Assistant General Manager of Marketing and Services decided to tackle rising costs with technology in the form of an 'office system'. The success of this depended on being able to achieve real improvements in productivity and to reduce, or at least to contain, the steadily rising headcount. Two initial pilot installations, one in the head office at North Harbour, Portsmouth and the other in a marketing centre in Warwick tested the functional and 'human' aspects of the proposed systems and demonstrated their potential value. (As explained above, IBM UK NOSS uses PROFS.)

The pilot installations were 'audited' before implementation, half-way through and at their conclusion. The first audit of full PROFS was conducted before the system went live. It measured current practice and expectations. Later audits measured achievements and identified trends. Some of the motivation for this work undoubtedly arose from the marketing need to demonstrate the value to be obtained from office automation and its 'auditabilty'.

The business case for PROFS implementation was approved in 1983. It depended on achieving a 7% productivity improvement and projected a two and a half year payback. This financial case was subsequently extended to provide for a larger investment, of some £70 million, a greater number of users and higher productivity gains.

The project aimed to achieve a 'critical mass' as soon as possible. By September 1985 there were 10 000 users of the system – clerks, managers, secretaries, professionals, receptionists – covering all jobs and all levels. Each year since then the project has expanded, either in terms of the numbers of users or of the function provided. By 1992 PROFS connections had been established with customers and suppliers, and home-based use of PROFS by employees was growing.

The objectives of the biennial PROFS audits were to determine the benefits actually achieved, to assess what use was being made of functions recently added to PROFS and to form a view of what further development was needed. Main audits of PROFS were conducted biennially, in 1986, 1988 and 1990. The pattern of each was similar and the results are summarized below. The audits were validated in being signed off by finance and functional directors.

Audits were conducted in four centres with different business functions, typifying the main users of the system. Some 400 users were involved in the surveys. In addition to systems statistics, data were collected by questionniares and interviews. Productivity benefits were analysed and collated by job type, location and by PROFS facility, such as memoranda, documents and directory.

Audit results

The use of PROFS increased from an average of 55 minutes per day per user in 1985 to 150 minutes by the end of 1988. This time had reduced by 7% in the 1990 survey. Of greater importance than raw usage was the steady increase in productivity.

Productivity targets were set for 7% in the original business case. Users reported that their productivity had continued to rise and by 1990 was assessed to have reached some 24%, on average. The general view among users was that PROFS could be still more productive when other office functions and enhancements were built in. The estimate of the potential had risen to a surprising 41% in 1990.

PROFS was a big project and was not without its problems. As each major problem was identified an 'audit' was conducted, the real problem determined and action taken. For example, during the annual budgeting process, local management were claiming that only 2% productivity had been achieved from the installation of PROFS, and additional headcount was needed. Central finance requested an audit. Using the same four-layer techniques as for the full audit, it was shown that there had been a 9% productivity improvement as result of PROFS, and demonstrated that there was no case for the requested headcount increase.

Based solely on the 1986 12% productivity improvement and on the 1988 20% improvement in productivity, the project broke even early in 1988, some three years after implementation.

There were other direct savings in terms of copiers, filing cabinets, postage and mail handling but these were not collated and recorded. Communications across the organization were faster and geographical constraints on work were removed, as individuals could work from any IBM location using a 'visitor's' terminal. Within IBM UK, time and space shrank.

The early PROFS audits revealed things of fundamental importance to users of the system. To be fully effective it was crucial to have PROFS all-pervasive throughout the organization; ease of access to and response from, terminals and printers; local expert support; further development of main line facilities, rather than 'bells and whistles'; and extension of PROFS coverage to non-IBM locations. Even in 1990, the top priority of users was to have a better understanding of PROFS.

How the audit results were used

From 1984 the productivity forecasts made in the original PROFS business case and in its extensions were taken by business planners and built into operating budgets, on a year-by-year basis. Of course, PROFS productivity projections were not the only factors to determine the level and allocation of resource committed each year to the operating plan. Product and marketing plans, sales channel management initiatives and business volume projections were all taken into account; but the planners banked on PROFS working. From 1984 to 1988 sales revenues and volumes increased some 170%, while the company headcount was substantially flat. PROFS laid the foundation in the 1980s for 'location-independent working' in the 1990s with the consequential and significant savings in real estate costs.

The working environment in IBM UK has changed dramatically over the last 11 years. The authors have personally experienced the benefit to be gained from global electronic communications across time zones, as the world wide IBM Consulting Group has been established. Within the UK, significant internal reorganization has been aided by PROFS. Laptop computers now provide off-site access to PROFS, enabling us to work effectively from home and other non-IBM locations. Much of our work is now 'paperless' with direct links to many suppliers and customers. Internal communications, from the CEO downwards, are more personal and have a fresh immediacy. On the foundation laid in the 1980s, PROFS function is being expanded to meet the justifiable business needs of the 1990s.

The projected benefits of PROFS have been continuously wrapped into business plans. Productivity improvements have been continuously required of functional line managers at all levels. Even while business volumes have increased, headcount has been reduced. Each audit has provided information needed to make further sound investment decisions. Confidence that value for money has been achieved has been built by careful completion of all five stages of the decision-making process.

Post-project appraisal is hardly worth the candle unless it is acted on. Project deliverables, where they are deficient, must, if it is worthwhile, be put right. Improvements and enhancements are normally possible at a marginal cost. Initial learning must be quickly completed and new standards become business-as-usual. The lessons learned and experience gained from all five stages of the decision-making process must be ploughed back to improve the next harvest of benefits.

References

1 Hashi Syedain, Managers an endangered species, *Management Today*, May 1991.
2 Bill Neale and David Holmes, Post completion Audits: The Costs and Benefits, *Management Accounting*, March 1988.
3 *Office Automation – The Barriers and Opportunities*, Touche Ross Management Consultants and Institute of Administrative Management, March 1991.
4 S. Zuboff, *In the Age of the Smart Machine*, Heinemann Professional Publishing, London, 1988.
5 Michael Hammer, Re-engineering work: Don't automate, obliterate, *Harvard Business Review*, July–August 1990.
6 Frank R. Gulliver. Post-project appraisals pay, *Harvard Business Review*, March–April 1987.
7 D. S. J. Remenyi, A. Money and A. Twite, *A Guide to Measuring and Managing IT Benefits*, NCC Blackwell Ltd, Oxford, 1991.
8 Mike Parker, in *Managing Information Systems for Profit* (ed. Tim Lincoln), John Wiley & Sons, Chichester, 1990.
9 *Office Automation in Government Departments*, Report by the Controller and Auditor General, The National Audit Office, HMSO, London, March 1991.
10 T. J. Lincoln, Evaluating the return of information technology, *Management Accounting*, April 1985.

Index